ALSO BY PETER DEMETZ

Marx, Engels, and the Poets
German Post-War Literature: A Critical Introduction
After the Fires: Recent Writing in the Germanies, Austria, and Switzerland
Prague in Black and Gold: Scenes from the Life of a European City
The Air Show at Brescia, 1909

PRAGUE IN DANGER

PRAGUE IN DANGER

The Years of German Occupation, 1939–45:

Memories and History, Terror and Resistance,

Theater and Jazz, Film and Poetry,

Politics and War

PETER DEMETZ

Farrar, Straus and Giroux

New York

Farrar, Straus and Giroux
18 West 18th Street, New York 10011

Copyright © 2008 by Peter Demetz
Distributed in Canada by Douglas & McIntyre Ltd.
Printed in the United States of America
First edition, 2008

Library of Congress Cataloging-in-Publication Data
Demetz, Peter, 1922–
    Prague in danger : the years of German occupation, 1939–45 : memories
and history, terror and resistance, theater and jazz, film and poetry, politics
and war / Peter Demetz.—   1st ed.
        p.   cm.
    Includes bibliographical references and index.
    ISBN-13: 978-0-374-28126-7 (hardcover : alk. paper)
    ISBN-10: 0-374-28126-2 (hardcover : alk. paper)
    1. Prague (Czech Republic)—History—20th century.   2. World War,
1939–1945—Czech Republic—Prague.   3. Bohemia and Moravia
(Protectorate, 1939–1945)   4. Demetz, Peter, 1922–   I. Title.

    DB2629.D46 2008
    943.71'2033—dc22

                                                                2007046188

Designed by Jonathan D. Lippincott

www.fsgbooks.com

1   3   5   7   9   10   8   6   4   2

CONTENTS

———

PREFACE

A few years ago, in *Prague in Black and Gold*, I wrote a history of my hometown from the sixth to the early twentieth century. I still remember how exhilarating it was to study the classic historians and what they said about kings, emperors, and the inevitable golem. It was harder to write the concluding pages about the funeral of T. G. Masaryk, first president of the Czechoslovak Republic, because on September 21, 1937, I had been there in the crowd, an eager boy of fifteen, sadly watching the flags, the casket on a gun carriage, and the soldiers marching by. Where was I to turn, writing about that event nearly sixty years later? There were reports in old newspaper files and the chronicles of professional historians, but overwhelmingly present was my own experience of that bleak morning, filtered through my eyes and ears, rising in my self.

These difficulties returned in full force when I decided to write about the years of the German occupation of Prague, 1939–45. Of course, I have relied on the narratives of historians and on newspaper reports, yet I was also constantly there, as I was not in the years of Charles IV or Rudolf II, in and of that world all these years, involved, walking, breathing, observing. Our grandfathers the existentialists are right: "to be" means "to be such and such," to speak a particular language, to belong to a specific ethnicity, to profess a definite religion. But matters were rather more complicated in Prague during those years if you did not march in one of the neat ethnic battalions so dear to schoolbooks. Then, you had to be a Czech, a German, or a Jew, pure and simple, and unfortunately people did not know what to do with half Jews like me, straddling languages and ethnicities.

I should like to define what I am doing here as an almost impossible effort to present synchronically a public narrative of the various societies of Prague during the German occupation and my private story. When I write about politics and cultural life in the protectorate, I take my cue from what historians would do, and yet I have not excluded the story of myself, working whenever necessary with a change of perspective, however sudden and abrupt. I do not want to present any coercive interpretation of how warring societies and individuals relate to each other in bitter times, and I prefer rather to put the public narrative and the private story (if, after Paul Ricoeur, philosopher of memory and forgetting, such a distinction can be made at all) side by side, hoping that the reader will occasionally feel a shock of awareness, even a physiological one, when considering the circumstances, which often defied inherited vocabularies.

When I concerned myself with the past of my family in order to tell my own private story, I discovered to my great surprise that I came from immigrant stock on both sides; a hundred years later only one of my cousins and his small family continue to reside in that ancient city Prague, once peopled by multitudes of my uncles, aunts, their in-laws, children, and grandchildren—a short and fragile encounter, considering the long span of Prague's history, yet brimming over with aspirations, individual fates, and tragedies. My South Tyrolean grandfather, who belonged to the minority of the Ladin peasants of the Gardena Valley, arrived in Prague on his trek to the north around 1885, and my Jewish grandfather, trying to escape the Czech anti-Semitism rampant in small Bohemian towns, came with his family as late as 1900, a remarkable coincidence of diverse origins, languages, and traditions found in the thicket of Prague's ancient urban community, continuously attracting people from all the many corners of the Austro-Hungarian monarchy.

I strongly believe that fin de siècle Prague had a touch of old New

York about it, with so many different people all living under one civil law and, a little later, in Masaryk's republic, under one constitution. The German occupation, driven by its own nationalism and triggering another one in response, for a while gravely undermined and almost destroyed the heritage of this multiethnic society, for centuries strongly alive and productive in Prague. And yet the city was indomitable, and the 3.5 million international tourists now visiting it each year hide rather than reveal that Prague with undiminished vitality and force again attracts new citizens, Russians, Poles, Ukrainians, a few Italians, Americans (nearly fourteen thousand in the 1990s but fewer now), and "new" Germans active in banking and business.

I dedicate this book, perhaps more personal than others I have written, to the memory of Hanna (1928–93). We fell in love shortly after the liberation of Prague in 1945, and we did not have to explain much to each other. Our Jewish mothers had died during the occupation, hers because the Jewish physician came too late, and mine in Terezín. And while many people returning to Prague from the concentration camps tried to emigrate immediately to America or Israel, we hoped that liberals of every shape would win in the elections of May 1946 and happily read newspaper articles by Ferdinand Peroutka, Pavel Tigrid, Helena Koželuhová, and Michal Mareš, all united in opposition to the Stalinists, who were daily expanding their power in Czechoslovakia. After the Communist putsch of February 25, 1948, we had to go too, and while earlier we had playfully discussed what kind of car we would acquire in the grand West (Hanna wanted a red sports car, and I a dark green one), the question was now how to get out of the country without being caught and sentenced to seven years of hard labor.

Hanna, working as a secretary at the Czechoslovak-British Society, was under growing pressure from the secret police to deliver information about what went on in her office. I had my own worries, having participated in the march of two thousand students to Hradčany Hill—the commanding site in Prague, where Hradčany Castle had housed the rulers of Czechoslovakia for centuries—entreating the president, Edvard Beneš, not to accept the imposition of a Stalinist government (he signed his capitulation while we were marching), and writing a dissertation on Franz Kafka and English literature. Hanna had to sell her mother's engagement ring so we could pay an aging Boy Scout late in 1949 to smuggle us through the woods and across the border to Bavaria, together with a few other students. And so it happened that we went through the refugee camps in West Germany, briefly worked for Radio Free Europe, and about two years later safely arrived at Idlewild Airport, New York, USA, with big rucksacks on our backs and a few pennies in our pockets. Prague, the ancient city, was of the past, but we did not cease to talk about its ambivalent charms, which were taking on, again, a golden hue.

In official Prague, meanwhile, partisan proclamations dominated for a long time. Only in the late 1960s and early 1970s did Detlef Brandes's magisterial work appear (in Germany), and Vojtěch Mastný's early study of the Czechs under Nazi rule (in the United States). Investigations of Jewish affairs ran into troubles of their own: the Communist regime, suspicious of Zionism, preferred "anti-Fascism" in general terms; thus Karel Lagus and Josef Polák's book on Terezín was published by the League of Antifascist Fighters (1964), and Arnošt Lustig, novelist and Auschwitz survivor, left for the United States (1969). Important studies of Jewish persecution during the protectorate— i.e., H. G. Adler's *Theresienstadt* and Livia Rothkirchen's fundamental *The Jews of Bohemia and Moravia: Facing the Holocaust* (after she had sporadically published in Czech earlier)—appeared abroad. Fortunately, by 1995, the Terezín Institute Initiative had published its first volume of international studies under the editorship of Miroslav Kárný, and many sequels have followed since.

In Czechoslovakia in the 1970s and 1980s, many ingenious authors preferred to write what is called *literatura faktu*, rather melodramatically combining documents and fiction, and these books—for instance, Miroslav Ivanov's bestseller on Reinhard Heydrich, in its fifth edition by 1987—were very much liked by readers. The "normalization," by which was meant the return of neo-Stalinism after the brief Prague Spring of 1968, threw new obstacles in the way of an entire upcoming generation of historians and political scientists, who fully emerged only after the Velvet Revolution of 1989 (Křen, Kuklík, Kural,

Kvaček, Moulis, Pasák, and others). It is enough to read Karel Bartošek's and Stanislav Kokoška's books on the Prague uprising of 1945 to see the difference: there (1965) a political treatise in spite of all protective camouflage and here (2005) a sober analysis of the events, based on international archival sources, including Soviet and American ones. It is a rewarding experience to see that younger Prague historians have joined their open-minded colleagues elsewhere.

I owe a heavy debt of gratitude to Sterling Memorial Library (Yale University), particularly strong on Slavic materials, the Czech National Library in Prague, where I happened to work first as a graduate student nearly sixty years ago, the Austrian National Library (Vienna), and the Library of the Adalbert Stifter Verein (Munich), where I enjoyed the dedicated assistance of the historian Dr. Jozo Džambo. It was a particular pleasure to work in the Czech Film Archives in Prague, where Ms. Jaroslava Šlechtová always readily answered my questions, and in the Prague Theater Institute, where Dr. Jitka Ludvová made it possible for me to study my father's manuscripts deposited there. I am greatly indebted to my agent, William B. Goodman, for constant encouragement and essential advice, and to Suzanne Gray Kelley, as usual my first American reader, who, patiently and tolerantly, smoothed the rough edges of my syntax (not to speak about the prepositions). It was particularly rewarding to work, once again, with my editor, Elisabeth Sifton, who gently watched over the changes in the text, taught me the art of the effective argument, and loyally reminded me of the expectations of my American readership. My cousin Ingrid Runggaldier, M.A., of the Language Office of the Autonomous Province of Bolzano, kindly checked on my Ladin narratives; my Prague cousin Petr provided me with important papers concerning the Bohemian history of the Brod family; and as far as documents and illustrations were concerned, I was able to rely again on the experience of Luba Rasine-Ortoleva, who had assisted me in the shaping of earlier books. I should not have been able to complete my research without the expert help of my two Prague assistants, Eva Hulanová, M.A., and Linda Skolková, B.A. Ms. Hulanová, then of the German Department (Charles University, Prague), helped me when I was writing Chapters I and II, and Ms. Skolková, librarian and electronic information expert, when I was busy with Chapters III and IV. It was enlightening and a pleasure to work with both of them, and I learned a lot.

I have particular reasons to express my especial gratitude to my wife, Paola, for her infinite tolerance, empathy, and quiet support.

New Haven, Connecticut, March 2007

PRAGUE IN DANGER

CHAPTER I

THE DAY OF OCCUPATION

President Hácha Travels to Berlin

Hitler never hesitated about his ultimate intent to create new "living space" (*Lebensraum*) for his nation in the east and to smash the liberal state of Czechoslovakia on his way. After Germany's annexation of Austria in March 1938, Prime Minister Neville Chamberlain traveled twice to the Continent hoping to appease Hitler's aggressive intentions and to prevent another destructive European war, but with a distinct lack of success. Czechoslovakia had signed treaties with France in 1926 and with the Soviet Union in 1935 precisely to protect itself against German aggression—the Soviet Union promised to intervene, but only if France acted first—but it remained exposed and vulnerable. Concurrent agreements among the Little Entente of Czechoslovakia, Romania, and Yugoslavia to defend against any aggression on the part of Hungary were of little use.

Within the Czechoslovak Republic, a virulently German nationalist movement, led by Konrad Henlein and fully supported by the National Socialists in Berlin, resisted Prague rule and demanded that the Sudetenland, where most of Czechoslovakian Germans lived, be united with the Reich. When, only two months after the Nazis' annexation of Austria, German troops readied to march across the border in May 1938, the Czechoslovaks partly mobilized, and the situation became increasingly ominous. The ambassadors of France and Great Britain delivered a note to President Edvard Beneš on September 19 demanding that the republic hand over its Sudeten territories to Germany in exchange for a guarantee of its new borders, this to prevent an immediate occupation by the Wehrmacht, and suddenly the Czechoslovak Republic and its (few) friends were isolated. On September 23, in a desperate gesture, Czechoslovakia once more mobilized its army and air force. Hitler's ally Benito Mussolini then proposed a four-power meeting to resolve the Czechoslovak crisis.

The famous conference convened on September 29–30 in Munich with representatives of Germany, Great Britain, France, and Italy in attendance, Czechoslovaks being notably absent. Chamberlain, French Prime Minister Édouard Daladier, Hitler, and Mussolini signed an agreement that conceded to all of Germany's demands. The Sudetenland was to be united with the Reich as of October 1; this and further concessions deprived the Czechoslovak Republic of a major part of its historical territory, its principal fortifications against Germany, and much of its iron, steel, and textile factories. Moreover, with the loss of the Sudetenland came the threat of further losses of border territories in the east, which Poland and Hungary coveted. A week after mobilizing, Czechoslovakia capitulated on September 30.

The Munich Conference not only deprived Czechoslovakia of defensible borders but also grievously weakened its democratic traditions. The country had emerged on October 18, 1918, from the disintegration of the Austro-Hungarian Empire as a liberal republic with strong parliamentary institutions, in contrast with many of its neighbors, and T. G. Masaryk, its founder and first president, together with his loyal associates, including Beneš, the young minister of foreign affairs, carefully watched out for political balances and the interplay of the different political parties. By 1926 representatives of the German liberals, Catholics, and Socialists had joined the government, and they stayed with it for more than twelve years. Masaryk's resignation in 1935 because of his old age coincided with the radical worsening of the European situation that year, and after the Munich Conference and the capitulation of the Czechoslovak government, continued German pressure forced Beneš, Masaryk's successor as president, to resign. Beneš left the country two weeks later in a private plane, on October 22, but he was as resolved as ever to renew the integrity of the Republic by monitoring changes in the European situation and by continuing to act, as Masaryk had done in his time, on the international scene. His Czechoslovak National Committee, established in Paris in 1939, was not a diplomatic success, but the Czechoslovak government-in-exile, which convened in the summer of 1940 in London, was eventually recognized by Britain and the Soviet Union and successively by all the Allies, as well as the United States.

Germany's operational plans against Czechoslovakia seemed for a while after Munich to be suspended. This hiatus was intended to reassure British public opinion and to avoid a premature conflict. But once the Sudeten question had been resolved in Hitler's favor, the Slovak problem came to the fore. The government in Prague that succeeded Beneš agreed in early October to federalize Czechoslovakia and make it the Czecho-Slovak Republic and to accept an autonomous government and legislature in Bratislava, Slovakia's capital. Hitler, with some delay, discovered the virtues of the Slovak separatists who were demanding independence and personally assured their militant leaders of his full, if belated, sympathies. Slovak nationalism surged, and by early March 1939 in Prague President Emil Hácha, acting within the constitution, had little choice but to dismiss four separatist Bratislava ministers and order army units stationed in that city to defend the republic, however hyphenated, if the separatists should revolt. His action may have played into the hands of Hitler, who promptly invited Monsignor Jozef Tiso, prime minister of the Slovak government, to Berlin and pressured, or rather blackmailed, him into choosing independence; the alternative the Germans offered to Slovakia was its occupation by Hungary, which had ever since 1918 been unable to accept the loss of Slovak territory. The trouble was that Germany's military clocks were ticking; secret marching orders had been given to the German troops massing at the borders of Bohemia and Moravia. At this juncture President Hácha asked the Führer for an interview to clarify the situation.

President Hácha's fateful trip to Berlin in March was not, for the Czechs, a matter that had been given careful diplomatic preparation, and it could not have been. The initiative and advance planning were all in the hands of the Germans, and the old man went straight into their trap. Hácha was not well informed about German intentions. He believed that in Berlin he would discuss matters concerning Slovakia, and the people around him, including his cabinet, were far too confident that Czecho-Slovakia still had a chance to survive if it did not challenge Hitler directly. They did not believe the reports issued by Colonel František Moravec, head of army intelligence, that Germany's military occupation of the country was imminent. (Moravec had received information from Czech journalists, from the French Deuxième Bureau, and from an agent, A–54, an Abwehr officer who was playing both sides.) Moravec, his duty done, packed part of his archives, gathered his officers, and boarded a KLM flight from Prague via Rotterdam to London, where he and the others landed at approximately the same time as Hácha's train arrived in Berlin.

On March 14, 1939, events happened fast. At noon the Slovak parliament in Bratislava voted on the foregone conclusion of Slovak independence, fully supported if not engineered, by Germany. The Foreign Office in Berlin notified its chargé d'affaires in Prague that President Hácha should come to Berlin immediately (Hitler, who originally wanted Hácha to travel by plane, gave permission that he come by train), and the signal was passed on through proper channels from the German Embassy in Prague to President Hácha, who happened to be having lunch with a Czech Catholic bishop and was looking forward to a gala performance of Dvořák's opera *Rusalka* at the National Theater in the evening.

The traveling party, quickly assembled after lunch, was rather small. There was the president; his daughter, Milada Rádlová (in her function as first lady); and Foreign Minister František Chvalkovský, suspected by many of political sympathies for Italian fascism, accompanied by an assistant from his office. There was also the president's secretary, Dr. Josef Kliment, who was to develop his own ideas of collaboration with Germany; the loyal butler, Bohumil Příhoda, who had served President Masaryk in better times; and a police inspector. After a few members of the government had taken leave of the president, the special train, still unheated, left the Hybernská railway station at 4:00 p.m. Mrs. Rádlová had the distinct feeling that a shot was fired at the windows of her compartment when the train left Czech territory (it might have been a stone thrown at the train). The travelers arrived a few minutes before 10:00 p.m. at the Berlin Anhalter Bahnhof, to be welcomed, strictly according to protocol, by a military honor guard; Dr. Otto Meissner, a minister of state; and Vojtěch Mastný, Czech ambassador in Berlin.

About midnight German Foreign Minister Joachim von Ribbentrop made a brief appearance at the Hotel Adlon. Hácha uttered a few ceremonious remarks about the difficulties of small nations facing a great power, and as soon as the foreign minister left, it was announced that Hitler was ready to see his Czech guests at the chancellery. By now it was about 1:00 a.m., because first Hitler had watched his daily movie, not a B western, as was his habit, but a rather sophisticated German comedy entitled *A Hopeless Case*, directed by Erich Engel, with Jenny Jugo, Karl Ludwig Diehl, and Axel von Ambesser in leading roles. In the courtyard of the chancellery, another honor guard (not army but SS) presented arms, and Hácha and Chvalkovský were received by Hitler and a motley group that included Hermann Göring, who had just returned from an Italian vacation, General Wilhelm Keitel of the Wehrmacht high command, the foreign minister and his assistants (among others, a translator, who was not needed because Hácha spoke fluent German), and Councillor Walter Hewel, whose task it was to provide a stenographic protocol of the proceedings.

Hácha, a gentleman of the old school, introduced himself to Hitler, but it is not easy to know what he really said in his quiet self-humiliation or whether he made attempts to discover if Hitler was open to argument. Journalists and historians have referred to different texts, quoting Hewel's stenogram (difficult to disbelieve, though Hewel was a Hitler loyalist who in 1945 killed himself in a Berlin street rather than be taken prisoner by Soviet soldiers), or Hácha's own aide-mémoire, written down a week later, on March 20, or an interview he granted to the Czech writer Karel Horký in April. Hácha wanted to present himself as a rather apolitical civil servant who had been long attentive to Hitler's ideas and to suggest that he had never been on intimate terms with Masaryk or Beneš. (This was true, but Masaryk had appointed him to his judicial position, and both presidents had fully trusted his handling of the law.) He also remarked that he had asked himself whether Czechoslovakia was happy to be an independent state ("ob es ein Glück für die Tschechoslowakei war, selbstständig zu sein"), not exactly a blasphemous idea if it had been articulated on another occasion; defended his recent intervention in Slovak affairs on constitutional grounds; and appealed to Hitler as someone who, being always aware of national problems, would understand the desires of the Czech people to have their own national life.

Hitler brushed aside Hácha's polite formulations, told him brusquely that he was not interested in Slovak affairs there and now, and announced that because of the Czechs' unabated ill-treatment of Germans, he had given orders to the army to march into Czech lands at exactly 6:00 a.m. the next day and to integrate what he continued to call Czecho-Slovakia into the Third Reich. Yet, he said, the Czechs would be granted "the most complete autonomy [*die vollste Autonomie*] and their own way of life [*Eigenleben*], more than they had ever enjoyed in Austrian times." The guests were unable to respond because Hitler started to shriek, declaring that any resistance would have the most terrible consequences. Hácha, still bent on an exchange of arguments, asked if disarming Czech forces could not be achieved in a different way, but Hitler insisted that his decision was irrevocable. The Czech president then expressed his doubts that it would be possible to notify all units of the Czech Army in the short time left (it must have been close to 3:00 a.m.), and Hitler told him that the telephones of his office were at his disposal. The Czech guests were brought to another room, and Hácha first called General Jan Syrový in Prague, the defense minister, to order that all possible resistance to German armed force should cease. Hácha and Chvalkovský made a number of other calls to the government in Prague, constitutionally in strange abeyance because its officers had tendered their resignations but Hácha had not yet accepted them.

By that time the text of a joint declaration had been circulated. The sixty-seven-year-old Hácha, totally exhausted, at first refused and then accepted a fortifying glucose injection administered by Dr. Theo Morrell, Hitler's personal physician and a great believer in injections of all kinds. Playing the good cop, Göring took Hácha aside and, rather than scream at him, told him quietly and almost delicately that he would really regret having to order the German Luftwaffe to bomb Prague and destroy that beautiful city, *die schöne Stadt*, just to show the French and British what German pilots could do.

Hácha at least said that he could not sign the joint declaration in the name of the government. It may be a somewhat later invention that a philological dispute developed about whether the fate of the Czech people actually lay in [*liegt in* . . .] the hands of the Führer or whether Hácha was putting it [*legt* . . .] there. Ultimately, Hácha, Chvalkovský, Hitler, and his foreign minister signed the formal declaration at about 3:55 a.m. The Czech president, who continued to believe that Germany's military occupation of his country would be only temporary, put the fate of his nation into the hands of the Führer (the rhetorical formulation had also been used by Slovak functionaries earlier that week). The text was immediately transmitted by telephone to Prague, and an additional protocol, based on a document prepared by General Keitel four days earlier, defined seven points of capitulation. There was to be no resistance by the army or police to Germany's occupation of Bohemia and Moravia, all aircraft were to be grounded and all antiaircraft batteries removed, public and economic life was to continue, and utter restraint on public media was imposed. Witnesses do not say how Hácha and his entourage spent the time until their special train left the Berlin Anhalter Bahnhof shortly after 11:00 a.m. on March 15, 1939, but it is clear that their journey was deliberately delayed by the German authorities (citing bad weather) for many hours to make sure that Hitler (who relied on a special train and his motorcade) arrived in Prague earlier than Hácha.

Emil Hácha: Judge and President

A protracted discussion of whether Hácha was a Fascist collaborator or a heroic patriot or both has long delayed a more nuanced historical analysis, but this has emerged in the writings of Tomáš Pasák and Robert Kvaček more than fifty years after the events. Yet the drama of March 1939, throwing Hitler, that vicious destroyer of all legal and humane order, against Emil Hácha, the highest judge and lawyer of his nation, has a Shakespearean dimension in which tragedy and the most cruel ironies are not absent. The more I have learned from Vít Machálek's resolutely defensive biography (1998) about Hácha's virtues and blindness, about his stubbornness and helpless self-pity, the more

I am inclined to see the fortitude of an aging jurist trying to save his nation rather than its state (as he said) and to sympathize with the terrible physiological and mental changes he went through in the last years of his life, spent in the castle of the Czech kings.

Hácha's forebears were southern Bohemian peasants and small landowners, master brewers and foresters, and it was his father who was the first in the family to leave the land to make a steady career in the tax service. His firstborn, Emil (July 12, 1872, at Trhové Sviny), went quickly through the schools, including a small-town gymnasium, and, exceeding his father's aspirations, became a student at the Prague Czech Faculty of Law, while his younger brother, Theodor, went to the United States, studied engineering at Cooper Union in New York (living on Long Island), and returned, a U.S. citizen, to a job in Prague (1904). Photographs of the time show the student Emil as a handsome and elegant young man, with his mother's full lips and energetic nose (they do not reveal that he was noticeably short), and considering his times, it is not much of a surprise that he did not neglect his literary and musical interests, listening carefully when Marie, a cousin on the maternal side and his future wife, played the piano and sang Wagner (Isolde).

Emil and Marie, later called Queen Mary by her intimate friends, were married on February 2, 1902, in Prague, and Milada, their only daughter, was born in early 1903. The young lawyer, at least in the first years of his marriage, was powerfully attracted to writing his own poetry and to studying literature (preferably English) even before he began to publish professional legal studies in the appropriate journals. His poems, commendable accomplishments rather than masterpieces, were attuned to the advanced art of the moment, whether it was called symbolism or fin de siècle. He cultivated Jaroslav Vrchlický and Jiří Karásek ze Lvovic, among the decadents, and admired the Belgian symbolist Émile Verhaeren from his Prague distance. In his poems, always addressed to Marie, he contrasted his dreams with the prose of his profession—"Two crutches, instead of wings/ my journey leads to ordinary plains/ I do not drink from sources rare/ and only gather dew drops in my hand"—and confessed how deeply enchanted he was by his bride: "Pre-Raphaelite women had your body/ your grand eyes and your hair's old gold/ I am imprisoned by your beauty and the music of your voice." In 1902 Hácha traveled to England to study both the legal system, so different from that of old Austria, and contemporary literature, and together with his brother, "the American," he translated Jerome Klapka Jerome's popular novel *Three Men in a Boat* (published by 1902 in Prague by Topič), Rudyard Kipling's poem "If" (by coincidence, also the favorite of Edvard Beneš), and Robert Louis Stevenson's essay on Villon, all published at about the same time. In 1903 he was busy reporting about current British writing for respectable Prague magazines, and in 1904 he published a long article on Conan Doyle, Kipling, Wells, and Bram Stoker, informing the educated Czech reader about what was happening on the British scene.

Yet a literary career was not to be—professional duties and legal researches intervened—and while Hácha retained a lifelong sympathy for British jurisprudence and literature (in an early letter to Beneš in London, after his own election to the presidency of Czechoslovakia on October 30, 1938, he respectfully promised on November 10, 1938, in English, that he "would do his best"), he was not to become a literary man, as he had perhaps hoped, but at least he tried to combine his legal work with an interest in modern sculpture, painting, and the graphic arts, which he collected as long as he could. It is less known that he liked to hike through the woods and swim in the waters of Bohemian rivers, the colder the better, far beyond his middle age. A cousin of his, a parish priest in Prague-Žižkov (on the wrong side of the tracks), inspired him to become a mountain climber who liked to spend many vacation days in the Austrian and Slovene Alps and to become a founding member of the Czech Society of Alpinists, all male and serious about their business.

After finishing his studies, Hácha had worked for three years in a lawyer's office, but he felt restricted there, and by 1898 he had joined the august administrative Council of the Bohemian Kingdom, where he worked, originally under the supervision of Prince Jiří of Lobkovicz, for nearly eighteen years, steadily advancing in duties and rank. His idea was to be a true "civil servant" of the British kind, loyal to the law but not to any political party. (A civil servant would feel offended if somebody asked him about his allegiance to any political party, he later wrote, during the time of the republic.) He was called to Vienna in 1916, made a

Hofrat (court counselor), and appointed a member of Austria-Hungary's High Administrative Court. Yet the loyalty to his homeland was not in question, and when the Czechoslovak Republic was established in 1918, he returned from Vienna to Prague to join the High Administrative Court of Czechoslovakia. It was President Masaryk who appointed him, on January 22, 1925, to be its chief justice, guarding the legal privileges of the nation's political, administrative, and economic institutions and of those individuals who felt deprived of their constitutional rights and turned to the court for redress.

By 1909 Hácha's legal studies had begun to appear in the appropriate professional journals, e.g., an essay on "Procedures of British Parliamentarism"; he had joined the Prague Czech Faculty of Law as docent and member of examination commissions; and after 1926, together with a committee of distinguished professors he edited the massive *Dictionary of Czechoslovak Public Law*, writing more than a dozen entries himself, among them the one on labor law. He also wrote in 1934 a comparison of new Prussian and Czech laws concerning the administration of communes, suggesting in no uncertain terms that whoever believed in democracy and representative institutions would be forever unable to accept the dictates of a führer.

The terrible events of the Munich Conference in late September 1938 affected the life of every citizen of the liberal republic, perhaps none more so than Emil Hácha, for they prevented him from retiring, as he had hoped, to be a lawyer's lawyer in a little town in southern Bohemia, dedicating himself to his studies, his art collection, and the memory of his beloved wife, who had died in February. The republic, or what was left of it, underwent momentous changes, especially when it became the federal state of Czecho-Slovakia. Its political parties, earlier thirty-two and more in number, agreed to constitute what was paradoxically called an authoritative democracy based on the consensus of only two party organizations, the Party of National Unity (conservatives and right-wingers) and the Party of National Labor (left-wing liberals, Social Democrats, and a few Communists). The army, having capitulated, was demobilized following German orders. When under German pressure President Beneš abdicated on October 5 and left the country for England on October 22, the constitution required that the Parliament (still functioning) elect a new president. Most people agreed that the candidate should be somebody of real stature, and the list was long and colorful; some people thought of the industrialist Jan Bat'a, Czechoslovakia's wealthiest capitalist, others of the famous composer J. B. Foerster.

It was Rudolf Beran, seasoned head of the conservative Agrarians and now chief of the Party of National Unity, who, believing that the new president would have to face important questions of law, order, and reconstitution, nominated (perhaps manipulated) Hácha, who originally resisted the nomination but was quickly accepted by others, including the Party of National Labor. On November 9, 1938, both houses of Parliament gathered, as they had in Masaryk's republic, in Prague's great concert hall, the Rudolfinum, and by noon it was announced that 272 ballots in favor of Hácha (including 39 Slovak ones) had been cast. Hácha was ceremoniously invited to the hall, sternly took the oath of his new office, and was immediately driven to Hradčany Castle, his new seat. He remained there, or at nearby Lány Castle, until May 13, 1945, when a dying man, he was carried out on a stretcher by Czech police and taken to Pankrác Prison, where he was to be tried for his crimes. His daughter, Milada, who was taken with him, was let go, suddenly and less ceremoniously, at Letná Park; being without a roof over her head, she went to the apartment of her half Jewish ex-husband, who took her in, no questions asked.

Yet there was one occasion (little known but for the researches of the untiring Vít Machálek) when the civil servant and high judge, at a dramatic moment, tried to intervene in the political process. A few days before the Munich Conference, Hácha had remarked in a private letter that Chamberlain's attempt to save the peace might, unfortunately, succeed at Czechoslovakia's expense; the republic had been fortunate in past years, but now? Hácha anxiously telephoned Beneš, apologized that he was using his valuable time, and suggested that the president interrupt his discussions with the French and British and send a representative to Berlin to discuss matters with Hitler personally, in the hope that the worst could be prevented. Beneš politely answered that he would consider Hácha's suggestion, though it ran counter to many years of Czechoslovakia's foreign policies. When the conference was over, Hácha remarked in another private letter that Beneš should have weighed his suggestion, because history itself would judge whether sending a delegate to Berlin was at least something to have pondered seriously: "one would say that he confronted the raging monster face to face." Hácha did not dream that he himself would confront that raging monster only five months later.

March 15, 1939: The Day of Occupation

The plan for occupation of the Czech lands by the German army and police had been well prepared on secret orders of October 10 and December 17 from Hitler, who told the army to get ready for an action of "pacification" without any mobilization of additional troops, and it went off without a real hitch, though the weather was inclement, with occasional squalls of snow. The Czecho-Slovak Republic disintegrated; on the morning of March 15 the Prague newspapers reported that Slovakia had declared its independence; it was followed by Carpathian Ruthenia, which was immediately occupied by Hungarian troops.

The actual invasion of the country had started in the early evening of March 14 and continued through the night and the morning of March 15, with German troops marching in from the north and the northeast as well as from the Ostmark—that is, Austria—through southern Bohemia and Moravia. Regular troops and SS crossed the border in the far northeast near Koblov, Petřkovice, and Svinov to take the important coal and steel town of Ostrava, though these actions were roundly denied by German diplomats or explained away as a step to keep open communication to Slovakia. After 6:00 p.m. the Germans also took the nearby town of Místek, where lonely Czechoslovak troops of the Third Battalion of the Eighth Infantry Regiment at the Czajanka barracks, a former factory, close to the bridge over the Ostravica River, opened fire on the invaders, the only instance of spontaneous resistance by regular troops during that evening and night. By the early morning of March 15 German divisions, possibly as many as 350,000 men belonging to the Third and Fifth Heereskommando, and a few sundry units of other corps, were sweeping in four columns through the country. At approximately the same time, units of the German Luftwaffe, under command of Generals Kesselring, Speerle, and Löhr, moved into Czech airspace and occupied Prague's airfield, Ruzyně. The invaders did not know that Josef Mašín, commander of the First Czech Artillery Regiment stationed nearby (and later shot as a member of the resistance), had been ready to disobey orders and to defend the airfield with his men but was overpowered in a confrontation with his superiors willing to give in.

By 7:45 a.m. German troops coming from the north had reached the Mělník radio station (established by the Czechoslovak Republic some years earlier to counteract Nazi propaganda and make more liberal views known to Sudeten Germans) and begun broadcasting as Prager Volkssender II (Prague People's Broadcasting Station II), announcing that they would soon reach Prague. A few German university students in Prague marched out to the city limits to be the first to welcome the Wehrmacht soldiers. German columns reached Prague shortly before 9:00 a.m., with an advance of police cars seizing the central police station, and behind them motorized infantry, motorcycles, and armored vehicles with mounted machine guns. Meanwhile, at the main railroad station, heavy artillery pieces and tanks were unloaded and positioned at nearby Wenceslas Square, in the heart of the city and in front of the saints' and patrons' monument, at exactly 10:42 a.m., as the *Lidové noviny*, a once liberal paper, reported with mock exactitude. Other columns appeared at the Ministry of National Defense in Dejvice and at Hradčany Castle, still watched over by a Czech military honor guard, though the president was absent.

"V Praze je klid [Prague is calm]," the newspapers said unanimously, a recurrent phrase that revealed nothing of the confusion, despair, and shock of the city's Czech citizens (or the resolve of the Fascists to take power immediately). Extant photographs show black masses of people gathering in the streets and on the squares to watch the German columns roll by. A few enthusiastic German women, forming pockets in the crowds, threw little bouquets of violets and forget-me-nots, as Czech women and men (children were in school) watched in silence. Pictures show tears, grim faces, many clenched fists raised in the air, but also, especially later in the day, a good deal of curiosity about German weapons and motorcycles. Czech policemen in their dark coats and bobby helmets, often barely hiding their feelings, were out in force, holding people back on the sidewalks and directing traffic; Germans were driving on the right side, as in the Reich, but willingly switched to the left, in the Czech fashion, for the time being.

General Johannes Blaskowitz, chief of Army Group Three and now of occupied Prague, issued a declaration (printed with red borders, multiple copies were affixed everywhere around the city) telling the citizens in both German and correct Czech that public and economic life was to go on undisturbed. The Czech chief of police immediately declared a curfew from 9:00 p.m. to 6:00 a.m., affecting all public places, including cafés, theaters, and movie houses, but allowed working people to proceed to and from work by the shortest route. (The curfew was lifted within twenty-four hours.) German officers were polite, and rapidly a number of white glove and heel-clicking visits were made. General Hermann Geyer, of the infantry, visited the commanding officer at the Ministry of National Defense, another general called on Dr. Jiří Havelka, chief of President Hácha's office at the castle, and still another ranking officer paid his compliments to the lord mayor of Prague, who was later executed.

Observers in foreign embassies noted that the occupation of Prague was, in the first days, a military affair, at least in comparison with what had happened in Vienna a year earlier. In Vienna, Jews had been beaten and forced by their Nazi fellow citizens to clean the pavements (occasionally with toothbrushes), but in Prague the armed forces dominated the scene for the time being, and while in Austria advance units of the Gestapo had quickly arrested 70,000 people on their lists, the Czech police, bound to cooperate with the German security service by a little-known agreement of January 6, 1938, and eager to get rid of German anti-Nazi émigrés and Communists, had a list of 4,639 people, of whom the Gestapo, in its so-called *Aktion Gitter*, kept 1,228 because they had been active recently, it was said.

Two short notices buried in the newspapers among the military and world news on March 16 and 18 revealed what was to come. These notices reported on meetings of lawyers and doctors, both of whose organizations had recently introduced undisguised anti-Jewish resolutions, although for the time being the Czech government wanted to avoid the Jewish question for as long as it possibly could. The Czech Bar Association announced that its non-Aryan members (the term "Jewish" was carefully avoided) must name acceptable Aryan substitutes to take over their affairs, and if they did not do so within twenty-four hours, the association would simply take care of the matter by its own authority. The organizations of the Czech medical profession did not hesitate either and declared that being aware of their duties to the nation and recalling the many ways in which Czech and German doctors had loyally worked together in the past, all non-Aryan doctors must be removed immediately from their jobs in public health institutions.

These announcements had been anticipated by the unchecked activities of small Fascist groups within the bar association and the medical organizations, especially the ANO (Akce národní obrody, Action of National Renewal) people, and though the occupiers had not yet exerted any pressure, these two professions, called to safeguard the justice and health of Czechoslovak society, did not hesitate to take matters into their own hands. The Gestapo, at any rate, noted in its internal report that apart from a few incidents, the Czech population did not show any resistance worth speaking of. That was to change.

Hitler in Prague

Hitler had talked to Hácha about the "autonomy" (*Eigenleben*) of the Czechs, whom he personally despised, but formal terms of the future had yet to be defined. As soon as Hácha left Berlin, Friedrich Gauss, head of the legal department of the German Foreign Office, compiled a memorandum suggesting that there be two "protectorates," one for Bohemia and one for Moravia, and a "general resident" appointed to represent the interests of the German Reich in both. Clearly, as Vojtěch Mastný has shown in his analysis, the Foreign Office wanted to avoid having this issue come up in another international conference like that in Munich the year before and "to preserve the fiction," as Gauss put it, that the arrangement was based on an agreement with the Prague government.

On the spur of the moment Hitler decided in the morning of March 15 that he wanted to go to Prague himself. He gathered a group of party functionaries, military men, and experts from the Foreign Office and further surprised his entourage by switching in the Sudeten region (Böhmisch-Leipa) from his special train to a motorcade that took him along icy roads to Prague. The procession was headed by Karl Hermann Frank, one of the leaders of the Sudeten German Party and soon to be an indispensable part of Hitler's administration. It was dark when the group arrived at Hradčany Castle at 8:00 p.m. A splendid buffet prepared by the fashionable restaurateur Lippert had been gobbled up by a group of German occupation officers who thought that it had been prepared for them, but Lippert was flexible; new provisions were sent immediately, and Hitler had a repast of Czech beer and ham, against all his principles. When President Hácha, unaware that Hitler had arrived earlier, later met with members of the Czech government in another wing of Hradčany Castle, he was informed about the presence of the unwelcome guest under the same castle roofs.

During that night of March 15–16 the German Foreign Office experts set to work to prepare the final version of the Führer's decree on the protectorate of Bohemia and Moravia. The text was ultimately edited by Wilhelm Stuckart, a Nazi Party member since 1922, participant in Hitler's putsch in Munich in 1923, organizer of the storm troops, and, as secretary of state in the Ministry of the Interior, an old hand at incorporating occupied territories.

The decree, which did not dwell on President Hácha's presence in Berlin the day before, in its thirteen articles defined the legal status of the newly occupied territories and enabled the authorities of the Reich to abrogate the rights and privileges accorded to the occupied if they considered it useful or necessary. Article 1 stated that Bohemia and Moravia, occupied by the Wehrmacht, now "belonged to the territories of the Reich." Its German nationals would become *Reichsbürger* whose German blood and German honor would be protected by law, while all other citizens would be nationals (*Staatsangehörige*) of the protectorate (Article 2). The protectorate was to be "autonomous and administer itself" (3), and its president would (4) "enjoy the rights of a head of state." (Later it was even confirmed that he was to be commander in chief of a small national militia, mostly charged with being his guard of honor.) The Czech government had tried to insist on the legal idea of the nation's autonomy, but the decree, asserting that the Reich would take over the territories' foreign policy and defense (6 and 7), also declared that a *Reichsprotektor*, with the seat of authority in Prague (5), would be appointed and charged by the Führer with guarding the interests of the Reich and seeing to it "that the lines of policy laid down by the Führer and the Reichschancellor be observed"; he would be authorized "to object to measures that are calculated to injure the Reich," to stop the promulgation of laws, decrees, and other orders harmful to its interests or as far as they "contradict the spirit of protection undertaken by the Reich" (12).

The decree was read over the radio by Foreign Minister Ribbentrop in midmorning of March 16. (Hácha heard the proclamation in his room in the castle.) Hitler appeared on a balcony of some building for a moment to greet jubilant Germans; inspected, in the castle courtyard, a group of Nazi students (in their role as victims of Czech terror); briefly received members of the Czech government and President Hácha in audience; and was gone again immediately. Magic Prague did not attract the Führer; he slept over in the Sudetenland and the next day went by way of Olomouc and Brno to Vienna, where he took lodgings at the Hotel Imperial and announced two appointments: Konstantin Freiherr von Neurath became Reichsprotektor of Bohemia and Moravia, and K. H. Frank his second-in-command as secretary of state.

The Third Reich, Suddenly

The Third Reich started for me when somebody outside our apartment in Brno, the capital of Moravia, shouted "Herr Pol[l]ak, hängens die Fahne raus; die Daitschn sind da! [Mr. Pol[l]ak, run up the flag; the Germans are here!]" I still don't know whether his name was spelled with two l's (possibly Jewish) or one (probably Czech), but I learned later that day that the local Nazi Germans, with a good deal of help from outlying districts, had seized power in the city in advance of the Wehrmacht, which had marched in by midmorning. On the preceding day Nazis had clashed with Czechs in the streets, and the night had been full of confused and restless noises. My stepfather, a surgeon and active Social Democrat of Jewish origin, had hurriedly left, and I did not know whether he had told my mother that he was going to try to reach London, as I suspected, rather than Prague, as he told me; he left her to her lonely and courageous insistence that she did not wish to go abroad anyway because she wanted to stay close to the members of her Jewish family, above all her mother, in Prague.

I was sixteen, going on seventeen, inquisitive about politics, girls, movies, and jazz (in that order approximately) but old enough to grasp that the harsh and dangerous times about which everybody had been talking had suddenly arrived. I did not love my stepfather (being appalled by his clinical way of talking about sexual matters), but I liked his political ideas and his practical commitment. He came from a little Moravian town but had learned his socialism during his student years in Vienna and was personally close to many Austrian Socialists who had escaped to Moravia after the Austrian civil war of 1934. He helped edit their newspapers and other secret publications in a Brno suburb and smuggled these publications in his doctor's car over the border to Austria, my presence in the little Tatra auto suggesting that we were merely on a family outing. I read the papers he subscribed to—the Moravian Volksbote, which was close to the traditionalist Dr. Ludwig Czech, then a member of the Czechoslovak government, rather than to Wenzel Jaksch, of nationalist leanings, as well as the monthly Der Kampf, in which Otto Bauer, the most famous theoretician of Austrian socialism, untiringly analyzed the situation in terms beyond my comprehension—and I was very proud when he received a postcard from fighting Madrid in which Julius (Julio) Deutsch, once commanding the armed Socialist Austrian Schutzbund and now a general in the Spanish Republican Army, sent his greetings. My middle-class Czech school friends did not know what I was talking about when I told them of this.

My political education was much advanced by the war in Spain and by the Munich Conference; I went to demonstrate in the streets in support of Republican Spain, and when Czechoslovakia mobilized against Germany after Munich, I immediately enlisted in the National Guard as a volunteer (I was too young to join the army), was given a 1918 rifle, was instructed how to present arms (evidently of essential importance in the situation), and marched up and down a hill not far from an outlying tram station to train for guard duty. My new Czech friends in school, including the girls, were rather astonished when I appeared one morning in early September 1938 in a shabby guard uniform, a long Russian czarist bayonet dangling from my belt. My mother had just transferred me from a German to a Czech school, and some of my Czech verb forms were still a bit deficient, so I had a hard time explaining how it was that I had joined the guard, well known for its Czech nationalism. I said I had joined up not because of my national persuasion but because the Czechoslovak Republic was in danger. I am still proud of that decision, which instinctively put the idea of the democratic republic before language and ethnicity, and when we in the guard were demobilized after a few days, I went again to demonstrate in the streets, demanding that the government in Prague, which had ordered the army to leave the border fortifications without defending them, immediately resign and give way to another, more courageous and soldierly body.

As soon as I received permission from my school, we moved to Prague to join my grandmother and all the aunts and uncles on my mother's and father's sides. We moved with Grandmother into a modern penthouse apartment near Charles Square, my mother and grandmother sleeping in the bedroom, I on the couch in the living room; there was space enough because my uncle, who rented the apartment, had left with my stepfather on the last train to London via Holland (I had guessed right), where he was to work in an ammunitions factory and as an inspector of the London Midland railways throughout the war. At a time when it was important to belong to a distinct group, Czech or German (we did not yet know anybody professing Jewish nationality), I did not have much of a chance to align with a definite ethnic group with a proper identity (never mind my week in the National Guard), and I was satisfied to be accepted by most of my new Czech school friends, whose political attitudes I shared (more or less), as a kind of irregular guy who tried to fit in.

It would have been exceedingly difficult to explain my special ethnicity (if I had one) in those years of either-or simplifications or requirements. My mother's Jewish family had moved from a Bohemian village to the small town of Poděbrady (the birthplace of Kafka's mother) and shortly after 1900 to the more secure city of Prague. (After an unemployed man named Leopold

Hilsner had been falsely charged with the "ritual" murder of a Czech ser-
vant girl, provincial Jewish shops were subject to attacks by Czech mobs.)
My father's family had left the Gardena Valley in the South Tyrol, now a
center of fashionable German and Italian tourism, because they had noth-
ing to eat. They were not South Tyroleans in the traditional sense but
Ladin peasants, a minority group speaking their own language who, little
anticipating the historical consequences of this decision, began to speak
German when they migrated first to Linz in Upper Austria and, by 1885,
to Prague; only my paternal grandmother continued to speak Ladin there.

These two families, so different in origin, religion, and idiom, went on
living in mutual distrust and condescension, the Jewish one in the New
Town, where a few of my uncles assimilated to Czech culture, and the La-
dini, with their baroque Catholicism, in a rabbit warren flat in the most
ancient part of the Old Town (where, paradoxically, Franz Kafka's family
lived around the corner). When as a boy staying with the Ladins, I did not
come back home from a visit to my mother's family, my Ladin aunt was
ready to call the police. She feared that Christian boys (I had been bap-
tized) might be killed "by the Jews" because Christian blood was needed.
If she had known that there was a Seder that evening and that I was recit-
ing (or trying to recite) the first lines of a Hebrew prayer at the supper
table, she would have gone out of her mind.

Improvisation and Accommodation:
Czech Fascists and National Solidarity

A good deal of improvisation was the order of the day during the first
weeks of the occupation. The curfew was lifted, young people had the
chance to go to the movies again (at the elegant cinemas downtown,
six American movies were shown, and one German musical), and German soldiers and officers in their greenish uniforms flooded Prague
shops to buy, at an advantageous exchange rate, candy, cakes with
whipped cream (a particular hit), souvenirs, and textiles. Some shops
adjusted their business hours to deal with the new masses of customers. Czechs had reasons to laugh at the affair of the Bayrischer
Hilfszug, a caravan of soup kitchens that came from Bavaria to feed

"the starving elements of the population until the new order could provide work and bread for everyone," as George F. Kennan of the U.S.
Embassy remarked. The Czech poor were ready to bite the German
hand that wanted to feed it, and Czech authorities sold to the Germans at a profit all the provisions that they previously had distributed
free of charge to the 180,000 Czech, Jewish, and German refugees displaced from the Sudetenland just months before, at the time of Munich. Prague was not a hungry city. Most German soldiers went for the
beer garden U Fleků on Křemencová Street, where Czech and Germans competed, though at different tables, to down gargantuan meals
and to quaff liters of freshly brewed beer ("pivo jako křen," beer as tasty
as horseradish, the Czech adage goes).

The new administrators were in no hurry. They traveled to Berlin
and returned again, discussing the question whether the new supervi-
sory jobs should go to people from the Reich or to Sudeten Germans
(preferably the former). President Hácha, suddenly changing into an
active politician of considerable skill, as if he wanted to undo what he
had done in his night with Hitler, had his chance to deal with the
Czech Fascists, also pushing for power. Occupiers and occupied came
to agree, within forty-eight hours, that Czech Fascists and other ex-
treme groups of the right must be excluded from political life. Berlin
wanted a Czech administration based on a broad consensus rather
than on the activities of "adventurers" (a term that both Germans and
Czechs used). In the past Czech Fascists had been radically anti-
German and pro-Italian, and only after Hitler had come to power had
they been willing to deal with German National Socialists. The essential political issue was to deflect, absorb, or paralyze the political energies of General Radola Gajda, hero of the Czechoslovak Legion that, in
Russia and Siberia, had fought in 1914–18 on the Allied side for a free
Czechoslovakia, and the rabid Vlajka (Banner) people.

Among Czech generals, often inclined to sedentary careers, Gajda
(originally, Rudolf Geidl) was a colorful bird, if not an adventurous
condottiere of sorts, and even his friendly biographers believe that in
the Prague context, he was an outsider shaped by his early experience
in the Balkans and in Siberia. It may have been the constant and not
entirely unjustified misgivings of the liberal establishment that ulti-

mately pushed him to become the leader of the Czech Fascists. Born
in 1892 of a Czech father, who was serving as a noncom at the Austro-
Hungarian Navy base at Kotor in Croatia, and of a possibly Italian
mother, Gajda dropped out of school, desultorily trained as a chemist,
and volunteered for the Austro-Hungarian Army. But at the beginning
of the Great War Gajda crossed the lines to join the Montenegrin
Army, soon in total disarray, and was saved by a group of amiable Serb
officers who helped him enlist in the Serbian division of the Russian
Army. In 1917 he joined the Czechoslovak legions, bravely fought at
Zborov and Bachmač against Austrian Army units, quickly rose
through the ranks, and after 1918 defied Masaryk's order to refrain
from fighting the Bolsheviks. It must have been surprising to many that
he served in Admiral Aleksandr Kolchak's left-wing Siberian government and then, after Kolchak had established his own local dictatorship in Vladivostok in 1919, conspired against him in a failed revolt of
disappointed Socialists.

One year later Gajda was home again. He bought a villa in Říčany,
near Prague, where he settled down with his Russian wife (technically
he was a bigamist, but he paid off his Czech wife, who promptly married a small-town lawyer) and his art collections, only to discover that
the new independent republic of Czechoslovakia did not really know
what to do with him. He was first sent to the French War College
in Paris, where as a student he condescendingly lectured to his military teachers, then as commander of an infantry division, to eastern
Slovakia, facing hostile Hungary, before, allegedly to be under closer
scrutiny, being appointed deputy chief of staff in Prague. Gajda's adversaries, including Masaryk, Beneš, and the officers of the French
military mission in Prague, did not cease to distrust him. Suddenly rising and spectacularly falling, by 1926 he was (on wobbly evidence) accused of spying for the Soviet Union and of organizing a revolt to
destroy the republic. Against the findings of an investigating commission of generals, he was stripped of his rank and most of his pension.
He responded by donning the uniform of a czarist general, adorning it
with the highest military decorations awarded him by France and
Great Britain (he returned the decorations after Munich), and assuming the leadership of the National Fascist Community, which he briefly

came to represent, twice, in Parliament. (In national elections in 1935 the Fascists received 167,433 votes.)

Czech Fascism was never a mass movement, but its small and agitated groups were in constant motion, collaborating with and opposing one another, trying to build unified organizations and splitting up again. In the late 1930s there were at least three of them: the National Fascist Community, gathered around Gajda; the ANO group (Akce národní obrody, Action of National Renewal), particularly aggressive among intellectuals; and the Vlajka (Banner) group, with which the ANO made common cause after February 1939. On March 3, 1939, days before the German occupation, Gajda was received by President Hácha, and this completed his rehabilitation. He was to be reinstated to his former military rank, and his pension paid back in full, but in return Gajda had to sign a document swearing that he would be loyal to the government; a trip to Germany, where he was to defend the Czech cause, was even discussed. But the situation changed rapidly, and he did not feel bound by his promise, or not immediately. On the eve of the German invasion Gajda presented himself at the German Embassy as its coming man, declared publicly he was the leader of the new nation, and after the Germans had arrived, he invited the Prague Fascists to meet at the Uhelný (Coal) Market for further action. Only three hundred showed up.

Gajda immediately paid a visit to General Eccard Freiherr von Gablenz, deputy commander of Germany's occupying force, who encouraged a Fascist committee in abstract terms. Within twenty-four hours, however, Gajda found himself outflanked by the concerted action of Hácha and the Germans. On March 17 he was invited to the office of the president, where he was informed that a unified new Czech citizens' organization, called National Solidarity, was being created, and that he was welcome to join it. (He was never appointed to the guiding committee, reserved for those who had served in the liberal First Republic.) On the next day, March 18, a joint communiqué of General Blaskowitz and the Czech government noted that public power was in the hands of the occupying forces and the legitimate Czech government; private organizations or groups of whatever kind (meaning the Fascists or the Vlajka people) were not allowed to intervene in public affairs. It surprised many that Gajda, who basically did not like Germans, wisely withdrew to a country mill, which he bought with his pension, and honorably helped Czech officers hostile to the occupation to escape via Poland to the west.

The Vlajka people had no scruples about collaborating actively with the occupying forces and serving as informers to the Gestapo. Originally a club of right-wing students at the faculties of philosophy and law at Charles University in Prague, established in April 1930, the Vlajka group and its periodical had emerged during the Depression years, enjoying the fleeting sympathies of the conservative poet Viktor Dyk and resolutely opposing the liberal establishment. Led by Jan Vrzalík, later a professor at a small-town school, it was at first demonstrably Fascist in the Italian sense, opposing Germans, Jews, Marxists, Freemasons, and nearly everybody else, but as soon as Hitler became chancellor in Germany, Vrzalík began to admire his power and turned the Vlajkas' spite against German, and often Jewish, left-wing émigrés in Prague. Vlajka students were among the ringleaders of the street battles that broke out in the fall of 1934, when Czech nationalists of all colors demanded that the ancient insignia (and medieval Carolinum Hall) of Prague's divided university, still in possession of the German faculties there, be handed over to the Czech faculties.

In the days of Munich and after they had played their cards as superpatriots, the Vlajka people flooded Prague with leaflets, demolished a few village synagogues, hunted down Jewish guests in city cafés, and firebombed Jewish shops and apartment buildings. When the Germans marched in, the Vlajkas entertained high hopes of assuming power immediately, meeting at the Prague restaurant Bumbrlíček and the Café Technika (a traditional student haunt) to work on a list of their people who would take over (among them Jan Rys-Rozsévač, their leader, as putative head of government). But together with Gajda, they were pushed to the sidelines, where the occupation regime used them to exert pressure on the government and to denounce, in their newspapers, liberals and Jews.

Hácha announced in his first speech that he was thinking of a unified organization that would represent all Czechs, and by March 26 he had appointed a steering committee to establish it and to guide its activities. The Národní souručenství (National Solidarity) was to be defined by its rather diffuse program of national togetherness and Christian morality, and this was enough to split the Fascist groups into those who wanted to join and those who did not. In practice, Hácha shrewdly relied on the strength of Czechoslovakia's republican traditions, and after consulting with the chiefs of the Party of National Unity and the Party of National Labor, now in the process of self-liquidation, he appointed people who had had strong records during the pre-Munich First Republic. The Agrarian Party leader Adolf Hrubý was chairman; Captain Šimon Drgáč, formerly of army intelligence, was secretary-general (within months, he was arrested by the Gestapo because of his work in the resistance); and Professor Miloslav Hýsek was appointed by Hácha to preside over the Kulturní rada (Board of Culture). Hýsek was a man who celebrated the Czechs as a "nation of readers" but as time went on, he had to pay for his illusion of his nation's cultural autonomy (as the critic Vincenc Červinka suggested) by praising the Nazi idea of a new Fascist Europe. People rightly perceived the Národní souručenství as a defense organization, dominated on the regional and local level by second-tier functionaries of the old Czechoslovak parties. In Moravia, Catholics were running the show (though Fascist pressure was heavy), and in Prague the local organization was dominated by officers of Beneš's National Liberal Party, continuing to exert massive influence through its Melantrich Publishing House and its newspaper *České slovo* (Czech Word), with a print run of more than a million copies a day.

The German Sicherheitsdienst (SD, the Security Service), remarkably candid in its internal evaluations of what was going on, reported that the Národní souručenství was not a movement of revolutionary renewal but relied on personalities well known from the past. That was exactly what attracted citizens to join it, of course, and within a month, it was reported, 97 percent of all Czech male adults had signed applications to become members. (If you wore the badge of the NS upside down, people whispered, it suggested SN, or Smrt Němcům [Death to the Germans].) Jews were excluded, and Vlajka informers discovered early that the NS considered it a task of honor to support the families of people whom the Germans imprisoned or sent to concentration camps. Although the NS did all this skillfully by using inconspicuous accounts at local bank branches to make support payments, the Gestapo in the course of events arrested 137 of its functionaries and executed 43 of them. Later it was announced that the NS would concentrate on cultural, not political, affairs, and by June 1940, after the arrests of the lord mayor of Prague, Otakar Klapka, and of the Prague secretary of the NS, Dr. Josef Nestával (who had successfully established a communications link via Bratislava and Budapest to Belgrade), all National Solidarity activities in Prague were quashed, though the national organization dragged on, its own shadow, until the days of open revolt.

Haven and Hell for Refugees

"We drove through the town around midnight," George F. Kennan of the U.S. Embassy noted early on March 16. "It was strange to see these Prague streets, usually so animated, now completely empty and deserted. We were acutely conscious . . . that the curfew had indeed tolled the knell of a long and distinctly tragic day." Kennan had watched fearful crowds seeking protection in the courtyards of the British and American embassies earlier that day, and he knew that among the people suddenly affected, none were more in danger than German-speaking anti-Nazi refugees (as the Aktion Gitter was demonstrating). Prague had once been their haven and was now their hell—whether they were Jews who had sought rescue in Masaryk's republic, or non-Jewish intellectuals and writers whose books had been burned in the Third Reich, or functionaries of the German left, Communists, or Social Democrats (defeated Austrian Socialists came to Brno after 1934).

In 1933, when Hitler came to power, the frontier between Bohemia and Germany had been porous, and in Moravia, railway lines were occasionally operated by Socialist crews. The Czechoslovak Republic then, with its strong parties of the left and its many German-language newspapers, theaters, and schools, was more attractive to Hitler's German enemies than Piłsudski's Poland or Horthy's Hungary. Unofficial estimates put the number of refugees from Germany at fifteen hundred (not all of them registered) every year after 1933. Efficient support committees had almost spontaneously sprung up in Prague right away. Among them were the Demokratische Flüchtlingshilfe (Democratic Refugees Support Organization) and the Jüdische Flüchtlingshilfe (Jewish Refugees Support Organization), and two years later the Communist Rote Hilfe (Red Help). These offered food, lodging, and meager pocket money in legal and sometimes in many illegal ways; they also helped German-speaking refugees confront Czechoslovakia's formidable bureaucracy.

Among the first wave of refugees were many who in the 1920s had left their native Czechoslovakia to write, publish, or edit important newspapers in liberal Germany and who now returned to Prague, cherishing their Czechoslovak citizenship, which enabled them to earn a kind of living in their profession, if they were lucky, and again to blend into the German literary world of Prague to which they had originally belonged. Most of these writers came early in 1933 and by 1937–38 or 1939 at the latest had left for England, the United States, or Palestine, where they usually continued to publish in German. The roaming reporter Egon Erwin Kisch, for example, close to the Comintern apparatus, often came to Prague to look after his aging mother in the old family home on Melantrichova Street; Bruno Adler published an important novel about the so-called Hilsner affair (the turn-of-the-century "ritual" murder) before going to England; the critic Willy Haas continued to edit literary magazines (he went to India in time); the novelist Hans Natonek was published in the liberal *Prager Tagblatt* and ultimately went, via Paris, to Arizona; Walter Tschuppik, who put out a weekly newspaper in Prague that was supported by the Ministry of Foreign Affairs, reached London only in 1940. Others less fortunate did not manage to escape in time and died by their own hand or in the camps. Ernst Weiss, novelist, playwright, and medical doctor, escaped to France only to commit suicide when Paris fell to the Germans in 1940; the newspaper editor Emil Faktor died in Lodz in 1941; and the poet Camill Hoffmann, long a member of the Czechoslovak diplomatic service in Vienna and Berlin, was deported to Terezín and, later, to Auschwitz, where he died in 1944. It was not merely a matter of sitting in the refugee café Continental exchanging the latest news.

As a way station of exile or a place to stay for a while before going on, Prague attracted many of the writers hated by Hitler's Reich. Some of them, like Bertolt Brecht, stayed just a few days, weeks, or months to breathe freely again. Erich Maria Remarque later wrote a novel about his Prague experiences. Others came to offer public lectures to friendly audiences; they included Lion Feuchtwanger and Heinrich Mann and his brother Thomas, who acquired Czechoslovak citizenship in 1936 and said then he would consider it a happy task to be a good German and a citizen of Czechoslovakia at the same time (he later became a U.S. citizen). Many others stayed for years in close and creative solidarity with their fellow refugees and Czech intellectuals and artists; among them were Friedrich Burschell, the German translator of Proust; the novelist Bruno Frank; young Stefan Heym, much liked by the brothers Čapek and later prominent in East Germany; Franz Pfemfert, defender of the avant-garde; and the Viennese writer Friedrich Torberg, who had grown up in Bohemia and knew Czech well.

Writers were joined by artists of the most different temperaments. From Berlin came John Heartfield (born Helmut Herzfelde), master of the satirical photomontage, who stayed for six years and helped edit the *Arbeiter Illustrierte Zeitung*, distributed all over non-Fascist Europe and the Soviet Union. From Austria came Oskar Kokoschka, who acquired Czechoslovak citizenship in 1935, had long conversations with President Masaryk, and painted his most famous modern portrait of Masaryk. Young Peter Weiss came to Prague to study painting at the Academy of Fine Arts, watched Masaryk's funeral (about which he wrote a moving essay), and left after four years for Sweden, where he later became one of the most important German playwrights of the postwar age.

The situation was complicated by the uncertain, if not divided, attitude of the Czechoslovak authorities toward this considerable group of German-speaking, politically active refugees, often organized by the Communist Party or manipulated by it. In Prague it was evident that the liberal Ministry of Foreign Affairs differed, in its views, from the conservative and nationalist Ministry of the Interior, run by the Agrarian Party. Masaryk, Beneš, and the Foreign Ministry were eager to demonstrate Czechoslovakia's democratic virtues on the international scene and often supported refugee writers, employing them on week-lies or periodicals subsidized by the government, while the police, di-rected from the Ministry of the Interior, looked askance at the political activities of so many foreigners in Prague and promptly intervened when German "neighbors" complained too vociferously.

As early as April 1933, the police prohibited preparation for an anti-Fascist workers' congress in Prague (it had to shift to Copenhagen and Paris) and later eagerly watched over an international exhibit of politi-cal caricatures arranged by the Czech artists' Club Mánes, removing everything that offended the sensibilities of the Third Reich. Their police actions were fully backed by the Czech conservative and right-wing press, in which anti-German and anti-Semitic arguments curi-ously alternated. As the 1930s wore on, pressure increased, and the Ministry of the Interior and the police began checking on the refugees' political activities, arrested many for a while, and prepared a new ad-ministrative ruling to restrict them to several districts in the interior of Bohemia and Moravia. (Liberal counterpressure was too heavy, and it was never promulgated.)

In spite of all the economic and mounting political difficulties, the refugees in Prague, whether living with friends, in collective apart-ments, or in the run-down castle of Mšec, which they restored with their own hands but had to vacate in 1937 to make room for the Czechoslovak Army, were remarkably headstrong and productive. Their presence in the city, much maligned by their enemies, constitutes a largely forgotten chapter of cultural solidarity between German and Czech intellectuals and writers. If in the short *Germinal* of 1848 Czechs and Germans had worked together for the revolution, which had then split into national branches by May 1848, in the mid-1930s they worked together for many years with a firm purpose in mind and learned from each other.

The cause of the refugees was supported, on the Czech side, by F. X. Šalda, the most important literary critic of his generation, who mobilized an efficient Czech Committee of Aid (with an office at the Fénix Palace on Wenceslas Square), and he was readily supported by

Professor Otokar Fischer, translator of Goethe's *Faust* into Czech; the writers Josef Kopta and Marie Pujmanová; the actor Václav Vydra of the National Theater; the painter Emil Filla, as well as Jiří Voskovec and Jan Werich of the Liberated Theater and many others. E. F. Burian, an inventive left-wing producer, introduced in his theater the renowned Voice Band, or collective recitation; it was taken over by the German Studio 34, organized by the refugees Hedda Zinner and Fritz Erpenbeck, who were important in the theater of the GDR after the war. The Bert Brecht Club, though strictly Communist-organized, in the name of the Popular Front arranged lectures on the Czech poet Jiří Wolker and even Masaryk, while the Club of Czech and German Theater Folk programmatically shared languages, texts, actors, and theaters. On May 23, 1936, the latter produced the (originally) bilingual comedy *The Czech and the German,* written in 1812 by the playwright Jan Nepomuk Štěpánek (1783–1844), in the Czech Theater of the Estates (President Beneš attended); the performance was repeated a week later in the Neues Deutsches Theater (New German Theater). This heroic feat had never been attempted before and was not ever duplicated in the long, uneasy history of Czech-German cultural relations.

Life was difficult for German-speaking refugees in Prague, but after Munich, when so many more Czechs, Jews, and Germans hurriedly left the Sudeten regions to seek protection in what was left of the republic, the situation turned desperate, and it was not made easier by the conservative, nationalist turn of the new Czecho-Slovak government. People tried to leave, legally and illegally. (A few young Jews even joined a group of Viennese going to the Dominican Republic to establish an agrarian collective there.) Some refugees left by way of the Beskid Mountains to Poland and thence to France, for the time being, or Great Britain (especially Czechoslovak Army officers and Air Force personnel), or down the Danube via Hungary and Romania to creaking freighters bound for Palestine, though strict British military rules prohibited this. Kafka's friend Max Brod took the last train heading to the Polish border on the evening of March 14, discovered the next morning that the railway station at Ostrava had been occupied by German troops during the night, but succeeded in crossing to Poland, and reached Jerusalem. It is said that he always kept the Prague telephone directory of 1938 on his desk.

The Destruction of Prague's Liberal German Institutions

The dramatic events of the years 1938–39 in Prague have rarely been described fully because views are often obscured by exclusive national sympathies, Czech or German, ignoring, if not obliterating, the Jewish contribution to the achievements of Prague's liberal institutions, especially those emerging from German cultural traditions. If the late 1930s were the most productive time of Czech-German cultural cooperation because of the presence of so many German-speaking intellectuals and artists (all, Jewish or not, agreeing with liberal Czechs and their antinationalist assumptions), they were also the years of the rapid breakdown and destruction of Prague's liberal German institutions. Their rise and tragic fall, among so many collective and individual tragedies, have left only a few traces in the consciousness of a fading generation and almost none in the written history. Munich was the beginning of the end of it; after it, the German theater closed, and the German university in Prague underwent its own Anschluss to the Reich. The *Prager Presse*, having been the German voice of the liberal Czechoslovak government associated with Masaryk, and the national-liberal *Bohemia* both ceased publication on December 31, 1938, and the *Prager Tagblatt*, famous for its economic reports and literary contributions, went through its own agony until it too was silenced by the occupation authorities on April 4, 1939.

It is little known that the New German Theater, built in 1888 and run by the Swiss Paul Eger since 1932, had closed its doors forever five days *before* the Munich dictate had been accepted by the Czechoslovak government. The Prager Theaterverein had been in debt for a while and was unable to support the institution any longer. It had produced plays by many authors forbidden in Nazi Germany, from Arthur Schnitzler to Bertolt Brecht, as well as important Czech plays in German translation by František Langer, Fráňa Šrámek, and Karel Čapek (for example, his anti-Fascist play *The Mother*, with the famous Tilla

Durieux in the lead), and could pride itself on employing some of the best actors and actresses of the time, émigrés or not. But it was its uneasy fate that it had to perform for a language island of only ten thousand potential ticket buyers, and state subsidies were substantially lower (12 percent) than those awarded to theaters playing in the language of the state. The difference had to be made up by private sponsors, big and small, many of whom were Jewish—for example, the family that owned the Petschek Bank and the heroic optician Moritz Deutsch, who had supported the theater for decades out of his own pocket. But times were uncertain, and when the theater ran out of money and stopped paying salaries and wages (actors and stagehands rightly protested in the press, but to no avail), immediate bankruptcy proceedings were avoided only because it sold its building to the state. President Hácha was wise enough to extend these proceedings ad infinitum; after the German Army had marched in by early spring, a new German theater was organized there by the Office of the Reichsprotektor.

The German university in Prague changed within a year to an institution of the Third Reich, while its Czech sister, inasmuch as it functioned under the occupation at all, remained loyal to the republic. The original university in Prague had been established by Emperor Charles IV in 1348, intending his universitas to serve "all inhabitants of his kingdom." Its two components, Czech and German, had parted ways in 1882–83, however, and the national conflicts were only intensified by the republican "Lex Mareš" of 1920 that declared the Czech faculties true heir to Charles's university. A strike of anti-Semitic German students in 1922 against the Jewish rector, Samuel Steinherz, and street battles in Prague about the university insignia in 1934 markedly intensified national and political tensions.

The days before and after Munich showed that the situation was untenable. When on September 18, 1938, the Czechoslovak minister of education requested the university's German professors to take a stand against the nationalist Henlein and his like, nearly half of them left Prague for Vienna and Bavaria, where they waited for orders from the Nazi organizations. There was much talk of shifting the university to the Sudetenland, but Hitler himself decided it should stay in Prague. On

November 9 the German professors, who had disregarded all requests by the Czechs to come back, returned triumphantly and immediately began remaking the university in their own image. Though the Czech government was to declare on January 27, 1939, that Jews no longer could serve the state, the German university did not wait so long and on its own, mostly through the deans, went about removing Jewish faculty and students (about 10 percent of the enrollment) during the fall and winter of 1938. Seventy-seven teachers were furloughed or dismissed, and since nearly half of these were members of the medical faculty, the university clinics were left in a deplorable state. On September 1, 1939, the German university became by law an educational institution of the Reich, and ten weeks later, after student demonstrations on November 15, the Czech university was closed down.

It did not come as a surprise to knowledgeable people that the *Prager Presse*, a newspaper established in 1921 and closely associated with Masaryk, was unable to survive Munich. Its editor in chief, Arne Laurin, was a critical mind of the first rank, and he had been valiantly supported by the translator Otto Pick (a friend of Franz Kafka's), who succeeded in persuading some of the best European minds, among them Albert Einstein, Hugo von Hofmannsthal, and Hermann Hesse, to contribute and to make its feuilleton pages instrumental in showing the German reader, if he would only open his eyes, the richness and vitality of liberal Czech and Slavic culture in the 1920s and 1930s. It may have helped, at least initially, that the *Prager Presse*, subsidized by the government, was paying in hard Czech crowns when inflation raged in Germany and Austria. In its melancholy leave-taking from its readers, the *Prager Presse* looked back on eighteen years in the service of the republic and rightly extolled its intentions of impartiality, its efforts to balance political opposites, and, above all, its systematic resolve to demonstrate the many virtues of Czech intellectual life.*

On the black day of December 31, 1938, simultaneously with the *Prager Presse*, the *Deutsche Zeitung Bohemia*, owned by the old Prague

---

*The literary historian Ladislav Nezdařil has demonstrated that of the 845 translations of contemporary Czech poetry published by the *Prager Presse*, at least 400 were contributed by Pavel Eisner; among them were poems by Vrchlický, Mácha, Nezval, Toman, Hora, and Sova. In this respect, not even the famous *Prager Tagblatt* could compete.

Haas family, ceased publication too. Its national-liberal orientation, so productive in 1828, when it was founded, and above all, in the revolutionary days of 1848, ninety years later had become a liability, if not an anachronism. Liberals were suspicious of the new nationalism, and new nationalists were turning to the Reich to fulfill their political demands; the difficulty of combining these increasingly divergent ideas was fully reflected in the *Bohemia*'s twentieth-century history. In 1919 it had been briefly silenced by Czechoslovak censors because it supported the idea of autonomy for the Sudetenland, and after 1933 it was confiscated in Germany because many anti-Nazi refugees contributed to its pages. The novelist and editor Ludwig Winder (later an exile in London) defined its loyalty to the Czechoslovak Republic "as being without any illusions but true and genuine."

The *Bohemia* left the scene with dignity and without bending its knees to anybody. "In the midst of the tragic fatalities of our time," the editors declared, "we should not bury ourselves in sentimentalities." It was the oldest newspaper in Czechoslovakia, the second oldest in the ancient dual monarchy of Austria-Hungary, and now many people—its writers, editors, printers, and machinists—who had been working for it for thirty or even fifty years were losing not only their daily bread but part of their lives' meaning. The editors were proud that the *Bohemia* had been the first "activist" paper to defend the participation of liberal and Socialist parties in the government of the republic, and those who called it a chauvinist publication were as wrong as those who believed it had become disloyal to German interests. "Activism was only the most recent shape of Bohemism," or the living community of the two nations, German and Czech, the editors said. It is moving to read that in its last issue the newspaper quoted to its readers the warning of the early-nineteenth-century German political philosopher Johann Gottlieb Fichte against false national self-aggrandizement, celebrated the German belief in liberty and the justice of laws, and predicted that the spark of freedom, now almost dying, would never be extinguished completely.

The *Prager Tagblatt* was younger than the venerable *Bohemia*, but it had early developed an efficient network of European correspondents who used the new technological possibilities of the telephone to report on political and economic developments at home and abroad, including the stock exchanges of Zurich, London, and New York. It had appeared as a fully fledged newspaper for the first time on December 24, 1875, and its original owner, a southern German named Heinrich Mercy, who had come to Prague via Milan, left it to his brother Wilhelm, and he in turn to his two daughters, one of whom became Countess Nostitz and the other Baroness Benies. The two were not absolutely resistant to the political pressures of the 1930s, for they did not renew the contract of the Jewish editor in chief, Sigismund Blau. Yet the *Prager Tagblatt* had a splendid history of editors and contributors, starting with Karl Tschuppik (after 1910) and continuing with Egon Erwin Kisch; Kafka's most loyal friend, Max Brod (1924–39); Emil Ludwig; Richard Katz; and Rudolf Thomas, and it always opened its pages readily to T. G. Masaryk, publishing his speeches, in and out of Parliament, and commenting on his political decisions with particular care and sympathy.

In the tragic months after Munich, the *Prager Tagblatt* loyally identified with Masaryk's republic, even long after the liberal German parties had dissolved, and it soberly reported on the inevitable changes, including President Beneš's abdication and his first days in exile. The editors tried to assuage its readers' justified fears and, on October 1, 1938, keenly analyzed the possibly "good side" of the "amputation of the republic," which would now become nationally and politically more integrated. Openly speaking about the "defection" of the "antidemocratic Sudeten Germans," they suggested that the new situation would ultimately strengthen the "democratic character of the republic" and that after a high tide of Fascism, democracy would emerge victorious again. The editors did not see any reason to change their cultural policies; the literary pages surveyed the production of the anti-Fascist publishers Berman-Fischer, Allert de Lange, and, in Amsterdam, Querido; discussed new books by Heinrich and Thomas Mann, Franz Werfel, and Stefan Zweig; and respectfully published a thoughtful commentary on the death on December 28, 1938, of the internationally celebrated Czech writer Karel Čapek, whom many perceived as symbolic of the First Republic, mentioning President Hácha's compassionate telegram to his widow.

The efforts of the paper to calm any fears ran counter to the beliefs of many readers, Jewish or not, that they must try to leave the country as soon as possible. The gap between the last pages of the paper, devoted to advertisements, and the editorial part was striking. The former made it clear that many readers wanted to be reeducated in crafts or technologies useful beyond the oceans, while on page three the Prague Jüdischer Freitisch-Verein (which gave free meals to the Jewish poor) undisturbedly announced its regular general meeting. Among the advertisements were one looking for a producer of handkerchiefs for overseas; one for the Meadow School, Bucks, England, which promised reduced fees for younger Jewish girls (only twenty-eight pounds, approximately $115, quarterly); one for a South American settlement looking for "capitalists" and artisans; and one from people ready to go to Panama and Palestine that offered commercial services. By midautumn these realities had penetrated to the middle of the paper, where Joseph Wechsberg (who later wrote for *The New Yorker*) wrote a number of instructive articles on how to book inexpensive passage to the United States, how to deal with questions about the necessary affidavits, and how to go about finding a first job there, always relying on the power of positive thinking and a clean suit. The most revealing signal of the terrible events to come was the suicides of the editor in chief, Rudolf Thomas, only recently appointed, and his wife, who, despairing of the future, took poison on October 10. While the published eulogies extolled his erudition and his universal interests, they were careful not to reveal that he and his wife had died by their own hands.

It was as if Thomas had had an inkling of what would happen to his newspaper on March 15, 1939, and after his Jewish colleagues no longer showed up in their offices. On the day of the occupation, the *Prager Tagblatt*, instead of being true to its distinguished past, immediately switched allegiance and, at the top of page one, printed a declaration addressed to the *Reichspressechef*, Otto Dietrich, saying that its editors and employees (*Gefolgschaft*) accepted his leadership, signing off with an unusual "Heil Hitler!" For at least two weeks the *Prager Tagblatt*, suddenly a kind of Nazi specter, represented the views of the occupiers, praised the occupation as an act of German history, reported on the Führer's trip from Berlin to Prague, and immediately registered the initial moves for the removal of Jews from public positions, the *Entjudung*. In the literary pages, instead of a writer from the Prague group, an Austrian blood-and-soil author named Karl Heinrich Waggerl made an ominous appearance (opening the gates to Bruno Brehm, Heinrich Zillich, and their like), and even in the ads unemployed "Aryans" now looked for loans or positions in industry. Paradoxically, the business pages remained unchanged, and while Hitler dominated page one, business people and economists had a good chance to study what was happening on the stock exchanges of Budapest, Paris, and New York and how cotton and oil were faring in Chicago. But if the management of the *Prager Tagblatt*, spitting in its own eyes, had hoped to preserve its paper in Nazi shape, it was mistaken, because the occupation authorities had other plans. On April 4 the *Prager Tagblatt* ceased to exist, and on April 5 the Office of the Reichsprotektor used its facilities to publish issue number one of the new daily *Der neue Tag* (The New Day), the official voice of the occupiers. The premises and printing presses of the Mercy enterprise were quickly taken over by the new Bohemia-Moravian Publishing and Printing Corporation. The last vestige of Prague's last liberal institution had been obliterated.

In My New School

The Academic Gymnasium, my new school, was an elite institution with a distinguished past, whether the language of instruction had been German, as in the old monarchy, or Czech, in the republic, and it was still located in the monastery of the Piarists, an old teaching order, in the center of town. My fellow students came from important families (one, an amiable and quietly elegant nerd, was the son of the chief of police; others were daughters and sons of lawyers and surgeons), and commuting proletarians from the outlying industrial suburbs were rare. More than ever, the old school prided itself on being a bastion of patriotism, tradition, and learning, with daily cultivation of Greek and Latin, and it was especially concerned with intense instruction in Czech literature, the most modern not excluded; the German occupation was not considered worth mentioning.

I was totally ignored by my math teacher, who knew about my background but did not want to create difficulties for me. Sensing that I would not understand his algebraic formulas in any language, he gave me a passing grade without ever speaking to me. I enjoyed reading new Czech literature in a class taught by a young and scholarly professor who noticed that I once compared Otokar Březina's mystical poetry to that of R. M. Rilke. Our teacher of German and history, fresh from Charles University, silently suggested a private truce with me as far as German was concerned; whenever she explicated a new German syntactical rule, she would briefly glance in my direction to see whether I would nod imperceptibly in agreement. Besides, she rarely ventured among us backbenchers because my friend Vladimír, sitting next to me, always stroked her hand softly when she put it on our desk. Fortunately for my academic career, my classmate Kari (Prince) Lobkovicz was graciously inclined to let me crib from his math examinations, and we became friends for life.

One day our professor of Czech literature announced that the school was continuing its tradition of encouraging students to write long essays on questions of literature or history to vie for prizes to be awarded by the school principal, and I quickly decided that I should compete. But I needed an appropriate topic. On my way home I remembered the writer Johannes Urzidil, who had paid my mother a visit before escaping to England. While paging through his book on Goethe and Bohemia, I had noted that Goethe had corresponded with a number of distinguished Prague intellectuals, among them Count Kaspar Sternberg, founder of the National Museum, and I decided to write my paper on Goethe and Prague, the "and" being rather fragile because Goethe, who went often to Bohemia's elegant spas, never ventured to Prague, rightly assuming that a trip to the Bohemian capital would only create political difficulties: Germans and Czechs would be watching too closely to see to whom he would be paying his respects. When my paper received second prize (the first going to a more patriotic one), I felt strengthened in my resolve to become a literary historian; I also learned from my professor that the principal had welcomed a paper on Goethe, greatest of German poets, in case the Nazi school inspector might check on the competition. (I could only pray that when he did, he would not proceed to my bibliography, consisting of the lonely name of Urzidil, who had just established himself in his London exile.) Sixty-five years later I gave a speech at an international Prague Urzidil conference and was present when a tablet reminding the world that Urzidil had attended the famous gymnasium in the times of old Austria was unveiled near the school gate, next to the new Prague branch of Jean Paul Gaultier, which had recently opened its shop in the building.

Movie Dates and Our "Corso"

In my new school, movie dates were important, and they followed a strict ritual from which a well-educated seventeen-year-old gentleman did not dare deviate. The young women, all from our school, sixteen or seventeen years old, and well coiffed, expected a tie, jacket, and clean shirt and tickets (only middle to back rows) to a fashionable movie (American, French, or Czech), preferably shown at the Cinema Juliš, at Wenceslas Square, or the expensive Cinema Broadway, nearby. Any sharing of expenses was considered unenlightened or a sign of inappropriate and unbridled intimacy, and the young man was also expected to buy the ice-cream treat, elegantly called Eskimo Brick, sold by the neatly uniformed usherettes during the long intermission. One could hardly touch the hand of the lady (or only fleetingly), admire her when she smoked a bold cigarette on the darkened street, and accompany her home by tram (another 2,40 Czech crowns [less than eight cents]).

Fortunately I was not entirely constrained by this middle-class ritual because there was always Libushka circling the box offices before the four-thirty showing of the less stylish cinemas—in the arcades of Wenceslas Square, for instance, the Aleš, or the Bio Skaut, in the upper reaches of Vodičkova Street (that's where I saw my first Marx Brothers movie). She was sixteen or less, pale, clad in a dress borrowed from her mother, looked a little older, but the ushers at the entrance were, in the afternoon, tolerant about age, as long as everybody had a valid ticket. It was a kind of blind date because Libushka was there to find any high school kid who would pay for a ticket and, equally important, for a little paper bag of cheap chocolates, which she munched incessantly. Whatever film it was mattered more than the escort. She sat in her seat erect, concentrated on what was happening on the screen with her almost protuberant eyes, and

*did not care at all whether I (hesitatingly) touched her knees or breasts—
a case of perfect mutual understanding. Years later I came to read Jan
Neruda's late-nineteenth-century story "At the Three Lilies" (in his* Tales),
*about a working-class girl of almost innocent sensuality haunting a cheap
Prague dance hall just to have the feeling of being alive. Neruda's fiction
and my memories of guileless Libushka (anno 1939) are one in my mind.*

*Hitler was threatening Poland, demanding Danzig, and we walked up
and down, preferably between 5:00 and 6:00 p.m. along our student
"Corso," the block that extended from the Café Juliš, an architectural
monument of Czech constructivism of the early 1920s, down to the Bat'a
corner on the left of Wenceslas Square, to parade our new ties and to cast
fiery glances at the girls in their newly ironed blouses with, perhaps, a dar-
ing flower in their hair. Yet a visiting flaneur, once he had left our "Corso"
and turned around to Národní Třída, on the left, or to Příkopy, on the
right, would have immediately noticed that people differed in their outfits,
and not only because of the many German uniforms in sight. Ethnicity
and ideology defined the dress code, and only those who tried to disappear
in neutral garb had something to hide (I knew).*

*German girls, with their short hair or long braids and their hefty shoes,
hefty at least in Czech eyes, did not wear rouge in the streets ("eine
deutsche Frau schminkt sich nicht [a German woman does not use
makeup]" the Führer had said), and if they came from the Sudeten region,
they more often than not wore dirndls or at least dirndl skirts of the Bavarian or Austrian kind, totally out of place in the industrial Bohemian metropolis, or the light brown uniform jackets of the Bund deutscher
Mädchen, with a black triangle on the sleeve indicating to which regional
organization they belonged. Younger Sudeten Germans, in the first months
of the occupation, continued to wear white shirts and black ties, once part
of Henlein's Sudeten Party uniform, and proudly walked in a sportif or
nearly military outfit of plump knickerbockers and ostentatious white
stockings (originally this was part of peasant attire, or so they thought).
Czechs preferred more formal wear, dark shades in suits and hats, except
on their weekend excursions to the Vltava woods, when they pretended to
be "tramps" or cowboys of the Wild West and dressed precisely according
to the theatrical descriptions they had found in the dime novels of the
early 1920s.*

Czech girls wished to be well turned out, like the young women in French and American movies, and for them a little rouge was not a sin but rather de rigueur, and so were high heels and expensive stockings; in the first years of the occupation they adorned their dresses and blouses with folklore Slavic motifs, or what was considered Slavic, called Svéráz (Our Own Way), in symbolic opposition to the German dirndls. Young Czech men of the lower classes developed their own burly elegance, with double-breasted jackets and extremely tight-fitting trousers; they called themselves potápky (diving birds) and congregated at the swing band cafés. They were later shipped off to forced labor in Germany.

Ethnic divisions were rather strict, and a Czech girl would not be caught dead dating a German. Veit Harlan, a less gifted ally of Leni Riefenstahl's, produced a film (never shown to Czech audiences) warning German girls from the provinces (the heroine played appropriately by his Swedish wife, Kristina Söderbaum) of poisonous young Czechs in Prague (impersonated in this case by a sleek Austrian actor) who want to rob them of their most precious possession and then leave them in the lurch. Needless to say, pregnant Kristina drowns herself, as she did in most of her movies; for good reason she was called, even by German moviegoers, the Reichswasserleiche (Reich's water corpse).

Yet these people often went to the same movie houses, were seen in the same expensive restaurants, though at different tables, and frequented other popular and attractive restaurants like the Zlatá Studně (Golden Fountain), a small roof garden high up on Malá Strana, where you could have a simple meal and admire the lights of the city below. (Veit Harlan had that right, but not entirely: in his movie the German girl and the Czech cavalier go there together, yet first he has to clear the place of all other guests before the hapless couple can be seated at the same table, all alone.) Prague, with its different ethnic and religious groups, had always been, at least latently, a double or triple city, Czechs and Germans and Jews preferring this or that café or living in this or that quarter. Czechs would have never gone to the Deutsches Casino (later Deutsches Haus); few Germans ever visited the Café Slavia, where Czech intellectuals congregated for decades; and members of the traveling Yiddish theater, so much admired by Franz Kafka, were certain to find a ready audience in the old Café Savoy. The occupation hardened the dividing lines into fatal

frontiers, and when, in the early summer of 1939, the first anti-Jewish city
ordinances were published, the modern city of Prague, which had been a
living space open to all only yesterday, again turned into a disorderly, if not
medieval, quilt of topographical restrictions and brutal exclusions.

The Appointment of the Reichsprotektor

Hitler's appointment of Neurath as Reichsprotektor was not much
liked by the Nazi functionaries, but it assuaged some of the misgivings
of the old guard in the Foreign Office by offering a seasoned diplomat,
well known internationally, a chance to return to a visible and responsible position—or so they and Neurath thought. On March 9, 1939,
Neurath had had a private supper with Hitler and used the extraordinary occasion to present his views on the Czech question: he recommended to Hitler that Germany be satisfied with controlling the Czech
economy and Czech foreign relations, granting in return a kind of autonomy to the Czech nation.

When President Hácha, on March 16, asked Hitler not to appoint
a Reichsprotektor from the ranks of the Sudeten Germans, Hitler was
still undecided on who would get the job. He possibly made his decision late on the same day or early on the next one; the story of the appointment has been reconstructed by John L. Heineman, Neurath's
American biographer, from postwar interviews and reports about Neurath's private telephone conversation after his meeting with Hitler.
Heinrich Lammers, chief of the Office of the Reichschancellor, and
Hitler himself were concerned about the international, especially
British, response to the establishment of the protectorate, and in order
"to calm the angry storm of indignation in foreign lands," according to
Lammers, Hitler was inclined to appoint "a personality who possessed
an importance and reputation abroad . . . who would be able to master
cleverly, in diplomatic fashion and with a certain quiet hand, the task
of bringing about the future peaceful cooperation of Czechs and Germans within the Greater German empire." Against Goebbels's strong
opposition, he concluded that "only Herr von Neurath was such a personality." Neurath was immediately notified that Hitler wanted to talk

to him in Vienna, at the Hotel Imperial, and met him there in private conference on March 18.

Neurath came to this conversation with Hitler with a few illusions of his own, and he dangerously underrated Hitler's cynical skills in using power. When Hitler offered him the position to assure calm and peace, Neurath at first declined (he later said), suggesting that he was advancing in age and lacked the administrative experience that was needed in Prague. After a few polite exchanges, Hitler impatiently remarked that he would have to offer the position to a Sudeten German, then, or to somebody from Ribbentrop's crew, if Neurath did not accept. But Neurath did, asking, however, for promises that he would be on his own and that other agencies of the Reich (he meant the SS and the SD) would not interfere. Hitler read him the essential sentences of the Führer's decree asserting that the protector would be the Führer's sole representative. Neurath did not ask for further guarantees, and he was promptly introduced to his new second-in-command and state secretary, waiting in the anteroom. This was K. H. Frank, the most radical functionary of Henlein's Sudeten Party and a rabid hater of Czechs.

On April 5 Neurath visited Prague for the first time to survey the scene and to demonstrate to the occupied people and to foreign observers that his appointment was not an empty, formal gesture. He was welcomed at the railroad station by General Walther von Brauchitsch, commander in chief of the armed forces, who had been flown in for the occasion, a gun salute was heard, the Czech lord mayor of Prague welcomed the protector, who would assure "the free development of all the rich talents of the Czech people," and a military parade was held, with heavy artillery, tanks, and representatives of the Czech government (not legally functioning) in attendance.

The day was not a real success. Children were kept at home from school rather than line the streets with their teachers. Their little paper flags, given to them to welcome the Reichsprotektor, were floating in the river, and rather than watch the proceedings, people animatedly promenaded along the fringes of Wenceslas Square and programmatically ignored what was going on. At a formal banquet the next evening the protector told his Czech guests that he had come to secure the happiness and well-being of Bohemia and Moravia within the Lebensraum of the German Reich, and he asked them to help him fulfill his "difficult task."

In private Neurath was more skeptical; to Gerhard Röpke, a friend and correspondent, he wrote that he had to restrain both the German anti-Czech elements and the Sudeten Germans, and when his daughter asked why he had accepted the job after "everything Hitler had done to him," he answered that "duty came first," that Ribbentrop was incompetent, and that he wanted to prevent the situation "from erupting into war." It was not to be, and only a few days after he had taken over administrative authority from the military, on April 16, the first signs of resolute opposition to the German occupation began to appear for all in the city to see.

CHAPTER II

THE BEGINNINGS OF
THE PROTECTORATE: 1939–41

Fresh Flowers

On April 20 the occupation regime celebrated Hitler's birthday, and many Czechs, in response, gathered at monuments to T. G. Masaryk, first president of the Republic of Czechoslovakia, and placed little bunches of spring flowers there. At the end of the year, on December 28, the birthday of Woodrow Wilson, similar bouquets were miraculously to appear on his monument, opposite the main railroad station, suggesting how people felt about the American president who had so efficiently supported Masaryk in his efforts to secure Czech independence.

In the uncertain months of 1939 after the occupation, Czech society spontaneously created its own ways of asserting autonomy by celebrating its history and language. (Czech historians had been always attentive readers of Johann Gottfried Herder, who believed that nationality, cultural achievement, and language were closely intertwined.) Large public demonstrations concentrating on symbolically meaningful events or figures brought tens of thousands of citizens spontaneously into the streets of Prague, and the new resistance groups began to understand that they should test their influence by organizing these public demonstrations as a coherent challenge to the occupying regime. Feasts of local saints and martyrs, pilgrimages to certain mountain chapels and churches, a soccer game against a German team: these were suddenly more important than ever, and the reburial in the spring of 1939 of the Romantic poet Karel Hynek Mácha in a Prague cemetery turned into a massive demonstration.

On May 6 and 7, 1939, tens of thousands of Prague citizens silently lined the streets to pay their respects to Mácha, who had died an untimely death at the age of nearly twenty-six in 1836 and whose earthly remains had been buried in the town of Litoměřice, where he had been living at the time. František Engliš, governor of the Czechoslovak National Bank, at the time of the Munich Conference had suggested to the government that Mácha's remains be exhumed before the German Army arrived in Litoměřice, which was in the hills near the German-Czech border, and reburied in Prague together with the other great poets, composers, and artists of the Czech tradition. A local gravedigger and his assistant, both Germans, did the job of exhumation, with a town physician attending. The remains of the poet were put into a metal coffin and, with the help of Czech soldiers who were leaving the area, loaded on a truck headed for Prague, first to the Strašnice Crematorium and then to the university's Anthropological Institute, where they were examined by Professor Jiří Malý and clothed in velvet and silk donated by prominent industrialists (among them Jindřich Waldes, who had made a fortune on snap fasteners and safety pins and who financially supported underground newspapers; he was to spend three years at the concentration camp in Dachau).

On May 6 a delegation of the Prague magistrate went to the gates of the Anthropological Institute and transported the remains, now in a simple oak coffin draped by the national flag, to the Pantheon, or central hall, of the National Museum, ceremonial fires burning at the gates. Many wreaths, most visibly one from President Hácha, were laid near the catafalque on which the coffin was placed, and in midmorning Jan Kapras, minister of education, and the lord mayor of Prague came to pay homage, followed, shortly thereafter, by Hácha himself, who remained in silent meditation. In the meantime the gates had been swung open, and a long line of citizens and schoolchildren passed by the coffin. By 5:00 p.m. the gates were closed again, and a motorcade, watched on its way by the citizens, left for the gates of the Vyšehrad cemetery, opened by Monsignor Antonín Stašek, guardian of the Vyšehrad Cathedral of Sts. Peter and Paul.

On Sunday, May 7, "all of Prague," "even the suburbs," ran up the national tricolor, the newspapers proudly reported, and the narrow streets up the Vyšehrad hill were packed with people of all ages waiting to catch a glimpse of the ceremonies. In the cathedral, the coffin was guarded by students with drawn sabers and, close by, a group of young girls in flowing white with spring twigs in their hands. By 11:00 a.m. official delegations had arrived, but since the gates were left open to let ordinary people enter freely, one could constantly hear, while the service went on, as a reporter remarked, "the tap of innumerable feet trying to be quiet and subdued . . . a secret ground note accompanying the church choir." A cello sonata by Dvořák was played by a member of the Philharmonic, and Monsignor Stašek in his sermon compared Mácha with the pilgrim wandering through the labyrinth of the world, searching for a *centrum securitatis*, the core of certitude, so difficult to reach. The national hymn of the republic, "Kde domov můj?" (Where Is My Home?), concluded the service.

The reburial was to take place in the early afternoon, and after a delegation from the university and representatives of the theaters (Mácha had been an amateur actor) and the Academy of Arts and Sciences (including the historian Josef Šusta and the famous sculptor Max Švabinský) had arrived, the coffin was blessed again, and the procession left the church to move to the Slavín, the adjacent part of the cemetery, where for many long decades the great of the nation had been buried. Václav Vydra, of the National Theater, recited the last verse of "Máj [May]," Mácha's most famous poem, and Rudolf Medek, a conservative writer and former officer in the Czech Legions, gave the funeral oration, praising Mácha as defender of the Czech language, the first who "had elevated her to poetic resonances," believing as he had in the immortality of his nation and its language. It was a moment of silent sadness when four Czech poets, unquestionably the most important ones of the century—František Halas, Josef Hora, Jaroslav Seifert, and Vladimír Holan—lifted the coffin and slowly lowered it on simple leather straps into the open grave, soon filled to the brim with fresh flowers.

Mácha's contemporaries would have wondered about his being reinterpreted by a soldier-legionnaire, because the poet was, in his own time and later, disliked by genuine patriots. The first important Czech poet born in Prague was no waver of flags, as were many of his minor colleagues, but a true romantic of the metaphysical, if not existentialist, kind. He was knowledgeable about the German Romantics, whom, along with Byron and, possibly, Leopardi, he imitated in his early poems written in German; his Vilém, hero of "Máj," happens to be the chief of an outcast robber band who has killed his father (out of jealousy) and, facing execution, prepares himself for "eternal annihilation." Recent interpreters have come to see lonely Mácha as a writer veritably *sûr l'abîme*, above the abyss, and admiration for his poetic genius, particularly loved by the modern surrealists, was not diminished but perhaps enhanced by the rumors about his intimate diary (long decoded but withheld from full disclosure), chronicling in technical detail his sexual encounters with his beloved Lori and their pillow talk (in German).

Erudite intellectuals gathered around the *Kritický měsíčník* (Critical Monthly), which devoted systematic attention to the linguistic and structural analysis of Mácha's difficult poetry, including his early verse written in German, were somewhat piqued by his new appeal to a mass readership and felt uneasy, to say the least, about the cheap newspaper articles about him and the attitude of many of their colleagues. In a remarkable commentary, Critical Monthly wondered about the anthropologists who did not know much of Mácha's life or work, the functionaries who followed his cortege in their tasteful automobiles, and the orators who so valiantly "exploited" his poetry. The critic Karel Polák, who bravely signed his critical remarks, suggested that Mácha fully deserved the new attention, but he also dared suggest that the interest was much belated and triggered by "noncultural, political events" for which the Czechs could not claim any responsibility. Critics, he said, were rather skeptical about "an official aesthetic of a national demonstration" to celebrate the most dedicated Czech admirer of beauty within a framework of valid ordinances and permissions. But politically, at any rate, Mácha's reburial was an extraordinary event, and the resistance groups, then in an early stage of formation and self-definition, had ample reason to consider what was going on.

In 1939, June 6, Jan Hus Day, commemorating the Czech martyr's death at the stake in Constance in 1416, was not only a day of "quiet reflection," as the *Lidové noviny* wrote, but also a new occasion for public and dignified manifestations. The indefatigable lord mayor of the city placed a wreath at the massive Hus monument on the Old Town Square, the historian Karel Vojtíšek delivered a festive lecture at the Czech university (still functioning), and memorial services were held at St. Nicolas (the Czechoslovak Hussite National Church) and St. Salvator (the Evangelical Church of Czech Brethren). After the services, people began to move to the nearby square and the monument; there were flags, girls in national costumes, legionnaires in everyday clothes, and a Hussite preacher who read from the Psalms. By 9:00 p.m. the crowds intoned the ancient Hussite battle hymn "Ktož jsú boží bojovníci [Ye Who Are God's Fighters]," which had once put the armies of German crusaders to flight. It was a spontaneous manifestation in defense of Czech history, lasting far into the night.

On June 8, two days later, a soccer game, Prague versus Berlin, was held in Letná Sports Stadium, the Czechs defeated the Prussians, 2–0, and patriotic fans had a chance to demonstrate in their own way with empty beer bottles. Other manifestations followed; on September 30 the resistance groups passed the word that to remember the Munich Conference, the day should be marked by a boycott of the tram system. Everyone except the uninformed Germans went about on foot for the entire day, trams clanging by. The German authorities did not know exactly what to say about this visibly successful boycott, explaining it as the result of a "Czech-Jewish" conspiracy or, conversely, as a demonstration by the Czechs against their having to use the trams together with Jews. The scene was set for October 28, the Independence Day of the Czechoslovak Republic, when more violent mass demonstrations arrayed occupiers against occupied and triggered political changes unforeseen by either side.

Konstantin Freiherr von Neurath: Wrong Place, Wrong Time

Prague's newspapers devoted a good deal of space to information about the new Reichsprotektor, clearly indicating that the appointment of this old-time diplomat, conspicuous on the international scene, suggested something hopeful about the situation. Their reports about K. H. Frank, the second-in-command, however, were restricted to a terse paragraph, his views on Czech affairs being well known from recent events in the Czechoslovak Parliament. Unfortunately the newspapers did not know much about Neurath's ambivalent and changing relationship to the National Socialist Party and the Führer, and even if they had known more, they would have been unable to publish the full record, which would not exactly have calmed the fears of their readers.

The Neuraths belonged not to an ancient aristocracy of vast estates or military glory but rather to a kind of *Dienstadel*, a modest German version of the *noblesse de robe*. One of the Reichsprotektor's forebears, originally from Hesse, a lawyer at the imperial court at Wetzlar (better known as the locale of Goethe's legal apprenticeship there than for its efficiency), was awarded the ennobling "von" late in the eighteenth century; it was the Reichsprotektor's grandfather who, serving the king of Württemberg, was elevated to the rank of *Freiherr* in 1851. Konstantin von Neurath (b. 1912) went through the prescribed local schools in Swabia, including the traditional gymnasium in Stuttgart and the law school of the University of Tübingen, but he could not join the German diplomatic service because he lacked a yearly income of twenty thousand marks, and he unwillingly resigned himself to serve in the mere consular corps. (His parents-in-law, Stuttgart bankers, did not want to increase their daughter's dowry, and ten thousand marks per annum were just sufficient to qualify for a consulate.) Neurath first served out a five-year consular appointment in London, was secretary of the International Copyright Conference in 1908, though he was not known for reading many books, and by luck and connections was allowed to shift to the diplomatic service in 1912 and told that he was to go, as first secretary, to the German Embassy in Constantinople in the spring of 1914. However, in early August he immediately joined the army, disregarding the wishes of the Foreign Office. He distinguished himself in combat, then had an emissary of the diplomatic service pick him up at the western front and take him on a dangerous journey to Turkey. He was not a great success there, negotiating as he had to do between conflicting interests of the Foreign Office and the German Military Mission.

He submitted his resignation (the first of many to come) and returned to Württemberg, where he became, in the family tradition, the king's chief of cabinet, combining the functions of a political adviser with those of a private secretary. When the well-ordered Württemberg revolution came in the fall of 1918, he calmly negotiated the king's abdication and royal pension and promptly withdrew to his gentleman's farm of Leinfelderhof and to the hunt, which he loved most. By 1919 he was back in the Foreign Office. He was one of the many diplomats not at all in sympathy with the republic yet ready to serve because he believed the German state was more important than its temporary shape, an idea that, to his misfortune, continued to guide him even after January 1933, when Hitler came to power.

After his return to the Foreign Office, Neurath served for nearly ten years as ambassador in Copenhagen, Rome, and London, and he learned to conjoin, without much conflict, his few conservative ideas with the requirements of his office. Though in his reports to Berlin he did not hesitate to make rash generalizations about Danes, Italians, and the English, and though liberals at home publicly criticized him for neglecting the writers Emil Ludwig and Gerhart Hauptmann when they visited Rome, his diplomatic style was to avoid dramatic confrontations, and he preferred to procrastinate rather than to force an issue. (In London, he enjoyed unexpected social success because he once, together with his father, had rescued a princess, the future queen Mary, from a fire, and in London the queen immediately recognized her childhood friend, "little Konstantin.") His years in Rome were of paramount importance to his political education: arriving in 1922, he had to deal with Mussolini, capo of the Blackshirt bands and the new Fascist statesman in spats and gray gloves, but the plans and actions of that principal were, so Neurath believed, efficiently tempered by dedicated Italian civil servants who thought they would outlive all Fascist disorder. However, Neurath did not believe that Italy would ever be a trustworthy ally, Fascism or not, and he rarely deviated from his belief that the fate of Germany would be determined in discussions with Britain and France rather than with Italy or the distant powers of the United States, Russia, or Japan.

When in the spring of 1932 Chancellor Heinrich Brüning's government fell, the aging President von Hindenburg, strengthened by his own recent reelection, resolved that the time had come to create a cabinet of conservative experts to run the country without the backing of the parliament, and he decided Neurath was the right man for foreign minister; Hermann Göring agreed. Neurath, who had turned down ambassadorships to the United States and the Soviet Union, on May 31 received a telegram from Hindenburg requesting him "to assume the foreign ministry in the presidential cabinet now being formed, which will be made up of right-wing personalities free from political party allegiance and will be supported not so much by the Reichstag as by the authority of the President." Neurath hesitated, as he usually did before any decision, and his wife tried to dissuade him from accepting the position, but Hindenburg knew, as did Hitler later, how to argue with Neurath. He appealed to his patriotic obligations, assured him he would be able to set foreign policy without the interference of nonexpert cabinet members or of the Reichstag, and mentioned that Hitler himself had agreed to Neurath's appointment. In Neurath's dealings with heads of government, a distinct pattern emerges: he hesitates or pretends to hesitate, the figure of authority speaks of his duty to the fatherland and suggests guarantees of independence that are, for all practical purposes, not of this world, and in his mind the idea of "self-sacrifice" takes hold.

Neurath had met Hitler for the first time in January 1932, and he was not fully aware that Hitler wanted to manipulate him to make Hindenburg open to the possibilities of a Führer government in which Neurath would continue to function as foreign minister. Neurath's impressions, as described by others, were those of the upper-class conservative who immediately noticed that Hitler was rather "common-looking" and "ill dressed," his most distinguished features being "his eyes which burned with unquenchable fire and his voice which had an extraordinary power of persuasion." Hitler preferred his usual two-hour monologue, but Neurath came away, strangely enough, with an impression of "sincerity" rather than fanaticism. Both men were in agreement about the sins, if not vices, of democracy, the necessity of undoing the consequences of the Versailles Treaty, and Germany's "sacred right to dignity and freedom" (meaning speedy rearmament), yet Neurath had his qualms about Hitler's impulsive brinkmanship and the dangers of a new war. However, when an emissary of the Führer came to see him in the evening and asked whether he would be ready to join a Hitler government as its foreign minister, Neurath responded that he was "in principle" yet wanted to hear more about the details of the offer. He did not let go of the illusion that he could modify or moderate Hitler's views, if not his actions, as did the loyal civil servants in Fascist Italy in the case of Mussolini. It was while trying, vainly, to do this, that he made himself culpable and was sentenced at Nuremberg in 1946 to fifteen years in prison.

As minister of foreign affairs in the successive governments of Chancellors Fritz von Papen, General Kurt von Schleicher, and Hitler, Neurath did show goodwill, carefully intervening in a few cases of colleagues endangered by anti-Semitic legislation. But he always covered his flanks, never resisted openly (as did Papen, who gave a famous anti-Nazi speech at Marburg on June 17, 1934), and arranged matters without much fuss; for example, when a half Jewish (according to the new laws) colleague in the East European department was let go, Neurath made arrangements to have his pension paid in foreign currency, enabling him to emigrate. An "honorary citizen" of Stuttgart and aware of his reputation as a good Christian, he nevertheless did little to help Stuttgart's Protestant Bishop Theophil Wurm when the Gestapo arrested him, though earlier he had supported him. And when the National Socialists demanded that the dueling fraternity Suevia, to which he had belonged with active enthusiasm, submit to the new principles and exclude its (two) Jewish members from the ranks, Neurath wrote an opinion saying that the two should sacrifice their membership for the good of the corps. The proud corps rejected his opinion and instead dissolved itself, leaving it to him and his son to administer its property (as he did religiously). He was not a man who had the full courage of his conflicting convictions; in November 1936 a new law about the Nazi organization for Hitler Youth, which was meant to dominate the education of boys and young men, was put before the cabinet, and it was not Neurath but Paul von und zu Eltz-Rübenach, a practicing Catholic and the minister of the post and transport, fearing that the law would radically diminish the function of parents, churches, and schools, who declared, in the presence of Hitler, that he could not agree with it, resigned on the spot, left the room, and closed the door behind him.

Neurath continued for years as minister of foreign affairs while Hitler, being a man of improvisations, played people and institutions against one another when he wanted to avoid binding decisions. Neurath had his hands full fighting competing party functionaries eager to formulate foreign policies in Hitler's name, and for a time he succeeded in defending his job and his colleagues in the Foreign Office. Alfred Rosenberg, the party ideologue and principal racial theorist, who had established his own foreign policy office within the Nazi Party as early as 1933, was an impractical and difficult figure, yet Hitler told Neurath that Rosenberg should keep his party office as a "harmless compensation." Joachim von Ribbentrop, the traveling champagne salesman who was avid to please Hitler, was more difficult to rein in. After Ribbentrop was named commissioner of disarmament questions in 1934, Neurath tried to neutralize him by putting him under the supervision of an experienced diplomat, but Ribbentrop promptly opened an office of his own, exactly opposite the Foreign Ministry offices on the Wilhelmstrasse, to organize his missions. (By 1935 there were 30 employees, and 150 a year later.) In June 1935 Hitler elevated Ribbentrop to be extraordinary plenipotentiary and ambassador of the German Reich on special mission and sent him to London, where he successfully negotiated new naval agreements with Britain. Within another two years, and in spite of his old game of sullen resignation, Neurath had to yield his job to this "awful fellow," who had been competing with him on the Paris and London scenes. In early February 1938 Ribbentrop was appointed minister of foreign affairs, and Neurath was made president of a secret cabinet council, which never functioned or, for that matter, even met.

Now, in April 1939, Neurath was ensconced in Prague's Czernin Palace, once the home of the Czechoslovak Ministry of Foreign Affairs. He rejected a list of Sudeten Germans proposed for his office, fearing they would complicate his dealings with the Czech government, and he filled the positions instead with people he knew from the Wilhelmstrasse. They were seasoned diplomats and bureaucrats but totally uninformed about Bohemian affairs: Hans Völckers, who had served in Havana and Madrid; Alexander von Kessel, at the central Berlin office;

and industrious Kurt von Burgsdorff, a Saxon who was not in sympathy with K. H. Frank, to run the office when Neurath himself became increasingly indolent.

Neurath might have done well in a different place at a different time, perhaps, but that was not Prague during the first years of World War II. He was qualified to serve as ambassador of a moderately monarchic Germany to a distant, possibly not too liberal, republic, but at the Czernin Palace on Hradčany Hill, he found himself between too many rocks and too many hard places: his Berlin masters, the Nazi police apparatus, including the Gestapo and the SD, the Czech government trying to represent a humiliated and recalcitrant nation, and an alliance of resistance groups taking their orders from London and later Moscow.

Czech and German Attitudes Toward the Anti-Jewish Laws

New policies to isolate Jewish citizens and deprive them of their rights did not start on the first day of Germany's military occupation. But hereditary Czech anti-Semitism has a long history reaching back to the first decades of the nineteenth century, and after the departure of President Beneš in October 1938, it emerged with new force, not at first as a prejudice based on racial assumptions, as in Germany, but rather as an illiberal and narrow view of ethnicity defined by habits of living and, above all, by language shared or not. Yet Fascist groups were ready to adopt the racial norms of the Reich, and within a few months even some conservative Catholics insisted that Jews differed from Czechs by origin, blood, religion, and idiom. In Masaryk's republic, anti-Semitism had been a matter for a few Fascist fringe groups: conservative petits bourgeois offended by Jews who spoke German and supported German cultural institutions, old-fashioned nationalists on the right wing of the National Democrats, and Agrarians who refused to see that the republic, anticipating European virtues, was a state made up of many nationalities, including Czechs, Slovaks, Germans, Jews, Magyars, Poles, Ruthenians, and Ukrainians, that it was not just the state of Czechoslovaks, a nation more utopian than real.

In the early months of what was now called the Second Republic,

the first democratic one having been destroyed at the Munich Conference, resentments coalesced in a new climate of enmity against Jews,
"Freemasons," and the left. Personal and public denunciations, unheard of earlier, were frequent. Jewish civil servants were pensioned
off; Jakub Deml, a defrocked priest and political narcissist, violently attacked liberals and Jews; and Karel Čapek, who had been Masaryk's
trusted friend in dialogue, was insulted by right-wingers and died in
December 1938, unhappily confronting the moral decay of his society.

Increasingly vociferous Czech anti-Semitism continued into the
protectorate, but there were many who did not want to be soiled by it,
and some members of the Czech government tried to delay the introduction of anti-Jewish laws for as long as possible, and not only, as later
historians believe, because they were eager to make Jewish property
and funds serve Czech society rather than the occupation regime. The
government had declared on December 1, 1938, that it hoped that
many refugees (including Jews from Germany and Austria) would find
a better future in nations of greater economic capabilities, yet it had
added that Czecho-Slovakia "would not be hostile" to Jews who had been
settled in the territories of the republic for a long time and "had established a positive relationship to its nation"; the Social Democrat Josef
Macek, speaking for the labor opposition, said the Jewish question was
not one of race but of nationality and that Jews who had become
members of the Czech nation would remain Czech. Unfortunately the
professional organizations of both lawyers and physicians did not
demonstrate equivalent patience when, on the very first day of the
German military occupation, they resolved to exclude "non-Aryans"
(a Nazi term) from membership and its privileges and forced the
hands of the government to deal with their resolutions at its first meeting on March 17 and then again on March 21 and 27. "Non-Aryan"
law offices were now to be run by "Aryan" substitutes, and "non-
Aryan" physicians were to be removed from public health institutions
and clinics run by insurance companies, though there were no laws
or ordinances yet to define exactly who these Aryans or non-Aryans
were.

The negotiations of the Czech government with the Office of the
Reichsprotektor concerning anti-Jewish legislation began in May 1939

and ended a year later, with the Czech government submitting to German pressure and accepting the definitions of the Nuremberg Laws of 1935; discussion of possible exemptions dragged on for one more year. On May 21, 1939, General Alois Eliáš, chief of the Czech government, addressed a formal letter to Neurath, saying that he wished to advance discussion of the Jewish problem and submitted a legislative document prepared by a government commission to define who a Jewish person was, the possibilities of exemptions, and the role of Jews in economic and public life. The document defined a Jewish person as someone who was born to four Jewish grandparents belonging to the Jewish religious community. If there were only three or two, it depended on whether the person in question, or his/her marital partner, had belonged to the Jewish community on or after November 1, 1918. The Czech government also suggested ample possibilities of exemptions. For example, in the case of deserving personalities, the president of the republic could grant an exemption, and all Jewish persons (of a clean record and not Communists) who had resided in Bohemia or Moravia fifty years or more could apply to be exempted. In the cases of those who were too young, the residences of their fathers would be included in the count.

Preliminary measures concerning Jewish businesses and enterprises, as discussed by the Czech government in its meeting on March 27, and the document submitted to the Reichsprotektor triggered a prolonged discussion between Berlin and Prague, involving the German Ministry of the Interior, the commandant of the German Security Service, the Czech government, and Neurath himself. The Office of the Reichsprotektor circulated the Czech document to its various departments, and on May 27, a meeting was held at the Czernin Palace to work out a German response. The meeting was informed of the view of the German minister of the interior, transmitted by Wilhelm Stuckart, that Jewish policies should be left to the Czech government and of Hitler's opinion, articulated in conversation with Neurath on May 2, that the Czechs themselves should take care of the Jewish question and German authorities should not intervene, "dass sie nicht hineinreden sollen." Walter Stahlecker, commandant of police at the Reichsprotektor's Office, argued that all Jews who had indicated in the census of 1910 or 1930 that their everyday language was German should be made Germans immediately and fall under German law without exception, but everybody else disagreed. Neurath himself cut the discussion short and, against his usual policy of procrastination and trying to guess at Hitler's final ideas, issued his own order concerning Jewish property on June 21; by implication it denied all Czech ordinances and asserted that the Nuremberg Laws, racial in character and intolerant as far as deadlines were concerned, were valid as the legal norm in Bohemia and Moravia. The Czech government again presented some of its differing views, covertly grumbling about "aryanization" as an instrument of "germanization," but it accepted the legality of the Nuremberg Laws on July 4, continuing, however, to keep the question of exemptions on its agenda. In late July the Reichsprotektor ordered that a Central Office for Jewish Emigration be established; it was run by Adolf Eichmann, who came to Prague from Vienna.

It is possible that President Hácha and the Czech government were thinking of the Italian racial laws of October 1938, with their ample catalog of exceptions, when they tried to exempt a few individuals from the new anti-Jewish legislation. However, the Italian laws based exceptions on the military and patriotic record of given individuals (including deserving members of the Fascist Party who happened to be of Jewish origin), while the Czechs thought in broader terms of persons whose achievements, as Hácha told Neurath, had been useful to society as a whole. Exemptions would be made on the basis of individual applications to be filtered through a complicated procedure; by August 1940 there were 717 applications, and 1,000 by October. The largest number came from industrialists and businessmen (328), physicians (196), lawyers (53), and Jewish wives of non-Jewish partners (86). After protracted considerations involving the Reichsprotektor, who remained aloof throughout, the government agreed on 41 persons to be exempted. Among them were Emil Kolben, once assistant to Thomas Alva Edison and the founder of the Kolben industries, important in Prague; the famous scholar of German literature at Charles University Professor Dr. Arnošt Kraus; and many Jewish wives of non-Jewish men well known in Czech social and artistic life. (One application that was

not accepted was that of Paul/Pavel Eisner, the most productive translator of Czech poetry and prose; he miraculously survived the war in
Prague.) But by October 4, 1941, all these efforts of Hácha and the
government had come to naught because Neurath's successor turned
down the entire list, arguing against its assumptions in "principle." In
the meantime the deportations of Jews had begun.

Not waiting for the Reichsprotektor to define who was Jewish according to the strict Nuremberg Laws, the Czech police directorate in
Prague (dominated by conservatives of the Agrarian Party) by early August 1939 had begun to issue ordinances limiting Jewish access to
public places, restaurants, and cafés. On August 4 the most elegant
and pleasant places were closed to Jewish patrons: for instance, the
restaurant on Slavic Island (Slovanský ostrov), close to the National
Theater; the restaurant and café Mánes, affiliated with the Artists'
Club; the restaurant on Sharpshooter's Island (Střelecký ostrov); the
Hanau Pavilion, a little above the city; the Švehla restaurant in the
Royal Gardens; and the National Clubs at Vinohrady, Smíchov, and
elsewhere. Restaurants and cafés owned by Jews had to be designated
as such; if other places (with the exception of those places on the
Aryan master list) wanted to, they could reserve a room for Jewish customers. Then the police turned their attention to the swimming pools
and bath establishments on the islands and banks of the Vltava River:
public baths were closed to Jews, and elsewhere a special schedule
was established to keep Aryan swimmers from mingling with non-
Aryan ones.

Many owners and managers of cafés and restaurants, Jewish and
non-Jewish, remained undeterred by these police orders, and announced in the *Židovské listy* (Jewish News), published by the Jewish
Community, either that Jewish customers were welcome in their
places or that Jewish sections had been established within them.
Among the first to advertise, on December 9, 1939, were the cafés
Tepna, on Wenceslas Square, and Jaro, close to the old Jewish district. Others followed within a few weeks. They included the café-
restaurant Seidling on Celetná Street; the Kávový buffet on the Old
Town Square, promising "fresh baked goods daily" (even in 1941); the
café Příkopy; the café Continental, which had earlier attracted

many refugees from Austria and Germany; and the indomitable café-restaurant Aschermann and its owner, Armin Walló, who advertised as late as February 1942. Surprisingly, the Národní kavárna (Café National), a few steps away from the Czech National Theater and a traditional hangout of surrealist writers, as of May 1, 1940, arranged afternoon teas, with music provided by Messrs. Löffelholz and Lederer (piano) and Schächter (violin) accompanying a "jazz singer" (Kaufmann). More serious music was offered three times a week at the café Nizza by the "well-known artists" Otto Sattler, Curt Maier, and Carlo Taube (couvert ten crowns, or about thirty cents), while the café Unitaria, near the Charles Bridge, advertised friendly afternoon card games of bridge, rummy, and skat, all supervised by Mrs. Elsa Weidbergerová.

Many other places established Jewish sections, among them the café Urban, whose room for "non-Aryans" was reached through the courtyard, the café Belvedere on Letná Hill, the Postillon Bar, and the café Zdar in the middle-class district of Vinohrady. The advertisements in the Jewish weekly included, as late as spring 1940, at least half a dozen notices from suburban cafés and restaurants that welcomed Jewish visitors willing to take a tram or train. These included the Garden Restaurant at Malá Chuchle, priding itself on daily dances from three to six in the afternoon, with a small orchestra consisting of Messrs. Schlesinger, Löwith, Stein, and Berkovič, and the Garden Restaurant Jezerka, at Michle, reached only by a lengthy tram ride from Wenceslas Square (you could select your own fresh fish from a water tank). The restaurant at the Hotel Amerika had other advantages to offer: though you had to take a train from the main station to get there, it had a garden with a good deal of shade, and you could play bridge. In May 1940 an ad for the Hotel Skalka restaurant appeared twice in the Listy promising a whiff of virtual peace: although it was not easy to reach the restaurant (first a bus and then a train), visitors, once they arrived, could enjoy "forest walks of fairy tale beauty," volleyball, Ping-Pong, and even swimming, and all that knowing there was a Jewish section to welcome them. But by that time new and even more stringent anti-Jewish regulations had been issued; thus the bridge parties on the riverbanks had become mere fairy tales reminiscent of olden times.

On September 1, 1939, when Germany's war against Poland commenced and citizens of the protectorate began to hope against hope that war would bring an early end to the occupation, Jewish apartments had to be registered, and on September 23 and 24 Jews had to deliver their radios to special collecting places. Inexorably, the machinery ground on. As of February 20, 1940, Jews were not allowed to attend cinema or theater performances; in March, their identity documents had to be stamped with the big letter *J*; on May 17 they were forbidden to linger in Prague's parks, gardens, or forests (at least the Jewish Community opened the garden of its old people's home), were not allowed to keep pigeons or to use taxis, and, in trams, had to stand at the rear end of the second carriage (if there was only one carriage, they had to wait for the next train with two carriages).

The Stories of One Jewish Family

I do not know when my mother's Jewish family settled in Bohemia, and the exact date is not important. They may have come in the thirteenth or in the sixteenth century, perhaps driven out of their Frankish communities by rabid Crusaders, who were burning the ghettos, or attracted perhaps by new economic possibilities in the Bohemian lands, where it was the habit of noble families to protect "their" Schutzjuden against kings and emperors who tried to squeeze Jews for as much money as the traffic would bear. My most ancient ancestors on my mother's side known by name and place were Adam and Eve—that is, Adam Brod of the Czech village of Horní Cerekev, who, according to a tax account of 1717, sold spices but mostly "went a-begging," and married Eva, of Moravia. They had five children, and Andreas, one of them, moved to the village of Lukavec, where he married Schönele and worked as a tailor, according to a tax account of 1740. Other sons who established their own families were glove makers, and my grandfather was one of the thirteen children of Isaak Brod and Anna, all born at Lukavec. I assume that my grandfather spoke Yiddish at home, Czech with his Catholic village neighbors and customers, and a good deal of German when he later came to Prague. Family myth, rather spurious, has it that as a young man he apprenticed himself to none other than Hermann Kafka, who (besides being father to Franz later) owned a textile shop at the Old Town Square, and then, having being trained well, moved to the little Czech town of Poděbrady, where he opened his own shop on the main square. The shop must have flourished, at least at first, because my mother and all her sisters and brothers were born there, but by 1900 he had closed the shop, or what was left of it, after virulent anti-Jewish demonstrations following Leopold Hilsner's alleged act of "ritual" murder swept through the Czech countryside, and moved his enterprise to Prague, seeking, as so many other Jews did at the time, security in numbers and the possibilities of a more civilized community.

I own only one photograph of this family, from about 1912, and the picture suggests order, moderate well-being, a certain quiet elegance (as far as the young ladies are concerned), and reasonable hopes for the future. On the left, a little apart from the family, sits Grandfather, the self-made man, serious, with a high forehead and an imposing military gray mustache of nearly Wilhelminian proportions, and his left hand, in an almost Napoleonic gesture, put between two buttons of his formal jacket. On the right is Grandmother, with a rather decorative coiffure and the trace of a smile on her attractive face. Close to her beside and behind are her five children, two of whom died in the camps, as she did, one of whom survived, and two of whom lived in exile in England during the years of the Nazi occupation of Prague. I have been told that she was née Zeckendorf (a gentleman of that name was a real estate mogul in New York when I arrived there in the 1950s) and married "down," and I remember that she sang to me the ballad about the two French grenadiers returning from Moscow in 1812, text by Heinrich Heine, "lass sie betteln gehn, wenn sie hungrig sind [let them go begging if they are hungry]," a sure sign that she had a middle-class education in German, though the song was not exactly a lullaby evoking happy dreams in my sleepy mind. She was certainly more courageous than Mama, I thought; once, when I was a boy, she took me for a walk on Prague's Císařský ostrov (Emperor's Island, in the Vltava River), a flat place of grass and sand, suddenly told me not to look while she squatted down, hitched up her long skirt, and urinated on the spot; she made me promise I would not say anything to my mother. Mama would have never done such a thing, and I was happy to have a secret to share with my grandmother.

In the middle of the family group I recognize my mother's oldest brother, Charles, or rather Karel, as he preferred to be called in Czech. Tall and earnest, he turned out to be the family millionaire, who established a respectable glass and bottle factory that flourished throughout the First Republic. I never knew much about Karel or his wife, Olga, née Kohn, from Písek in southern Bohemia, because they lived in a distant world of rich industrialists, but I remember my cousins Ivan and Jan, their well-groomed sons, from rare Sunday excursions to Prague parks and playgrounds. I assume that Uncle Karel kept somewhat aloof from us because he was a politically conscious Czech Jew who had grown up speaking Czech more or less exclusively, subscribed to the liberal Lidové noviny (not the Prager Tagblatt), went to the Czech National Theater and never set foot in the Prague German Theater, where my father, worlds apart, produced the most recent wild and woolly plays by Berlin expressionists. Sometime in the summer of 1936 or 1937 Ivan and Jan came to Neubistritz, a little town in southern Bohemia, where I spent my vacation, and I urged them to come with me to a meeting of the local Social Democrats, who were discussing the latest attacks by the Falangists in Republican Spain. Uncle Karel was appalled by my aberrant behavior and my efforts to drag his sons away from the swimming pool—not only because the meeting was Socialist (I had grievously underrated his class attitude) but because it was conducted in German rather than in Czech, more fitting for my cousins' ears.

One day the handsome young man of the family photograph of 1912 had to walk on crutches because he had slipped on a stairway and broken both his legs. Listening more carefully to family gossip, however, I learned that he had been courting a married woman, had been surprised in her bed when the husband suddenly returned home, and had had to jump from a balcony down to a lawn, where he was later picked up by the city ambulance. Family gossip had little to say about the husband involved, but my mother knew everything about Aunt Olga's justified rage, assuaged only by Uncle Karel's taking her on a luxurious cruise on the Adriatic— on a Yugoslav ship, of course, as befitted a Slavic patriot. It was a different kind of life from ours.

Another day four or five years later, the entire family was deported to Auschwitz, where Uncle Karel, Aunt Olga, and Jan died in the gas chambers. Ivan survived, marched to the east to join the Soviet Army, and *returned with the Soviet-organized Czechoslovak Army Corps under General Ludvík Svoboda. He later told me, in a café on Forty-third Street in New York, that escaping, he took shelter in an abandoned farm, found some canned fruit (the first he had seen in years), hungrily gulped it all down, and was immediately afflicted by terrible diarrhea, which kept him the entire night on the ghost farm before he trudged farther east. His father might have been surprised to learn that he married a German woman named Isolde and happily lives with her in West Germany.*

The girl who puts her hands dreamingly on Uncle Karel's shoulder and looks impatiently into her future is my aunt Fritta, and the uninitiated observer cannot see that the frontiers of language and culture cut right through the idyllic gesture on the family photograph. Karel was a proud Czech, while Aunt Fritta (possibly taking her cue from her mother's German upbringing) became a famous actress on the stages of Frankfurt and Berlin; her first husband was the playwright Paul Kornfeld, who established the psychological drama of the Weimar period on the stages of Berlin, Frankfurt, and Munich (he died in the Lodz ghetto). When I was a boy, Tante Fritta's imperial visits from Berlin were special occasions; once my mother refused to accompany her on a city shopping spree because Aunt Fritta wore pants, in the manner of Marlene Dietrich, and Mama believed that in Prague trousers were in bad taste. I had a good time because Fritta gladly added to my meager pocket money, paying me half a Czech crown per hour if only I kept my mouth shut; she was hoity-toity about language and could not stand my Prague German, in which all major consonants were pronounced in the Czech way and with t and d and p and b unfortunately interchangeable.

I later read that Fritta had been the heroine in first performances of Brecht's plays, performing opposite the famous actor Heinrich George (later a super-Nazi) and lived on Breitenbach Square in Berlin in a colony of artists and intellectuals. Everybody there had the habit of calling neighbors by initials only, and I discovered much later that when Fritta talked about "der L.," she actually meant the famous Marxist critic Georg Lukács (about whom I gave my first public lecture at Yale thirty years later). Fritta moved among the prominent of Berlin society, but in the spring of 1933 she had to leave too, and the Prague family gladly welcomed the stagestruck girl of yesteryear and her second husband, Friedrich

Burschell (the German translator of Proust), back home. Fritta and Friedrich came to live in a dark little apartment in the suburb of Dejvice, not particularly fashionable, and when they departed again, they left many books on our shelves, including a few novels by Franz Kafka in the Heinrich Mercy & Son edition (now rare); my father wondered why I perused the books of that Kafka Franzl so eagerly. Fritta and her husband moved to Majorca, of all places, and wrote wonderful letters about their sunny exile, until General Franco's navy occupied the island and they had to move on to England, where they rented a cold house at Oxford and Friedrich commuted to London, where he worked for the BBC German Service throughout the war.

I visited them when I studied at University College in London shortly after the war, and Uncle Friedrich always admonished me to bring my candy ration to Fritta, who immensely enjoyed the meager sweets. She was often asked to return to the stage or take part in television productions, but she was honest and confessed that she felt incapacitated, after so many years, by stage fright. Ultimately she moved to Munich, where she died in a small apartment filled with books and memorabilia of the Weimar time.

The little boy with big ears standing close to Grandmother as if needing special protection grew up to be my uncle Leo, who had an uneasy time among languages, historical changes, jobs, and countries. He went to German and Czech schools to train for commercial life but switched to the Prague German university to become a lawyer and, after receiving his degree (a family first), for many years worked for the legal department of the Riunione Adriatica di Sicurtà, the renowned Trieste Insurance Corporation, doing business in all the lands of the former monarchy, his office being in its imposing building (Le Corbusier called it, somewhat condescendingly, an Assyrian palace) located on the corner of Jungmannova and Národní Třída. (I watched President Masaryk's funeral from there.) I suspect that Uncle Leo really wanted to be a journalist and writer more than anything else, and he was responsible for much of my advanced Prague education, taking me to entertaining movies, from the Marx Brothers to Fred Astaire, and to the polemical performances of the Liberated Theater and its glorious songwriter Jaroslav Ježek, whose blues melodies haunt me still.

During World War II, Leo worked in a factory and for the railways *near London. He returned to Prague almost immediately after the end of the war to take a position with the Association of the Jewish Communities of Czechoslovakia. He promptly lost his job after the Communist takeover of February 1948, as a Jew, a "Western émigré," a bourgeois lawyer, and somebody unwilling to join the almighty party; he was constrained to earn a living as factory help and a crane driver on construction sites. In the early 1960s, when conditions somewhat changed, he had a chance to work as a learned tourist guide, taking foreigners to Hradčany Castle, to the Jewish town, and to the New Jewish Cemetery, where Franz Kafka was buried. By 1969 he had moved again, with his wife, Elisabeth, and his son to Fürstenfeldbruck, in Bavaria, where, one of the last writers of the renowned Prague Jewish group, he spent late and happy years writing essays, features, and lectures for Czech, Austrian, and German audiences. I am not surprised that his son, Petr, after his studies in the United States and in England, worked for the BBC in Prague and once a month spends a long weekend at the Munich Staatsbibliothek to study the history of his Jewish forebears.*

The girl in the middle of the picture with the six buttons on her dress and the rounded white collar is my mother's younger sister, Irma, who looks a little as if she did not want to belong to the group and carefully avoids body contact with Grandmother. She was a šička (seamstress), with a minimum of schooling, like my mother, and I remember her, with her red hair, light-colored eyes, and all, as a tall, self-willed woman who ran a salon for stylish Prague women who still preferred to have their dresses made to measure and by hand. There were the usual family rumors about her chic life, but she did not change her boyfriends very often and remained attached to a married Slovak or Hungarian industrialist from Bratislava, who usually picked her up to travel with him to the most fashionable places of the late 1920s and early 1930s. My mother (who often went to little spas in Moravia or Silesia) only sighed when she would tell me that Irma again had gone, of course—to Nice, Juan-les-Pins, or Biarritz. In 1941, Irma was deported to Terezín, worked there as a much-needed seamstress, returned from Mauthausen in May 1945, strong and resolute as ever, and married and cared for Milan, a diabetic Czech workingman whose legs had to be amputated. Aunt Fritta invited her in the 1970s for a trip to Austria, where I met her, but it was not easy to talk. Irma died, eighty-three years old, in her native city.

My mother's family had fully participated in the modest fortunes of Bohemian Jewish society in the advancing nineteenth century. It was, as far as I remember, closer to the liberalism of the age than to ancient spiritual and religious traditions, and I cannot really recall that they strictly adhered to inherited ritual, inside or outside the synagogue. Kafka once suggested that his father was a four-holiday Jew, attending synagogue only four times a year (including the emperor's birthday), and his characterization may be equally fitting to most members of the Brod family (unrelated to the family of Max Brod, Kafka's closest friend). I am certain that my Jewish grandfather honored his ancient religion in his village community, and he and his family were happy with memories of the old way of life, reading to each other Vojtěch Rakous's famous Jewish stories, in Czech, about Modche and his wife, Resi, and their lives in the Bohemian countryside.

As the nineteenth century advanced, matters were complicated, at least as seen from the outside, by questions religious and linguistic, as was each individual decision, or rather habit, made by each member of the family to speak either Czech or German rather than the Yiddish still spoken in the village communities. The Czech Jewish movement, going back to the physician Siegfried Kapper, who started to write Jewish poetry in Czech rather than in German as early as 1843 (to the ire of Czech liberals), was of importance to the Brod sons, who, trying to sort out whether they belonged to the Czech- or German-language communities, were not yet attuned to the promises of Israel. Zionists were few, and even many younger intellectuals, including Max Brod, preferred to profess a "cultural" Zionism, discussing Martin Buber and exploring Jewish traditions on the spot rather than to be pioneers in Palestine, as long as political events did not force them to leave.

The Resistance Groups and October 28, 1939

In the summer of 1939 resistance groups began to define their hopes and means, more often than not in continuation of what they had thought and done in the preceding days of the Second Republic, after the demobilization of the army, President Beneš's abdication and flight to London, and the disappearance of the old political parties, including the Communist one, from public view. Memories of 1917–18 and a certain fluidity among the groups were still the order of the day, and the resisters often worked hand in hand, if not in personal union, with new official organizations created with German compliance, the chief censor, for instance, being the head of an effective unit providing information to London and the chief of government secretly financing underground resistance organizations. For a while contact with people in foreign countries was still possible, though on a reduced scale; consular services continued to function, managers of important firms traveled to sign contracts, noted scholars attended foreign conferences to deliver papers, and other people, occasionally pretending to be on vacation, went over the borders to Slovakia, Poland, and Hungary. London exiles, Moscow functionaries, and the opposition in Prague agreed that it was best, for the time being, to avoid open and violent conflict with the occupying power; and a pragmatic repertory of action recommended by the Czech exiles in London on September 1, 1939, listed the gathering of information first, followed by unobtrusive sabotage and (though it was not said how) spreading active propaganda among restive Austrians and Bavarians thought to be dissatisfied with Hitler's Reich.

Among the ranks of the opposition, perhaps the most salient members were officers and other professional soldiers, who went on living and working in close contact with one another even after the demobilization of the Czech army. The government was confronting the difficult problem of how to place thirty thousand of them in the civil service (not to speak of what to do with the civil servants displaced in the Sudeten, Slovakia, and Carpathian Ruthenia). Former soldiers were grouped in particular offices, administrative institutions, and a seven-thousand-man Government Army (Vládní vojsko) that had mostly ceremonial purposes. But soldiers who opposed the German occupation favored the organization, or rather reorganization, of their earlier command structures in a projected secret army that would function in Prague and in other regions of the protectorate. A body calling itself Obrana národa (In Defense of the Nation, DN) was military rather than political, and its actions were taken by command, not discussion, especially when it was a matter of moving its radio transmitters daily to escape detection or guiding thousands of young men across the border to join military units in France and Britain.

The first DN commanders were Generals Sergej Ingr, soon to leave for London himself, Bedřich Neumann, and Josef Bílý, who, unlike most of his colleagues, had studied at the Imperial War College in Vienna. The orientation of the DN was strictly nationalist and on the right, and though it resolved to serve the republic and to respect President Beneš's authority, it foresaw at least a temporary military dictatorship in Prague after Germany's eventual defeat. Unfortunately the Gestapo was successful in crippling the DN, though its officers preferred suicide to providing names and places, and when London, in September 1941, demanded that it participate in planning an armed revolt, General Bedřich Homolka, its commander in chief of the Prague region, had to respond that he would need arms and men in order to comply.

Another important resistance group had already been established when President Beneš left Czechoslovakia in October 1938 and asked his personal secretary, Dr. Prokop Drtina, to keep together his friends in order to gather information for the Czechs going into exile. He wanted the group to be headed by Chancellor Dr. Přemysl Šámal, *ancien combattant* and chief of the old "Mafia" that had worked for Masaryk and Beneš in Prague in 1917–18; whether it was a wise move to put such a highly visible figure in charge of a secret organization may be a different question (Šámal paid with his life), but Beneš was always enamored of the idea of legal and historical continuities. The group called itself Politické ústředí (Political Center, PC) and professed a strong belief in the democratic and liberal institutions of the First Republic. Politically it expressed this in its changing committees made up of representatives of the five political parties that had been the republic's establishment, among them the Agrarian Ladislav Feierabend, a member of the protectorate government *and* the underground, and the remarkable Dr. Ladislav Rašín, who, against the will of his party, the National Democrats, declared his loyalty to Beneš. The PC group was charged by the exiles in London with collecting information, which it did exceptionally well. Its radio transmitters, whenever they worked, were run by Professor Vladimír Krajina, a plant biologist and former soldier (though his colleagues at the DN demanded that they edit his communications), a particularly active group of railway men smuggled endangered people over the borders, and a circle of journalists made it their special task to keep colleagues in the official newspapers informed about what was really going on in the world.

A third organization was taking shape on the liberal left, bringing together trade unionists, people active in the Workers' Academies, younger intellectuals who disdained the traditional parties, and Christians of Socialist orientation or from the communities of the Czech Brethren. Members of this group, which later called itself the Petitions Committee: We Remain Loyal—this was a reference to words in President Beneš's moving speech on the occasion of Masaryk's funeral and a manifesto written by intellectuals in May 1938—had been active in support of Republican Spain, and they continued to believe that they could appeal to dissatisfied Germans in the Sudeten and the Reich (a belief that the anti-German secret army did not share). The Petitions Committee expected a definite shift to the left in Czechoslovakia's future, but it was to reject the ideas of the Communists, who, after Hitler's attack against the Soviet Union in June 1941, demanded a social revolution without respect for the liberal traditions of the First Republic.

By the fall of 1940 these military, liberal, and Socialist groups had begun to act together under a Central Leadership of Home Resistance (ÚVOD). They also had personal contacts with Czech Communists, who had valiantly supported the republic, at least in the later 1930s, but matters were not made easy for the latter by the abrupt political changes dictated by Moscow, upon which they totally depended. The KSČ, one of the strongest Communist parties in Europe, had been dissolved by government decree in December 1938, yet its finances were in good shape because it had had the brilliant idea of selling its printing presses to Czechoslovakia's archcapitalist Jan Baťa (who had introduced American principles of production to his shoe factories); the party reported to Moscow in September 1939 that it could rely on tens of thousands of dues-paying members in the factories. Nevertheless, reorganization was difficult after the German occupation; top functionaries left for Paris and Moscow, and many party activists were arrested on March 15 thanks to Aktion Gitter, and others on September 1. A party declaration in August supported "firm national unity" and spoke of allied "German anti-Fascists" of Communist, Socialist, Catholic, and Protestant persuasion. Yet Hitler's nonaggression pact with the Soviet Union, signed that month, changed the prescribed view of the coming war, which now was clearly going to be an "imperialist" one. On the other hand, party members had to change their beliefs overnight, and the apparatus admitted that there was "some confusion" among the rank and file and suggested that measures be taken "to enlighten the masses." Some observers believe that after the German-Soviet pact the Communists were inevitably isolated from the other resistance groups, because they were involved more with Moscow than with their political allies at home. In any case, for some time, at least until May 1940, the Communist apparatus and the German security forces in Prague avoided confrontation. It is also true that the Communists favored the demonstrations of October 28, 1939, and that during the night of February 12–13, 1941, nearly the entire Central Committee of the party was arrested by the Gestapo, which then tried to use the Communist transmitters to broadcast fictitious messages to Moscow, but in vain.

Thinking About My Mother

The young girl in the family photograph, standing there a little apart, round cheeks, dark eyes, and a full shock of hair (reddish, as it turned out), was Annie, my mother, sixteen years old at the time, and rather steadfast in her life, at least compared with her sisters, Irma, the one with the gentleman friend, and Fritta, the bohémienne. My mother never enjoyed the privileges of a higher education as did her brothers; girls were supposed to work and to contribute financially to the well-being of the family, and my mother, who was apprenticed, after elementary school, to a seamstress, learned the trade and kept a keen eye on elegant ladies' dresses. Basically, she was a proletarian working girl, at least from eight in the morning till six in the evening, and then she returned to her lower-middle-class family to help in the house. She did not show much interest

*in her religion, as far as I remember, nor was she ever interested in poli-
tics. What she knew about literature, and especially about the theater, she
learned from my father, who no doubt gave her long speeches about his literary hopes and plans on their dates, which went on for four or five years
before they married.*

*My father met my mother, according to family lore (possibly of his in-
vention), one morning in the early summer of 1914 at the corner of
Wenceslas Square and Štěpánská Street. My mother was going to work,
and my father—God knows what he was doing there that early in the
morning, but he had dropped out of school, hoping for a job in the theater.
Family reports affirmed that my father was immediately enchanted by my
mother, the Jewish girl, and all my aunts, on both sides, unanimously said
it was because there had been few Jews in the Tyrol and none in the lonely
Ladin valleys and my dad was hopelessly attracted to the exotic redhead
with the freckles. I wonder in what language they originally talked to each
other, Mother with her fragmentary German, Dad with his insufficient
Czech? Perhaps they developed their own Prague language of love.*

*It is not difficult, at least for the literary historian, to know where the
young people went on their dates, because my father always wrote a poem
about the latest Sunday excursion, either on the riverboat to Zbraslav or
on foot up the Kleinseite hill, and it was regularly published in the* Prager
Tagblatt: *impressionist verse in the beginning but expressionist pathos
later, in the most recent avant-garde mode, with a lot of exclamation
marks. Knowing my mother, I think she was not much impressed by the
avant-garde style. She went on sewing, and when war broke out in August
and my father had to join the Imperial Army for a few weeks of basic training in Szegedin, in Hungary, she duly went there to visit him. It was her
first trip beyond Prague ever. Since my father was employed by the Prague
Theater, a public institution, he was quickly reclaimed as irreplaceable
and returned home without being sent to the front.*

*They married after the war, against strong reservations by both fami-
lies, one arguing against the Jewess (Grandfather used a stronger term),
the other against the goy, but to little avail. After I was born, all religious
and ethnic arguments were suspended, if not discontinued, because both
families in their own ways had welcomed the republic, the Jews because
the new constitution recognized Jews as a nation of their own (Masaryk*

was for them a new incarnation of the old gentle emperor), and the Ladins because they did not feel they belonged to either Germans or Czechs (though they now spoke German) and rather foolishly assumed they could stay above the fray. Yet there were at times unforeseen questions and difficulties. When I was eight years old and joined in the celebrations of the republic, enthusiastically waving a tricolor on the street, somebody (undoubtedly a German nationalist) told my father he should take better care of me, working, as he was, for a German institution.

In our Prague beginnings, my mother called me Chuliminda (a freely invented intimate Czech name) and fitted me with a Lord Fauntleroy suit, complete with little white gloves, to play in the sand with other astonished children on Žofín Island, near the National Theater. More often than not, she left me to a slečna, the poor daughter from a working-class family who kept my Czech alive, and in the evening departed for the theater to be present at the most recent production for which she had sketched the dresses for the ballet or the diva. I found a number of portraits of her, the queen of the theater or press ball, once in a silken and shining green dress to set off her fiery hair, and I often wondered how sure she was of herself, given her incomplete education, being on equal terms with the visiting stars of stage and screen.

Occasionally, though, I felt called upon to show what I myself could do. Once we were on a walk through the meadows near Marienbad with the film star Elisabeth Bergner and her mother; the ladies discussed a new play using psychoanalytical ideas but could not remember the name of the playwright. Twelve years old and dragging my feet, I piped up from behind and suggested that the author was, of course, Grete Urbantschitsch (I had seen the play on my father's desk). In the summer we often went to well-known provincial spas in Bohemia or Moravia, and to Karlsbrunn or Gräfenberg in Silesia, or to the famous Austrian Südbahnhotel in Semmering, in whose splendid restaurant I had my first crush—on an Indian princess at the next table (I put little love letters under her napkin, but I am afraid she never read them). A group of elegant ladies often went for healthy walks up the Pinkenkogel, an unheroic hill near the hotel, and my mother would don firm shoes and woolen stockings for the occasion. I noted eight years later that she put on the same shoes and stockings when she had to join her transport to the ghetto of Terezín.

My mother was too shy to be a self-conscious bohémienne *like her older sister, Fritta, but she was not a housewife either who would be interested in cooking according to the famous recipes of Magdalena Dobromila Rettigová, which always start, "Take 12 eggs and . . ." I am afraid my mother was no cook at all; in good times she could rely on the help of an experienced girl, or two, from the Czech countryside who did the housework and also had their essential function in my prepubertal restlessness. On Tuesdays, when the washing was to be done, the girls went up to the top floor, where big wooden tubs were ready and hot water steamed in marvelous clouds. The girls, clad only in their thin, wet undershirts, were not cross when with suspicious regularity I appeared in the clouds of steam or hid under the tables. They laughed easily, around the tubs, and chased me.*

I think my mother's troubles began in the mid-1930s; I noticed that she had to lie down frequently in a darkened room, I had to change cold towels on her forehead, and she complained about terrible headaches. This all coincided, so it happened, with my father's prolonged and unexplained absences from home. I am almost certain that it was my mother who instituted divorce proceedings because she did not want to live with an absentee husband known to travel with young actresses eager for his advice. My mother showed admirable energy: one night I heard a great commotion in the apartment, with my father screaming and weeping, but my mother called the police and had him removed from the premises. To survive financially, she then established a salon for ladies who appreciated her well-tailored dresses, and I became one of the youngest readers of Vogue *and* Harper's Bazaar *in prewar Czechoslovakia.*

A few years later my mother told me that she would have had a chance to go to the United States, showing me a little photograph dedicated to "My dear Annie" by Conrad Veidt, who, on a tour and in a brief encounter, had suggested she join him in Hollywood. My mother confessed that she had refused because I was still in school, and it was too late to tell her that I would have loved to have been educated in America. Whenever I see Conrad Veidt as the German Air Force major in Casablanca, *for me a cult movie for my own reasons, I sadly think of my lost career as a Hollywood scriptwriter. The real problem, in the political situation of 1936–37, was that by divorcing my father, my mother deprived herself of an "Aryan" husband and the meager protection of a "mixed" marriage by* which she would have survived, even if, in the later years of the protectorate, one of the partners in mixed marriages was removed to the Prague Hagibor Stadium or to Terezín in the spring of 1945, when the Soviet Army was inexorably approaching.

There were confused thoughts in my mind, but my mother wanted to restore her life, and in 1937 she rather suddenly married Victor Mandel, a well-known physician from a little Jewish community in Moravia, trained as a highly qualified surgeon at Vienna's renowned General Hospital. In his student years there he had joined the Socialists and did not cease to support them after they had been defeated by the Austrian Army in the civil war of February 1934. I did not know much about my mother's plans, at least not in the beginning, but I joined her on little walks with Victor, who, on Tuesday and Thursday afternoons, worked at the clinic for railway men, where we picked him up for our suburban perambulations; my mother did not want people to know yet. Later she no longer hid her feelings, and since Victor owned a car, we went on frequent weekend trips with him to the Czech or Austrian countryside, and I was permitted to join them at breakfast, mostly in little village inns.

I have to thank Victor for my early political education, and when I was considered for a comparative literature professorship at the University of Vienna many decades later and came to sit, at an official banquet, next to His Excellency Prime Minister Bruno Kreisky (a prearranged coincidence, I guess), he was surprised that I knew an inordinate amount about his comrades of 1934 and their escapes from Austria to Czechoslovakia. Comrade Kreisky left his Czechoslovak exile in time to go to Sweden, but Victor escaped only on the last train to London, leaving my mother alone and unprotected. At that moment, strangely enough, my father emerged, suddenly and almost from the middle of nowhere, and began to support her again, materially and in many other ways. It was a strange situation, to say the least.

The Fall Demonstrations of 1939

The Prague demonstrations of October 28, 1939, to celebrate Czechoslovakia's independent republic were the first ones to be guided, at least in part, by the resistance groups, which did not entirely agree what should be done: whether, as Beneš suggested, to be content with symbolic action or to undertake a general strike. Radio communication with London unfortunately did not work, for technical reasons, but some decision had to be taken. Prague citizens were surprised by a surfeit of handbills suggesting that people should wear black ties (an idea later rescinded so as not to make it easy for the German police to arrest demonstrators) or their dark Sunday best, refrain from smoking or drinking (to avoid the state tax), shopping, using the trams, or working. Alas, October 28 was a Saturday, when working hours were short anyway, and the few attempts to strike were easily put down by the threats of the managers. Action was on the street and squares in the city center, and though the Czech and German authorities knew in a rather general way about the plans of the demonstrators, both the government and the Office of the Reichsprotektor were resolved to play them down. Neurath, in his best diplomatic manner, left Prague for a long weekend, the better to be able to ignore what would happen, but his state secretary, K. H. Frank, and Walter Stahlecker, commander of police, waited for their opportunity to intervene and to show that Neurath's diplomatic procedures were totally wrong.

The day started rather quietly, with workers and employees arriving at their jobs on time (only construction sites were empty), but by 9:00 a.m. many people, especially of the younger generation, had gathered on Wenceslas Square, wearing little ribbons in Czech colors or, occasionally, riding caps, which Masaryk had very much liked. German students whom Frank used as agents provocateurs suddenly appeared on the scene and made it their sport to tear away ribbons and push the patriotic caps rudely from the demonstrators' heads. In the later morning Czech demonstrators, singing or chanting slogans—"We want freedom! Long live Beneš!" (and also "Long live Stalin!")—spilled over to the Old Town Square, where Czechs and Germans battled each other as the Czech police tried to look the other way.

At the railway station, droves of people arrived from the suburbs and outlying villages to join the melee. By 1:00 p.m. a vociferous group had gathered in front of the Gestapo building at Bredovská Street to demand the release of prisoners, but by that time the commandant of the German security forces had notified the Czech minister of the interior that the SS Leibstandarte (bodyguard) would march down Wenceslas Square, as it did every Saturday, and if passage was not cleared, the SS would take care of the problem. Czech and German police began to push demonstrators away from Wenceslas Square and into surrounding streets and squares.

At 3:00 a group of demonstrators attacked the Hotel Palace, nearly opposite the main post office on Jindřišská Street, where Gestapo people were billeted, and succeeded in freeing a man whom the Germans had arrested, and Wenceslas Square, at least on one side, again filled with a tide of returning demonstrators defying the police. By 5:00 p.m. Frank had visited President Hácha at Lány Castle and told him in no uncertain terms that Hitler would not tolerate demonstrations in the protectorate and declared that if the Czech police would not act more resolutely, the SS Leibstandarte would take over immediately. A little later German and Czech police (the latter under pressure from the government) again removed the demonstrators from Wenceslas Square; a few shots were fired, and people were dispersed, but demonstrations went on near the railway stations and elsewhere until about 8:00 p.m. Four hundred people were arrested that day by Czech and German police, and fifteen demonstrators were brought to hospitals. On the upper reaches of Žitná Street, Otakar Sedláček, a workingman, was instantly killed by a bullet through his heart, and Jan Opletal, a medical student, was shot in the abdomen; he lay critically injured in a hospital. From that day on Frank, possibly conspiring with Heinrich Himmler, who came to Prague on November 2 and suddenly promoted Frank to SS group leader, personally and in recurrent telephone calls to Berlin worked to discredit Neurath for not having shown an iron fist to the unruly Czechs.

Jan Opletal died on November 11, and his fellow medical students wanted to be present when his coffin was transferred from the Hlávka dormitory, where they all were housed, to the railway station, whence it would be taken to the Moravian village of his birth. Guarantees that the funeral would proceed in a dignified manner were offered to the Czech police by functionaries of the official Student Union, a branch of National Solidarity, and by the dormitory director. Permission to proceed was granted by the Czech and German authorities, who ignored a meeting of the students at the U Fleků beer hall held to organize it all. The Gestapo was just waiting for its chance.

On the morning of November 15, more than three thousand students paid homage to Opletal at the University Institute of Pathology, and in the chapel a preacher of the Evangelical Church of the Czech Brethren read from the Bible and thanked Opletal's parents for the exemplary education of their son and the student groups for their presence. The coffin was carried in silence to the waiting hearse, but when it was placed in it to be driven from the Albertov medical district to the railroad station, students, male and female, began to intone the national hymn, a sign of trouble brewing, and then marched, over five hundred strong, up to Charles Square, where they clashed with Czech police and had to take refuge in the Technical University building. The police allowed them to leave only in small groups, but these groups coalesced again in a procession that tried to break through to the city center, demonstrating for "Czechoslovakia" and "Freedom." Frank, who wanted to see for himself what was going on, found himself surrounded on the corner of Národní and Spálená and ordered his car to a halt; his driver was roughed up by the excited crowd, which gave him a broken nose and a bloody right eye, and alas, his wristwatch was gone in the melee. In small and combative groups, students continued to demonstrate, throwing German streetcar signs into the Vltava River, congregating on the Old Town Square at the Tomb of the Unknown Soldier, and singing old national songs in front of the Faculty of Law, where they briefly battled Czech police and a carload of SS officers, who arrested three of them. By noon everything was over, at least in the streets of Prague.

Yet Hitler, after the rapid triumph of German forces in Poland over the preceding ten weeks, was unwilling to tolerate Czech defiance of any kind, and before the demonstrations had hardly ended, he demanded that Neurath, Frank, and General Erich Friderici, of the Wehrmacht in Prague, immediately come to Berlin to discuss the situation. Historians continue to conjecture what was resolved on that occasion, and when. Defenders of Neurath, among them the historian Gustav von Schmoller, note that in the morning of November 16 the closing of the Czech universities was discussed, while in the afternoon, in a meeting attended only by Hitler, Himmler, and Frank (Neurath and his entourage being excused), other measures were approved. Neurath was foolish enough to put his special plane at the disposal of Frank, who wanted to fly back to Prague immediately. Neurath and his chief of staff took the train the next morning, and when they arrived in Prague, they were confronted not only with the announcement that all Czech universities were to be closed for three years but with the fact that nine student functionaries had been shot and more than twelve hundred students transported to a concentration camp. Notice of the first, on red paper, was posted on street corners all over Prague, and it bore the name not of Frank but of Neurath; he fully and officially accepted responsibility when General Alois Eliáš, new prime minister of the Czech government, in an evening audience asked for confirmation of these brutal measures.

Of the nine men who had been shot at Ruzyně at 7:00 a.m. on November 17, eight had been active in National Solidarity or in the national or local organizations of the Student Union, and Czech police reports noted that many of them had, in the First Republic, belonged to right of center political parties, either the National Democrats or National Unification (Národní sjednocení), both aggressively opposed to Beneš's and Masaryk's policies. Dr. Jan Matouš, for example, had been appointed by President Hácha to chair a Czech-German Friendship League, and Jan Černý, twenty-five years old, had been sent to Berlin to establish contacts with appropriate German student organizations there. That is to say, eight of the nine were, to say the least, committed to policies of the government-sponsored National Solidarity and were in no way active in the resistance. It has never been discovered why the Gestapo included, among these men, Marek Frauwirth, a Slovak citizen, born in Poland of a Jewish family. He had finished his studies earlier, returned on March 15 to Slovakia, and yet had come back to Prague, where he had worked in occasional jobs at the Slovak Consulate, possibly (as Josef Leikert surmises) helping people to escape via Bratislava to Belgrade. The Czech police believed that he was a Communist.

While the executions were being prepared, German police surrounded five of Prague's most important student dormitories and two more in Brno (though no Moravians had yet demonstrated), and the arrested Prague students were brought to the Ruzyně Prison, where they were scrutinized one by one. The ones under twenty years of age were let go, along with Slovak citizens and students from Yugoslavia and Bulgaria; those who could show membership in the Fascist Vlajka group were also sent home. The rest, twelve hundred strong, were immediately transferred to the concentration camp in Oranienburg, and later to Sachsenhausen. By 1943, on the protracted insistence of Hácha, intervening with Neurath and later with his successor, many of the students were let go in small groups, but the Czech government had to pay a heavy political price for their release. Fifteen of them died in the camps, and three who survived—Zdeněk Mikeštík, Adolf Skalka, and František Stavělík—heroically died on the Prague barricades in May 1945.

My Father's Family

The Ladins are an ethnic group that linguistically goes back to the first century B.C., when the expansive Romans, under the emperors Drusus and Tiberius, began to occupy and administer the Alpine rims of their empire, where the local Rhaetian population assimilated to the spoken Latin of the newcomers. Alpine valleys divide, and speakers of Ladin (Romansh) in modern times live in the canton of Graubünden in Switzerland, where their Rhaeto-Romansh constitutes Switzerland's fourth official language; in the Friuli region of northern Italy (Pier Paolo Pasolini used the local idiom in his early poetry); and in the Dolomite valleys around the Sella Massif in the South Tyrol, once Austrian and now Italian.

My father's family originally lived in Gardena Valley (Grödnertal), not far from Bolzano (Bozen), and when I thought that their Ladin sounded like Old Provençal, my philological instincts were not entirely incorrect. Of course, there is no "Ladin" in the sense of a unified language, for even in the Dolomites alone Ladins use at least five separate idioms, according to village and tradition. In the autonomous province of Bolzano, in northern Italy, nowadays 60 percent of the population are German South Tyroleans, 36 percent Italians, and 4 percent Ladins who, I guess, under-

stand their fellow Ladini in other provinces quite readily and easily switch to Italian or German, if they do not prefer English when American tourists come.

My father's forebears owned a homestead called da Tlousel, first mentioned in a parish book of the sixteenth century. The owner was listed as Melchior de Metz da Tlousel; explications of his Ladin name, derived from de Mezz, meaning "in the middle (of the valley)," do not require any etymological detour via the French city of Metz. Living was not easy, harvests on the high slopes were meager, and the mountain peasants had to develop other than agricultural skills to survive. There was weaving, the preparation of waterproof loden cloth, glove making (reminiscent of what my Jewish ancestors did in their Bohemian villages), and a good deal of bobbin lace. By the eighteenth century, some families had taken up carving religious figurines, kitchen utensils, or toys from the precious wood of the zirbel, mountain pine, and a hundred years later everybody was busy working with the plow, feeding a few cows, and handling the carving knife. The peasants discovered that there was a market for their carvings far beyond the mountains, and many enterprising sons and daughters began to travel, selling Gardena carvings abroad. There were groups of Ladin merchants in Naples, Venice, and Trieste; a Johann Matthias Demetz ran a sales office in Padua, Johann Aldosser resided in Lisbon, members of the Runggaldier family could be found in Nuremberg and Klagenfurt, and Peter de Mez in Philadelphia. When my grandfather Josef Anton Demetz da Tlousel (b. 1857), who had married Maria Josefa Insam, a Ladin girl who briefly worked in a textile shop in Innsbruck, decided to move first to Upper Austria and later to Prague, he came too late and went bankrupt because in the new age of mechanical toys the market had changed, and nobody wanted to buy wooden toys anymore.

I know far less about my father's family than about my mother's, and since I came to live on her side rather than among the Ladins, huddled together in the little Týnská Street, close to the Old Town Square, and looked at askance by her folk, much has become a myth. At first, it seems, my grandfather prospered, acquired an adjacent solid house at the Týn Court. His name was put in ornamental stonework in front of the entrance, but in 1945 it was believed too German and was removed. He became treasurer of the long-established Prague Club of Italians (Ladin or

Italian, no difference). I remember as a boy paging through his many hand-painted catalogs of wooden figures of saints, drums, and trains produced in a distant valley. After his bankruptcy the house had to be sold, and the family moved to a kind of railroad apartment in the late medieval building at No. 6, in front of Týnská, close to the Old Town Square (now gloriously housing a wing of the Metropolitan Gallery of modern Czech painting). When I was young, the old building was a rather disreputable affair. On the ground floor was a beer place whose urinals stank to heaven, and in the gate of the next house an aging prostitute waited day and night for customers. (She was quite motherly, however, when I collected my pocket money and became one of her customers.) My mother certainly did not like that my father continued to pay the rent for the hapless Ladin family and kept a wary eye on my dubious Týnská excursions.

My photograph of 1898 does not attest to happiness among the Ladin immigrant children living in the Old Town, not far from where Franz Kafka was born. My grandfather and grandmother do not appear in the faded picture, but there are five children (out of seven) dressed in curious provincial costumes and looking rather bewildered. On the left stands Aunt Mathilda, who rented rooms and died of cancer (I remember being at her bed, one of forty, in a ward of the Prague General Hospital), and at her side is Aunt Anna, usually called die anbrann'te Tant (our singed auntie), because she went blind early and, at Christmastime, developed a habit of coming dangerously close to the burning candles on the tree (a bucket of water was always ready). Aunt Anna lived in a home run by hospitable nuns and survived by selling stockings and shawls that she knitted herself; I have to confess that I do not know when she died (possibly in the last years of the war). The little girl next to her actually happens to be my father dressed in female clothes, according to the fashion of the day for small children, and next to him stands Uncle Felix, who stuttered and, fortunately, found a steady job in a bank. (When he was arrested in 1945 as "German," my father got him out, and he camped for a year in our kitchen before he joined his daughter.) Leopold, on the right, must have been the secret of the family; he was retarded, put in an institution or died early, because I do not remember that his life was ever mentioned by anybody.

Aunt Paula does not appear in the photograph because she was born later. She was not fortunate either; wanting to escape from the family, she met an army officer and died of a botched abortion in 1917. Uncle Karl does not appear because he was born in the new century, and though he was spared the physiological burdens and afflictions of his many siblings, his later life was difficult for other reasons. He was a gifted artist, had a small atelier somewhere on Hradčany Hill, which I liked to visit because of its attractive disorder, and made a living by sketching advertisements and posters for a few well-known enterprises. He was, to judge from the misgivings of my mother, a ladies' man, the ladies being those who sat in the late afternoon at the café Juliš (on the first floor) waiting for well-heeled beaux; his tastes ran to statuesque girls who had just arrived from the countryside. Unfortunately he was rather foolish; one afternoon in 1941 he was sipping coffee in the lobby of the Hotel Zlatá Husa (Golden Goose), on Wenceslas Square, and, making light conversation, told a man at his table that the war was lost and the Reich would never be able to fight the United States. The other guy did not share his opinion, showed him his Gestapo identification, arrested Uncle Karl on the spot, dragged him to prison, and sentenced him to twenty years for high treason. He was sent to the infamous Small Fort (Malá Pevnost) at Terezín, where guards tortured political prisoners at will, and was later transferred to a prison in Dresden. On February 13, 1944, he was liberated by the devastating attack of Allied bombers on the city. The historian Frederick Taylor writes that many of the prisoners roaming through Dresden changed into everyday clothes at the burning railroad station, where they found disemboweled pieces of luggage, and I hope that my uncle was one of them and did not have to make it, in his prisoner's garb, through the woods on the border with Saxony (where I happened to be working in a labor camp for half Jews) to Bohemia and Prague, where he hid for three months in the old Týnská flat. When the Czechs rose against the Germans in early May 1945, he hastened downstairs to help build barricades but was denounced as German by a neighbor; he was rescued only by the testimony of his Terezín fellow prisoners. He spent his last years living on the small pension of a Nazi victim in Nuremberg (of all places) and died there quietly. He was the only one of my father's family ever to go back to Gardena, and my distant cousin Hubert, whom I visited there in 2003, vividly recalled the visit of that curious old man.

Writing About My Father

It is not easy to write about my father, and my questions, doubts, and admiration combine with a recurrent melancholy about a life that hoped for much and was later totally distorted by circumstances of place and time, not to speak of history. I understand why he wanted to get away from the Týnská family, though he almost religiously continued to support his mother (who worked in the kitchen in long gray skirts, a rosary around her hips, muttering in Ladin) as long as she lived, and he tried to help his sisters and brothers, who had their own burdens to carry. Other young people ran away with the circus, but he was attracted to the rich world of the theater, did not finish school (I suspect), and was hired on the spot (1914) when he presented himself to Heinrich Teweles, an erudite critic and director of Prague's German Theater, as resident writer (dramaturg). Of course, he wrote poetry, eagerly read what the most advanced writers published in Berlin (Prague German writing was rather conservative, he thought, with the exception of Franz Werfel's poetry, which he adored), and, under the weary eyes of Teweles and the German Theaterverein, which included the pillars of Prague's German Jewish society, began to introduce new expressionist plays to a hesitant Prague audience. By 1916 he had convinced Teweles that a new repertory series of Kammerspiele (chamber plays) should be produced at the old Theater of the Estates, and he established a new publication titled Blätter der Prager Kammerspiele (Publications of the Prague Chamber Plays) to defend his dramaturgical decisions. I wonder how much he knew about his courageous ally Karel Hugo Hilar, on the Czech side, who produced new plays from the post-1914 advanced German repertory at the Vinohradské divadlo.

Prague's comfortable German Jewish middle class liked Arthur Schnitzler, but my father made theater history by producing Walter Hasenclever's Der Sohn (The Son), a play that spoke for an entire restless generation, in the middle of World War I (it premiered on September 30, 1916) and before it appeared in Dresden or Berlin. In Prague the radical son was played by Gerd Fricke and later by melancholy Ernst Deutsch. The young régisseur intrepidly went on with most of Frank Wedekind and a new play by Max Brod (in spite of his personal skepticism about the author) and continued his pioneering experiments by staging Ernst Weiss's Tanya, an almost mystical play about revolutionary Russia, with Rahel Sanzara (October 11, 1919), and a spate of later Hasenclever plays, done with surprising cinematic techniques. He was briefly joined by Georg Wilhelm Pabst (later one of the great movie directors) and by the composer and conductor Alexander Zemlinsky, dominant in musical life and in German opera, who challenged Prague audiences by performing Arnold Schoenberg and Erich Wolfgang Korngold, of later Hollywood fame.

I do not believe that my father was overly disturbed by the events of November 16, 1920, when a Czech mob, which had first vented its rage against Jewish institutions in the old quarter and which was led by eager actors of the Prague National Theater, stormed the Theater of the Estates, bodily removed my father from his office, and occupied the building in the name of the Czechoslovak nation. It was used henceforth for Czech performances. (President Masaryk, however, never entered the building thereafter because he believed that the occupation was unconstitutional and not in the best interests of the republic.) I guess that my father, growing up in the Týnská Ladinia, did not feel partisan about local national conflicts. He moved into a new office and, in agreement with Leopold Kramer, his new director, who had come from Vienna, established in 1922 a Kleine Bühne (Little Stage) to continue experimental productions; the three-hundred-seat theater was in an old building at Senovážné náměstí, Heuwaag Square.

My father was very happy when he was invited in the mid-1920s to run the German theater in Brno, capital of Moravia, where he thought he would be free and on his own. My mother was particularly pleased, she told me later, that he moved out of the shadows of the Týnská family and devoted himself to her own; in Brno they settled comfortably in a spacious apartment on Úvoz, under the mighty old Spielberg, Brno's hilltop castle-fortress. His job was not easy because he had to provide a complicated triple repertory: drama in one old place smelling of fish on the Vegetable Market; operetta in another; and on Mondays and Tuesdays on the stage of the Czech theater, grand German opera performances for a demanding clientele that often compared the local fare with performances in nearby Vienna. (I was allowed to attend opera performances for the first act, after which the fräulein took me home to bed. My cultural deficiencies in the opera field have never been repaired.)

Only later did it dawn on my father that it had not been his wisest decision to leave Prague for the Moravian provinces; he was of an apolitical mind, committed to literature and the arts (his Turandot *production, with Julius Patzak as the unhappy prince, became famous although he had a deaf ear for music of any kind), and in the new job he was suddenly responsible for public decisions made in a narrow space where German nationalists clashed with a prosperous German-speaking Jewish middle class in a Czech context. He found himself involved in these conflicts, which he had long avoided in Prague but could not avoid in Brno. Moreover, the events of October 1928, or rather their consequences, proved to be inescapable for decades to come.*

When he announced, for October 30, 1928, a festive performance to celebrate the first ten years of the Czechoslovak Republic, a delegation of nationalist German students, mostly from the local Technical University, appeared in his office to protest his decision and to demand that the performance be canceled and that subscribers not be forced to attend. My father did not give in, so the German students organized a public demonstration, interrupted the performance (at which the Czechoslovak hymn was played), and in the tumult tried to read a proclamation against celebrating the republic and making any attempt to pressure German subscribers to participate. The Czech police intervened, and five nationalist students were arrested. In January 1931, my father being the principal witness against them, these five were sentenced by a district court for disturbing the public peace and, according to the law protecting the republic (Paragraph 14), for rioting "against the state, its origins, against its independence, constitutional unity and its democratic-republican form." The court insisted that the sentence was unconditional and that the five had to serve their short prison terms, but when they returned a few years later to the scene as fully fledged Nazis, my father (married to a Jewish wife) did not have much of a chance to continue as usual.

My father's contract was not renewed in 1933, when Hitler came to power in Germany, and thereafter he was unable to work in the theater as a dramaturg or artist. My mother explained to me one day, after he had left home, that he was looking for a job somewhere else, and when he developed a curious habit of coming one day and going another, my mother divorced him. I heard conflicting news about what he was doing, briefly working as secretary in a union of theater directors, jobbing in private business, and for some time (I was pricking up my ears) working for the Mělník radio station.

In the first year of the protectorate he found a job as assistant at the Cinema Broadway, on Příkopy, Prague's most elegant movie house, which meant unlimited free tickets for me and my buddies. Unfortunately one day he was unceremoniously fired by its SS Treuhänder (trustee, appointed by the Office of the Reichsprotektor) because, it turned out, he had sided in an occasional dispute with the Czech cashiers and ushers against the German trustee. There was always a dark spot under the candlestick, he reasoned, and he accepted the invitation of a former colleague to work as administrator of the Rose Theater in Berlin, the last private enterprise of its kind in Prussia, flourishing on presenting folksy comedies written in local dialect.

Its glory did not last beyond September 1, 1944, when all German theaters were closed because of the war, and my father, now in his fifties, was in danger of being mobilized in the Volkssturm to defend Berlin against the advancing Allies. He lived in a cheap hotel room, Berlin was bombed nightly, but he did not feel like defending it, and since it was impossible to run away, he developed an ingenious plan to remove himself for medical reasons. His plan was to "fall" in the darkness into a gaping bomb crater and injure himself slightly, but when he jumped, the crater proved rather steep and he broke both legs (Volkssturm, adieu). His girlfriend brought him from Berlin to a Prague hospital, where his Czech fellow patients and the doctors kept him, well bandaged and, for show, on crutches long after they were needed, as a kind of honest German pet until the May uprising in 1945, when he went home, seven minutes across Charles Square, limping a little, a picaresque hero of his time.

A Literary Discussion in 1939

At the beginning of the protectorate, "autonomy" of national life was very much on the minds of many people in the Czech government, the schools, the media, the theaters, and the film studios, where production was ordered to go on under German supervision. Yet given the

Reichsprotektor in the Czernin Palace and the Gestapo, people rightly found it hard to believe in any political autonomy, and the idea was revised to refer to Czech culture in the broadest sense. People turned to the past to discover what constituted Czech traditions and the ways their historical defenders upheld them. The avant-garde of the recent First Republic, so rich in its achievements, gave way to an inclusive historicism of a deeply committed kind that inspired a new interplay among writers, critics, and readers. Historical plays and movies became fashionable, and publishers turned to the Czech classics of the patriotic nineteenth century, read now by widening audiences "as if driven," a critic remarked, "by an instinct for self-preservation." Few wanted to realize that the new historicism paradoxically repeated what the Germans themselves had done when fighting the French invasions of the early nineteenth century.

The European Literary Club, which had published important translations of works from France, England, and the United States for the educated middle classes, announced in February 1939 that it planned a new series under a Slavia imprint; it actually began its *Národní klenotnice* (National Treasury) with a volume by Alois Jirásek, a nineteenth-century master of the historical novel. Other publishers followed suit, and patriotic novelists, poets, and historians of the previous century were published en masse; among them were František Palacký, with his massive *Dějiny národu českého* (History of the Czech Nation); the Prague women writers Božena Němcová and Karolina Světlá; the realist Jan Neruda; and the Romantic poet K. H. Mácha. While the initial print run for a new Czech novel was at the most 1,200 or 1,500 copies, these classics appeared in editions of 10,000 to 20,000, which were quickly sold to eager readers. Eight different firms published 14 various volumes by Božena Němcová in 1939 and 28 in 1940, of which 70,000 copies were sold, and 37 different titles by Jan Neruda were published in the two years 1939–41. Yet older interests persisted: in 1939, 134 translations from English were published, and 127 a year later, 43 from French (32 in 1940), 9 from Russian (10 in 1940); and new novels by Pearl S. Buck, Dorothy L. Sayers, and John Steinbeck (as late as 1941) were read by many not easily swayed.

Albert Pražák, a professor of Czech literature at Charles University and later the chairman of the Czech National Council, which directed the armed rising against the German occupiers in May 1945, articulated, for many, his grave doubts about the new historicism. In a widely read essay in *Kritický měsíčník* (1939), he suggested that looking to the past in difficult moments of the present was a Czech tradition. Historicism, he said, was flooding the movies, the theater, and art exhibits; when we are anxious, "we ask our ancestors for advice," and even Mácha "dreamed in ruined castles about the future glory of his nation." Yet the question arises whether people do not look for "the idyll of old times" in order to avoid present troubles and to avoid looking ahead to confront what is coming. Pražák suggested that the new historicism implied a good deal of provinciality and demanded that Czechs keep attuned to what was new and alive beyond their borders. He even asked if Czechs should not study more carefully what was going on in Italy (possibly he was thinking of Alberto Moravia and Elio Vittorini) and Germany, and developed the idea that it would perhaps be useful to establish a periodical titled *Die tschechische Geisteswelt* (Czech Intellectual Horizons), to acquaint Germans with what was going on in Czech thought and literature. (The idea was not implemented because it was too late.) The most important reason why the interest in the past should be redirected, however, was the young and creative generation of writers and poets, alive, active, and highly talented, a guarantee of the nation's future, who should not be ignored.

František Kožík was thirty years old when in late 1939 his fictionalized biography of Jan Kašpar Dvořák, known to the world as Jean-Gaspard Debureau, the greatest of French pantomime players, was published; it turned out to be the country's most popular novel and bestseller, selling nearly fifty thousand copies almost instantly and with new editions, inconspicuously revised, continuing to appear throughout the century and all changes of regimes. Kožík, an editor at Brno's radio station, was the darling of the reading middle classes and the bane of intellectual critics, especially after he won first prize in the European Book Competition of 1939, and his book, in spite of all international difficulties, was published in many translations, including an American one by Dora Round that appeared under the imprint of Farrar & Rinehart in 1940. Kožík's *Největší z pierotů* (The Great Debureau) was a good read that satisfied many expectations, historical and patriotic, precisely because it was a rather eclectic affair, carrying its sources lightly and, perhaps, with youthful carelessness. Kožík had been in Paris for a brief vacation in 1937, and his France much resembled that of *La Bohème*, Act One; he entertained his reader with stories of suffering and success, theatrical revolutions, plucky Parisian street girls and vampiric courtesans, and a good deal of sentimental nostalgia for Bohemia, which Debureau-Dvořák had to leave behind when he was a boy.

Debureau's father is a restless Czech soldier of the Imperial Austrian Army that fought against revolutionary France. In France he meets a French girl who returns with him to winter quarters in Bohemian Kolín, on the Elbe River, and gives him many children, among them his fifth son, Jan Kašpar, born in 1796. Life is not easy, and when rumor reaches the family that Jan's French grandmother has left them a house in Amiens, they decamp for France again with all the children, now an ever-hungry band of musicians and acrobats, only to find that the house is in ruins and must be sold for a pittance. They perform all over France and ultimately in Paris, where young Jan Kašpar has a chance to join the pantomime troupe at the Théâtre des Funambules, much enjoyed by people of the suburbs and, increasingly, by younger intellectuals tired of anachronistic tragedy. Jan Kašpar Dvořák, now Jean-Gaspard Debureau, as clumsy and sad Pierrot, becomes the star of the troupe, admired by Romantic writers and celebrated by the critic Jules Janin as a true "artist of the people." Yet he is not happy. He marries poor Desirée, who gives him a son but betrays him with a fan painter, and for Marie Duplessis, whom he calls *la dame aux camélias*, he is but a fleeting affair. Napoleon, Victor Hugo, Charles Nodier, Georges Sand, and Honoré de Balzac, among others, make cameo appearances; Debureau, of all people, fires the first shot of the 1848 Revolution, and when he is aging, his son Charles takes over as the famous melancholy Pierrot.

The Czech novel was a rather simple and sentimental narrative, but it is remarkable that young Kožík, in the Moravian provinces, felt powerfully attracted to the figure of an artist who persists in his art, though he does not speak. Not much later, in German-occupied France, the character became central to *Les enfants du paradis*, one of the best French movies ever made (1941–43, script by Marcel Carné, with Jean-Louis Barrault in the starring role). Perhaps it was the right moment to celebrate such a figure.

Největší z pierotů, and not just the bestseller, immediately challenged Václav Černý, a learned university professor of comparative literature, indefatigable critic, and editor in chief of *Kritický měsíčník,* which took as its prime mission to uphold the highest critical standards even in difficult times. As early as in mid-1939 a review of new books by young poets briefly mentioned Kožík, who "promised good intentions but does not convince," writes "descriptive poetry" that can sometimes be read with pleasure, but more often substitutes sentimentality for poetic commitment. Černý's review essay about the novel, rare in its rage, does not lack scholarly erudition or legitimate insight, but it may be that it uses all-too-heavy artillery to demolish Kožík's airy cardboard and mirror construction. Černý grants that the author has resuscitated the forgotten life of a Czech artist who had "beauty and a certain greatness," but he feels piqued, if not provoked, by the great honors bestowed on the artless book. Unfortunately, he continues, Kožík did not grasp the rich possibilities of his subject— that is, he neither concentrated on the inner drama to show how Dvořák became Debureau nor, from a more sociological viewpoint, showed how his career intersected with French intellectual developments from the time of Napoleon to the 1848 Revolution. Psychologically, Kožík's Dvořák was just a "little man," the hero of a "populist novel," and Dvořák and Debureau the artist remained forever separated from each other; from a sociological point of view, Kožík totally misunderstood French intellectual history, especially Romanticism, which was, in its beginnings, royalist, reactionary, and Catholic and only later espoused the revolution. Worst of all was Kožík's style, since he preferred maudlin melodrama and the easy way out. But success and art are two different matters, Černý insists, and Kožík's novel did not bridge the gap between the two.

In his later memoirs (1995), Kožík suggests that at first he wanted to respond to this criticism by confessing all his sins of omission but that his publisher (who also happened to publish *Kritický měsíčník*)

wanted a polemical answer to the review. The young author, disregarding the warnings of his best friends, wrote two articles published in the
Lidové noviny in late April 1940, accusing his critic of pedantry and of
deriving a certain "pleasure for doing evil." Kožík could not hope for
gentle treatment; even before he wrote these responses, critics and experts of *Kritický měsíčník* had castigated him for pandering to "success, popularity and advertising" and condemned his new play about
Shakespeare (he was writing fast) as "superficial and confusing." Černý
wrote another longish article against Kožík's novel, coming within a
hair's breadth of accusing him of plagiarism (from Sacha Guitry's play
of 1918 and from a story by Egon Erwin Kisch in his *Prague Pitaval*,
written in German and published in 1933) and attacking him for describing Théophile Gautier's famous waistcoat as red rather than pink.
A little later he also panned Kožík's new novel about the Portuguese
poet Camões, noting that most of the Portuguese names in it were obviously misspelled.

   Uninformed about this little culture war in Prague and perhaps life
in the protectorate, Kožík's American publisher cast him into a heroic
role; his brief biography on the book jacket duly noted that he was director of the drama section of the Brno radio station and added, somewhat poetically, that he was now, possibly, somewhere in France with
the Allied armies "and deprived of the chance of seeing his book ever
printed in his native language or land." What happened was somewhat
different from this surmise: after the success of his novel, Kožík was
transferred from Brno to Prague, and since he was well known, the
Germans included him in a group of European journalists and writers
who in 1943 were sent to the forest of Katyn, near Smolensk, to confirm that the thousands of dead Polish officers whose bodies had been
discovered in mass graves there had been murdered by the Soviets.
(This was true, but acknowledged by the Soviet authorities only fifty
years later.) After 1945 Kožík was investigated by a writers' commission
for participating in this alleged slander of Soviet officers, was sentenced to four years of silence (soon reduced to two), lost his job but
never ceased writing, and by 1955 was back at work, since the Communist minister of culture had read his book in Moscow during the
war and liked it. While Černý had been deprived of his professorship,

been relegated to a menial job in the state library, and only briefly returned to the university after 1968 (he died in 1987), Kožík, good-natured, inoffensive, and perhaps a little unworldly, continued to write children's books, as well as historical plays, film scripts, and fictionalized biographies (including ones of Comenius, Tristan and Isolde, Charles IV, etc.). He listed 107 publications in his bibliography and died peacefully at the age of eighty-eight in 1997.

A Political Test

My first political test came in late 1939 or early 1940, and I have to confess that I failed it miserably, at least when I compare my experience with later stories I heard of some of my Czech friends who seemed to have slept with well-oiled machine guns under their beds throughout the years of the protectorate, permanently ready for the final battle. Perhaps there were mitigating circumstances to consider, but do not heroes act, disregarding them all, including complicated family affairs?

Our arrangements were rather fragile, to say the least, because the owner of the apartment in Prague where I lived with my mother and grandmother, my Jewish uncle Leo, had left for England in 1939, and then my Aryan father had appeared out of nowhere but with German papers and took it bravely upon himself to support his former Jewish wife, the mother of his son. Since the apartment was likely to be listed as Jewish, he found an Aryan straw man who took it over and kept his mouth shut about his Jewish and half Jewish tenants, who enjoyed the nightly luxury of listening to the Swiss Radio Beromünster, famous for its balanced reports, or the BBC, because the radio was registered in his name. These idyllic circumstances were interrupted, one evening, by my Ladin aunt Mathilda, who said on the phone that I should see her immediately, it was a matter of life and death. Obediently I climbed up the wooden stairs in the ancient house at the Golden Ring, only to be told that she had found a Browning in the room she had rented once to a clerk in the Polish Embassy and that in the name of all the saints (and there were many) I should get rid of the fatal weapon; if it were found, we all would be hanged or shot, people were being executed for less.

Had I been the hero I wished to be, I should have tried to pass the weapon on to Maria, sister of my friend Kristina, who, so nearly everybody assured me, had joined a secret Communist cell in the social security office where she worked. Alas, instead of arming Maria and her Communists, I put the weapon in my schoolbag and walked to Charles Bridge— it was evening, and I was a student on his way home—where I leaned against the dark and lonely parapet, not far from where St. Nepomuk was once thrown into the river by his tormentors. I opened my bag and, after looking around, let the Browning drop into the water, as dirty as my conscience.

My self-esteem was only restored four years later, when I found myself in a German prison cell in Poland, in a place called Opolno, with a little blackboard on the wall that neatly listed my name, date of birth, a file number, and the reason for my imprisonment. It said, "Illegal activity," and I was, at least for the moment, strangely and fleetingly proud of myself.

History in Suspense?

A deceptive calm descended on the streets and squares of Prague after November 17, 1939, and even the broadcasts from London suggested that people should be cautious and not provoke the occupying force directly in mass demonstrations or in the open. Neurath did not want to see any irritating changes in the government, but after Ladislav Feierabend, minister of agriculture, escaped to England in January 1940, Hácha appointed Count Mikuláš Bubna-Litic his successor and opened the door to other conservative members of the Czech gentry and aristocracy to fill important positions in the National Solidarity organization. Within months the Czech Fascists again believed a propitious moment had come: a group of Vlajka people attacked the Prague district office of National Solidarity on August 8–9, 1940, and an SS group supporting the Fascists clashed in brief conflict with the Czech police protecting the attacked. In the press and on the radio, a new group of journalists and commentators—among them Emanuel Moravec, a disappointed military man, Vladimír Krychtálek, and Karel

Lažnovský—made their appearance, trumpeting the glory of the Reich and the happy inevitability of active collaboration.

Times were difficult and confusing, and since many people lacked reliable information, "whispered news," *šuškanda*, made the rounds, usually introduced by the skeptical phrase *jedna paní povídala*, "a woman told me," predicting Stalin's immediate intervention and the defeat of the Wehrmacht within forty-eight hours. When Czech children were to be inoculated at school against diphtheria, the *šuškanda* insisted that these German injections would harm them, and many mothers appeared in the schools to rescue their children from the danger.

Rationing had been introduced on October 1, 1939. In the beginning, every *Normalverbraucher* (normal consumer) received nearly 3 kilos of bread per week, 350 grams of sugar (as opposed to only 300 in the Reich), 500 grams of meat, and 155 grams of fats (270 in Germany). Additional ration coupons were given to people doing heavy labor (*Schwerarbeiter*) and very heavy labor (*Schwerstarbeiter*), children, and pregnant women. People doing heavy labor in war industries received (for instance, in the weeks from December 23, 1940, until January 19, 1941) additional rations of 500 grams of meat, 120 grams of various fats, and nearly 2 kilos of bread, while the additional distribution for people doing very heavy labor amounted to 700 grams of meat, 455 grams of fats, and 2.5 kilos of bread. Children from eighteen months to ten years were also entitled to special coupons and received, in the same period, 125 grams of butter and half a liter of milk per day.

The trouble was that the protectorate also had to deliver to the Reich thousands of tons of provisions (e.g., from spring 1939 to spring 1940, 18,700 tons of vegetables, 64,800 tons of sugar, and 5,200 tons of fresh fruit), and the original fairly high level of rations could not be sustained for long. In 1939, 37.02 kilos of meat were distributed to each protectorate citizen, but by 1941 the ration had decreased to 28.86 kilos, and by 1943, to 25.02. The yearly distribution of milk increased from 130.97 liters in 1939 to 145.82 in 1940 but decreased steadily later (1941: 112.56; 1943: 65.05). There were 151 eggs available per capita in 1939, but just 86 in 1941, 70 in 1942, and 64 in 1943. Only the distribution of sugar, amply produced on the fields of

Moravia, showed remarkable stability: 33 kilos per capita in 1939, 25.78 in 1940, 31.04 in 1942, and 32.09 a year later. As Václav Král has shown, quoting the official statistical yearbook, distribution of all major provisions, with the exception of sugar, notably declined from 1939 to 1945: bread by 23.73 percent, meat and butter by 50 percent, fats by 55 percent, and milk by 75 percent.

Other goods, such as soap, shoes, clothes, tobacco, and alcohol, rapidly disappeared from stores and were sold on special coupons and available from time to time only on *Sonderzuteilungen* (special distributions). Discrimination started early. Jews were restricted to shopping between 11:00 a.m. and 1:00 p.m., and then from 3:00 to 4:30 p.m. to buy what was left; on October 1, 1941, the Ministry of Finance excluded Jews from buying tobacco in any form or shape. The Prague city government had hastened to issue a decree demanding that Jews return their *šatenky* (clothing coupons), as early as October 10, 1940, and it then ordered them to buy their clothes at junk shops (the Ministry of Commerce decreed on January 23, 1942, that Jews were forbidden to buy caps). As for food, Jews were excluded from buying apples (January 18, 1941), an additional ration of sugar (June 13), and marmalades or jams (August 29). On October 23, 1941, the Ministry of Agriculture excluded Jews from acquiring all kinds of fruits, whether fresh or dried, cheese, fish, chicken, or game, and they were not to buy onions (November 8), alcoholic drinks (November 21), coffee (Christmas 1941), or garlic (January 15, 1942); by December 12, 1942, Jewish children were not to receive any honey.

Over the years people increasingly looked to acquiring wares *pod rukou* (underhandedly), *pod pultem* (under the counter), or by *šmelina* (on the black market). Most Prague Czechs were fortunate to have kind relatives in the countryside who could provide an illegally killed chicken or a Christmas goose, but it was necessary to get off the slow train from central Bohemia at a peripheral little railway station, perhaps at Braník, and quickly switch to the No. 14 tram there. Czech police conducted irresolute searches, and nice slice of bacon usually did the trick. Even if you did not have a grandmother or aunt at Těchobuz or Čerčany, there was always a good chance that if your grocer knew you, he would let you have things, albeit at slightly inflated prices.

Waiters, especially at the more elegant places, would hand you the menu (clearly indicating how many ration coupons you had to surrender for each chateaubriand) and politely suggest that you were free to order anything if you paid for it; if you agreed, he ceremoniously took out little silver scissors from his tailcoat, cut a few ration coupons from his own reserves, and later brought a discreet bill that did not indicate the purchase but that he handed over with a bow (a ritual that was a sure hit with your date). The occupiers, in the meantime, tried to convince the occupied of the culinary virtues of *Eintopfgericht* (a kind of thick stew of potatoes) but did not succeed in impressing a nation used to a traditional Sunday lunch of *vepřo-knedlo-zelo*, or pork, dumplings, and cabbage.

Until the fall demonstrations of 1939 Hitler seemed surprised by the relative quiet of the protectorate, and after Germany's occupation of much of France in mid-1940, when people in his Ministry of Foreign Affairs and leading functionaries of the Nazi Party districts adjacent to the Czech and Moravian lands considered the question of what should be done with it, it was Hitler himself who insisted on keeping it, because he thought that war production was successfully functioning there. Memorandums from the Berlin Foreign Office wanted to correct the borders agreed to at Munich so as to widen the economic hinterland of a few Sudeten towns (nearly a hundred thousand Czechs would then be shifted to the Reich), and party bosses in the Sudeten and in Niederdonau (Lower Austria) had their own demands; Gauleiter Hugo Jury continued to press for southern and central Moravia to be added to his Austrian party domain, making him, in practice, lord of Olomouc and Brno. When these internal discussions heated up in the late summer, the Prague Reichsprotektor thought it necessary to protest against such efforts to reduce his power, and on September 23 both Neurath and Frank were received in Berlin, where Hitler assured them that he had personally resolved that the border of the protectorate would not be changed, though Jury, in Austria, was not easily convinced.

The high-level conversations about the future of the protectorate did not merely touch on questions of administrative borders but, in secret, considered the future of the Czech people within the German Lebensraum. Both Neurath and, surprisingly, Frank suggested that

germanization of the Czechs, or at least of those who were racially acceptable, should be prepared immediately but that action should be
postponed until after the war. Hitler himself, on September 23, stated
that "assimilation of a greater part of the Czech people was possible,
provided that Czechs who were racially useless will be eliminated."
Frank was put in charge of preparations, and the Chief Office of Race
and Settlement began to organize expert anthropological, legal, and
statistical investigations, one of which came to the conclusion that
Czechs were racially superior to Sudeten Germans because 45 percent
of them were Nordic or Dinaric types, while among the Sudeten population only 25 percent were; they also analyzed finer points of racial
theology, pondering the problem of whether a Czech buying the services of a German prostitute was culpable or not (he was not, because
the issue of the honor of the blood was not in question). A meeting in
the Prague Office of the Reichsprotektor, attended by a general of the
Wehrmacht, decided in early October 1940 that half of all Czechs
could be assimilated but that the other half must be deprived of power
or settled somewhere outside the protectorate. It was not surprising
that the (non-Communist) Czech resistance in Prague refused to understand why a soldier of the Czechoslovak Army being trained in England was allowed to speak on the BBC to the Czech nation in his
German mother tongue.

The Gestapo, a state within the state, constantly intervened in
Czech affairs by systematic waves of arrests, starting with the Aktion
Gitter on the first day of the occupation and continuing with mass arrests of intellectuals and political representatives on September 1,
1939, the day Poland was attacked. In the fall the incarceration of students followed, and in May 1941 a roundup of younger and older Social Democrats, including Antonín Hampl and the Agrarian Rudolf
Beran, who had only recently been prime minister. (He was put on
trial, released at Christmas 1943, and tried again after May 1945.) The
Gestapo was rather inventive, often with the help of informers, in discovering the organizational structures of the resistance, and it almost
brought to a halt the activities of the PC, the Political Center. It arrested nearly five hundred members of In Defense of the Nation in
Prague and the provinces, and slowly and deliberately it collected evi-

dence against those members of the Czech government who were in touch with London. Meanwhile, until Germany attacked the Soviet Union in June 1941, the Communist Party went on dreaming about its "most important ally," the indefatigable and revolutionary German working class.

CHAPTER III

TERROR AND RESISTANCE

Reinhard Heydrich in Prague

When Hitler attacked the Soviet Union on June 22, 1941, the Czech citizens of Prague began to hope again, and resignation gave way to joyful, if muted, expectations. The Communist Party changed its policies overnight; while it had refrained from battling the occupiers after the Hitler-Stalin pact of August 1939—all wars being equally "imperialist," it was said—it now joined the resistance, though on its own, as it were. The Office of the Reichsprotektor acknowledged, not to overstate matters, that "events resembling strikes" were taking place. Telephone lines and railway brakes were cut more frequently, a German children's home was firebombed, and a boycott of the protectorate newspapers, which Radio London had suggested for the week of September 14–21, was markedly successful, with more than 60 percent of all newspapers having to be returned to the distributors unsold. Neurath himself reported to Berlin that anti-German enmity had "stiffened," and K. H. Frank called a meeting of his men to discuss the situation. It was decided that he write an (anti-Neurath) memorandum to Hitler, who called for a meeting at his headquarters in Rastenburg, East Prussia. Frank, Himmler, and Neurath were to be present, but it was SS General Reinhard Heydrich who gave the most detailed analysis of the situation, prepared for him by the Prague SD chief, Horst Böhme. When Neurath was late, his plane delayed by bad weather in Berlin, he lost his chance to defend himself, and Hitler appointed Heydrich, who in addition to keeping his Reich Security command became "acting" Reichsprotektor—for the time being, it was said. Neurath was sent home to Württemberg on sick leave (he reappeared as a war criminal before the Nuremberg court in 1946), and Heydrich arrived in Prague on September 27, 1941, without further ceremony. K. H. Frank once again was second-in-command.

The story of Reinhard Heydrich's life and death usually takes an analytical turn sooner or later. British, French, Czech, or German biographers are inclined to seek and to discover a single and exceptional trauma in his early life to explain everything that comes later, rather than to satisfy themselves that his ambition, along with his ruthless capacity for systematic work, can be explained in a variety of ways, whether it was Heydrich's suspicion that many of his contemporaries believed that he was half Jewish, his feeling of being a middle child neglected by his parents (he had an older sister and a younger brother), or his attempts to compensate for being disrespected by his fellow cadets, who laughed at his weak body and his falsetto voice, calling him the billy goat, not to speak of his dishonorable discharge from the navy. He rarely left his desk, incessantly worked on his files, and was finely attuned to the changing intentions of Hitler and Himmler, his immediate superior. But though engineering the death of millions, he never pulled the trigger or killed anybody himself, unlike the two SS men who were commanded to abduct an engineer, Formis by name, who ran a secret anti-Nazi radio station at a little Bohemian hotel near Prague, to Berlin. (Formis was, to the great consternation of the Czech police, inadvertently shot on the spot.) Heydrich was the ultimate terrorist untiringly active at his desk, and when Göring asked him to chair the Wannsee meeting about the final solution of the Jewish question, it did not come as a particular surprise to anybody in the Berlin bureaucracy.

Reinhard Tristan Eugen Heydrich was born in Saxony, in the town of Halle, in 1904 to parents of differing background and temper. His father was a tolerably gifted singer, musician, and composer of modest background; his mother, a strict Catholic disciplinarian of upper-middle-class upbringing and attitudes. Reinhard, an intent and quiescent child, entered the local Reformrealgymnasium in 1914, always wanted to be first in class, and early excelled in chemistry and physics (he later had a working knowledge of English, French, and Russian). Vacationing at Swinemünde, on the Baltic coast, he admired the (rather small) German fleet and in March 1922 enlisted as a cadet officer in the navy, trained on the tall ships *Niobe* and *Schleswig-Holstein*, and ultimately became a signals and radio officer. He was not popular with his fellow cadets, who disliked his music and his efforts to outdo everybody in fencing, swimming, and shooting. Though he was occasionally invited to play his violin at parties of his superior officer, Wilhelm Canaris (chief of German military intelligence), he lacked the social polish required of a cadet officer, especially when mingling with British officers and their polite ladies on foreign shores. At any rate, he was commissioned lieutenant by 1925 and promoted to *Oberleutnant-zur-See* three years later.

Heydrich was not, as many believed, of partly Jewish origin, but hometown rumors persisted and were not silenced by an official investigation later undertaken by the Nazi Party. His paternal grandmother in her second marriage had chosen a locksmith named Gustav Robert Suess (the name sounded like Jud Süss to small-town racist ears), and matters were not made easier by his father, who liked to entertain his friends by imitating what he believed were Jewish habits of speech and gesture and by addressing his mother as Mrs. Suess when sending her monthly check for support (it was the postmaster who started the rumors). Even in school young Heydrich had a chip on his shoulder if only because of what people believed, and some of his later biographers assumed that it would make for a more darkly split and demonic figure if one could speak of the Jew in him or of Jewish self-hate in the highest levels of the Nazi hierarchy. It is certainly not impossible that he joined the navy because he wanted to escape from his artsy father and his Catholic mother, and his decision to marry Lina von Osten, of a genteel family (though her father was a mere schoolteacher) on the island of Fehmarn, in the North Sea, may suggest that he wanted to get as far away from Halle as possible. When he met Lina at a navy ball, he did not know yet that she was a politically conscious member of the Nazi Party, and her brother an early admirer of Hitler, whose rhetoric had fascinated him, Lina's brother, at a mass meeting.

Yet the young officer was still to receive "the heaviest blow of his life" (as he told Lina) when in 1931 he was dishonorably discharged from the navy, where he had hoped to find a home and a mission. The trouble was that before encountering Lina, he had met a well-connected girl from Berlin-Potsdam, and when he thoughtlessly sent her the announcement of his engagement to Lina, the girl had a nervous breakdown because she felt entitled to be his future bride (she had spent a night at a rooming house resisting his advances, she claimed); her father, a shipyard director, demanded that the navy establish a court of honor to determine the outcome. Heydrich was foolish enough to take the proceedings lightly, if not with a certain disdain, offending the officer judges, who unanimously sent him home in disgrace and without a pension. It was a real turning point; Lina stood by him, and his mother turned to his godfather, Karl Freiherr von Eberstein, who had close contacts with the Munich Nazi leadership. Eberstein recommended him to Himmler, who asked him to establish a Sicherheitsdienst, Security Service, within the SS to ferret out internal enemies potentially hiding in the elite formation or elsewhere in the party organizations. It was just the job he needed to prove himself, and he started out in a shared office and with a borrowed typewriter in August 1931; he married Lina, a swastika above the altar, four months later.

During the 1930s Heydrich rose to run the entire security system of the Reich by skillfully using his Bavarian base against the Berlin organizations. He had to weather the storm about his alleged Jewish ancestor, and when Hitler became chancellor in January 1933, he was not among the first to be rewarded, but he made himself particularly useful by charging ahead against the conservative Bavarian government, hitherto unwilling to submit to the new Berlin masters, and by organizing mass arrests of Bavarian Catholics, Socialists, and Communists. In June 1933 Hitler's office commissioned his Security Service (SD) to be the sole intelligence service of the party. Heydrich moved to Berlin, and within two years he had succeeded in outflanking both Göring and Fricke, the new minister of the interior, who had their own security organizations. Heydrich built the SD according to his own predilections; admiring the British Secret Service, he gathered people with impressive academic credentials in his office and did not hesitate to "turn" agents in competing organizations if it suited his purpose. He developed his own theory about terror tactics and applied it in Bavaria and, later, in Prague: in Bavaria, in 1933, more than sixteen thousand functionaries of political parties inimical to the Nazis were taken into "protective custody"; more than twelve thousand were released again after he made sure they would spread the story of their frightful experiences.

This was not enough for the adventurer. He liked to be admired on the international scene, and as a pilot he flew with or without special dispensation. Through an Austrian intrigue, he had himself elected president of the International Police Organization, a forerunner of Interpol, and at a Budapest competition he was declared Germany's best fencer, though the competition was won by a Hungarian. When war broke out, he went on flights over Poland, Holland, England, and Scotland, was awarded an Iron Cross First Class, which Hitler discovered (by chance) on his tunic, and, on his own, flew from Moldavia over Soviet territory, was brought down by enemy fire, and had to be rescued by his men. He disliked the rough guys of the SA as well as the ideologues Streicher and Goebbels, and he doggedly pursued the changing anti-Jewish programs as defined by the party: when it was a matter of removing Jews to Palestine, he established contacts with Zionist agents (possibly imitating Mussolini, who had for some time favored anti-British Zionism) and delegated Adolf Eichmann to study the situation in the Near East; when it was proposed to ship Jews to Madagascar, he sent Eichmann to the Tropical Institute at Hamburg and considered all the possibilities, including that of removing all Polish Jews to that island off the African coast. Yet the course of war changed all this, and (as Günther Deschner has shown in his sober biography) Heydrich shifted from being a "policy maker," planning the forced Jewish emigration to Palestine or Madagascar, to being the "precise executor of commands" or, more aptly perhaps, to organizing mass murder by the Einsatzkommando butchers under his rule.

Hitler's policies had a high degree of improvisation, and in the first years of the war the anti-Jewish policies of the Reich went in different directions, often at the same time. Heydrich continued to busy himself

with Madagascar plans, and in the late fall of 1939 his underlings began to explore the possibility of creating a Jewish settlement in Poland,
centered on Nisko, on the plains of the San River. Nearly five thousand
Jews from Katowice (Poland), Vienna, and Moravian Ostrava (in the
protectorate), and Prague were transported there, while Hans Frank,
the governor of occupied Poland, complained to Göring about the economic problems that the resettlement was creating (the Nisko plans
were dropped). In March 1941 Hitler issued his guidelines about "special areas" in the rear of the front, and Heydrich gathered three thousand men to follow the regular troops. In September 1941 Jews were
sent to Minsk, Lodz, and Riga (in Riga all thirty-eight thousand were
shot upon arrival), and his special commandos duly reported to him
that three hundred thousand Jews had been killed.

In 1935 Professor Carl Jakob Burckhardt, the Swiss delegate to the
International Red Cross, traveled to Berlin to investigate disturbing reports about German concentration camps and met Heydrich officially;
he described him as "slim and blond," particularly noting his fine "Pre-
Raphaelite hands, like lilies." He did not say anything about Heydrich's
perversely suspicious mind, yet when Heydrich arrived in Prague in
late September 1941, he proclaimed martial law within hours, and a
wave of executions began that lasted for many weeks. He had prepared
the list of victims before he left Berlin.

Protectorate Jazz

It is not easy to remember that while the occupation regime perfected
its machinery of terror, daily life in Prague went on with a semblance
of gray regularity. The proverbial trains were running on time (at least
until the partisans and Allied pilots attacked the railways in the last
year of the war), and citizens were busy on the black market, but they
also read new volumes of poetry, eagerly bought theater tickets, and
went to movies more often than before (there were three performances
daily in every movie house). Young people, especially, did not inevitably
turn to the patriotic past but preferred to listen to, or play, jazz music,
old and new.

Many gifted students, now deprived of their university courses, joined existing and fresh music groups in Prague as well as in the provinces (even in distant Náchod, as Josef Škvorecký has shown in his wonderful novels). Jazz became essential in creating the illusion, if not almost the physiological feeling, of freedom. Young people excitedly listened to transatlantic musicians on records offered by RCA (His Master's Voice), Decca, or Parlophone, and many American musicals, among them the *Broadway Melody* movies of the mid- and late 1930s, were shown to packed audiences in Prague downtown cinema houses until Pearl Harbor. The expectations of young Czech people did not differ much from those of many young German and Austrian "swing kids," especially in Vienna, Berlin, Cologne, or Hamburg, whether in uniform or not.

Even before the establishment of the republic in 1918, jazz had touched Czech sensibilities with the performances of black tap dancers on the European circuit, syncopated versions of classical pieces, and at Prague's most popular cabarets—above all, the chic and sinful Montmartre, where famous Emča Revoluce (Emma the Revolutionary) danced to the tune of "Alexander's Ragtime Band." Innovative musicians took jazz from the cabarets to popular cafés, independent little theaters, and radio stations, and in 1935–37 Jan Šíma's Gramoklub orchestra once more related jazz to the contemporary avant-garde of the left, if for the last time.

In the 1920s and early 1930s the glories of jazz, such as it was known, were also defended and used by younger Prague composers and writers. Among the earliest to attempt a synthesis of concert music and jazz was Erwin Schulhoff, of a well-to-do German Jewish family, approximately a contemporary of Franz Kafka's. He studied composition and piano in Germany and was attracted by the radical Berlin Dada group, above all by George Grosz, whose merciless pictorial precision could be followed, Schulhoff believed, by the incorporation of recent jazz into chamber music, opera, and piano compositions, e.g., his Suite for Chamber Orchestra, using ragtime, shimmy, and step rhythms, performed for the first time in Berlin in 1922.

In the 1920s Schulhoff returned from Germany to Prague and Ostrava, where he played for the radio station and independent theaters, came to know the avant-garde composer Alois Hába, the conductor Václav Talich, and Leoš Janáček, wrote music for the surrealist poet Vítězslav Nezval, and produced "Cinq Études de Jazz" (1926), "Hot Music" (1928), and the jazz oratorio "H.M.S. Royal Oak," a new version of the Potemkin story, with the difference that while the Russian sailors had mutinied because of their mistreatment by czarist officers, Schulhoff had their British comrades do so because an admiral prohibits jazz on board ship. In the early 1930s Schulhoff turned against his own past and to socialist realism, acquired Soviet citizenship in spring 1941, and was promptly sent off to the fortress of Wülzburg in Bavaria, where he died in August 1942. Only recently have his many achievements been rediscovered by Czech and German historians of music.

The first to celebrate jazz as a music of liberation, in a Czech book of considerable importance, was the young composer and theater enthusiast E. F. Burian, who after the war looked somewhat askance at his youthful enchantments when, after his return from a German concentration camp, he directed the Prague Theater of the Czech Army in accord with the demands of the Communist Party. Written in 1926–27 and published in 1928, Burian's apologia for jazz proceeds from a late futurist belief that Romantic music has seen its day, together with "the perfume of violets" and the "stupid little moon" (the images could have been Marinetti's). He demands that the "revolution" of music enter "the phase of action" and that jazz, the rhythm and the sound of the century, replace discussion of Bach or Beethoven. Burian wants to challenge and provoke (with illustrations of Josephine Baker in the nude), but he knows a good deal about the new French composers, Ernst Křenek's jazz opera, and even Erwin Schulhoff, and he patiently explains the technical principles of syncopation and improvisation, calling upon a number of American witnesses, among them Irving Berlin, "that fairy-tale millionaire," Jasbo Brown of Chicago, George Gershwin, W. C. Handy, and Paul Whiteman.

The advances of Czech jazz in the 1930s and the high quality of its later achievements closely relate to Jaroslav Ježek's work for Prague's Liberated Theater. As a boy Ježek, whose eyesight was always in grave danger, was educated in a home for the blind, where he also received his first musical education. He went on to the Prague Conservatory to study piano and composition with Josef Suk and applied himself to Ravel, Hindemith, and Schulhoff. To conclude his studies in 1929, he submitted a Piano Concerto, in which he combined tradition with a fox-trot, tango, and shimmy, and he duly discovered Gershwin's *Rhapsody in Blue,* praising its "perfection of form, the sensuous substance of its seductions, and the exoticism of its colors, sounds, and rhythms." Ježek worked for ten years for the Liberated Theater as in-house composer and bandleader; he called his small orchestra a swing band as early as 1934, kept an eye on Joe Jenčík's ballet of six girls (none too fragile), and, when the anti-Hitler theater was closed by government edict shortly after Munich, left with its founders for New York, where he died, of a kidney ailment, in 1942. He was the true genius of early Czech jazz, and some of his intelligent songs and blues (e.g., "Tmavomodrý svět [The Dark Blue World]," 1930, or "Kdepak je ten klobouk [Where's That Hat?]," 1933) were never forgotten by successive generations.

Czech swing during the war years enjoyed the advantage of uncertain German policies and the ambivalence of Goebbels himself, who axiomatically believed that Germany had lost World War I because the nation back home had been left to hunger, despair, and frustration; as a consequence, though jazz was officially prohibited in Germany after 1933, it could be heard all over Berlin's chic bars and nightclubs, especially around the time of the Olympic Games in 1936, and, since controls were less than perfect, even in the grand dance halls like the Femina. Goebbels was opposed to the dogmatic ideas of Alfred Rosenberg and other provincial Nazi ideologues for pragmatic reasons. He knew the tastes of soldiers and, in 1941, wrote an article, published in the official weekly *Das Reich*, in which he said that atonality and the preponderance of rhythm over melody "offended the ears," yet grandmother's and grandfather's waltzes could not be the end of all musical developments. "Rhythm," he continued, "was one of the basic principles of music," and "the melody of the world" was now determined by the "thousandfold hum of machines and the droning of motors." He was not opposed to "rhythmical dance music," as favored by the fighting and working nation (and, as it turned out, by Luftwaffe pilots, who loved to listen to the BBC), but he avoided the term "jazz." He even organized a special jazz orchestra whose broadcasts were directed at

British soldiers and tolerated the repertory of the radio programs designed for German soldiers, especially in Belgrade and Oslo, rich in
"rhythmical dance music." These radio programs were run by the army
rather than by his Ministry of Propaganda anyway. Troop entertainment was geared to the expectations of soldiers, who demonstrated
deplorable lapses of taste: when an orchestra was sent to entertain
infantrymen near Calais, they wanted to hear that famous New York, or
rather Yiddish, tune "Bei Mir Bist Du Shein," above all.

It was a member of the older generation, R. A. Dvorský (born in
1899 as Rudolf Antonín in the small town of Dvůr Králové), who
brought the age of swing to Prague's popular music of elegant entertainment and the fashionable five o'clock tea, though he was never
disloyal to his conservative taste or to occasional patriotic and folksy
evergreen tune. He began as a self-tutored amateur, as many musicians
did, worked as a clerk in a local brewery, and went to Prague in 1918
to play the piano in popular cabarets. He founded his Melody Makers
in 1925 and later his Melody Boys, originally a group of five but in time
many more, and quickly attracted very gifted singers, among them the
Allan Sisters and Inka Zemánková, as well as Kamil Běhounek, master
of the accordion, and the composer and pianist Jiří Traxler. Dvorský
himself, well bred, erect, most often in white tie and tailcoat, a little
resembling a member of the old aristocracy, was the first in Prague to
use a microphone when singing with his orchestra, and his suave performances in Karlsbad at the Hotel Richmond and in Prague at the
Barrandov Terraces, near the studios of Prague Film and the Lucerna
Bar (both owned by the enterprising Havel family), were broadcast
early on. When he performed at the grand Lucerna Hall, his concerts
appealed to thousands of fans of all generations, his repertory skillfully
combining American and British dance tunes, a few pieces by the German jazz musicians Theo Mackeben and Peter Kreuder, and in conclusion, a march by František Kmoch, the most beloved Czech folk
musician of earlier decades. Young people also flocked to hear Jaroslav
Malina (b. 1912), who with his big band regularly performed at the
café Vltava and was willing to conform to popular expectations, though
he could not compete with Dvorsky's refined, eclectic elegance.

Karel Vlach belonged to a younger generation eager to swing and respond to new jazz outside the country, brought closer by the radio stations of the Allies' advancing expeditionary forces. He had been born in 1911 in Žižkov, a plebeian district of Prague, as a boy played the violin and the saxophone, borrowed from his brother, and worked as a gofer and traveling salesman for a well-known (Jewish) notions firm before he was told by its Nazi "trustee" that it would be perhaps better for him to switch to music entirely. He had established his Blue Music and his Blue Boys in the late 1920s and by 1939 was performing with his Karel Vlach Orchestra at the Vinohrady National Casino, where his performances enchanted students especially and were broadcast nationally.

During the war years he settled at the café Lloyd on Příkopy Boulevard and worked with the best singers, the dramatic Jiřina Salačová, the ever-present Allan Sisters (now four in number), and Inka Zemánková. Vlach was Prague's answer to Benny Goodman, and he showed much courage employing and protecting composers and arrangers who had been attacked by Czech Fascists, especially Bedřich (Fritzek) Weiss, who was sent to Terezín in 1941, and Leopold Korbař (famous for his "Hm, Hm, You Are So Wonderful"), who was removed, together with Vlach's crooner Arnošt Kavka, to a camp for half Jews in 1944. Not everybody knew that the famous "Vlach Stomp" was written by Theodor Ferstl, a jazz kid from Vienna who was stationed, as a soldier, in Prague and died on the eastern front. In his later years Vlach was more fortunate than Dvorský: while Dvorský had to fight a bout of TB in 1944 and was later imprisoned by the Communist authorities, Vlach shifted his orchestra to Prague theaters, first working with Jan Werich (who was favored by the new regime) and later at the Theater of Musicals, where he played for the staid audiences of the 1970s and 1980s (he died in 1988).

The protectorate kings of swing had to compete increasingly with smaller groups that concentrated on jazz pure and simple and on the liberating art of improvisation, often taking their cue from *le jazz hot* from Paris (especially after December 1941, when matters American were officially removed from the scene). Emil Ludvík was a university student who had established his Hot Quintett by 1939, programmatically turning against "commercial café music," and he drew young enthusiasts and real experts to his concerts, often transcribed on Esta Records. He had his moment of glory when he was invited to perform at Lucerna Hall on October 13, 1940, perhaps with the striking detail that of the twenty-four pieces he presented, at least twenty-two were American imports, including Hoagy Carmichael's "Stardust," W. C. Handy's "St. Louis Blues," and Duke Ellington's "In My Solitude."

The difficulty was that Ludvík's and other groups were made up of young people and students who were the prime target of the occupation authorities, eager to send entire age-groups to German armament factories. And then there was the Prague German Walter Paul, who played for Jaroslav Ježek and for Ludvík and who died in German uniform in the east. In 1942 the Ludvík orchestra dispersed; a few of his people formed another group, the Elite, but not for long. Others who continued were the courageous Harlem Jazz Group, founded in 1941 in the Prague suburb of Spořilov (far out), and the Malostranská Group, which echoed Django Reinhardt in Paris and *le jazz hot* and survived in one form or another at least for a time.

The situation was fluid—for many reasons, musicians changed places or were mobilized for the armament industries—and the career of Inka Zemánková, first of Czech jazz singers, shows this pattern. Inka, originally Inez, was born in Prague in 1915 but spent most of her early years in little towns in eastern Bohemia. She was taken by her widowed mother to Bratislava, where she was trained in the ballet of the Slovak National Theater; when her mother died, she was moved by friends of the family to Prague, where she joined the jazz fans at the café Metro and began to sing for Bobek Bryan's band, mostly in Moravia, and later for R. A. Dvorský and Karel Vlach. Her fame was almost instantaneous when she performed in Martin Frič's film *The Blue Star Hotel* armed with a big straw hat, as well as in other forgettable movies. She moved with the grace of a trained dancer, and though her voice had a definite nasal quality, it was difficult to decide whether her diction was in imitation of English vocalists or her own; she was fortunate that she could rely on texts and tunes by the most talented composers, among them Alfons Jindra's "Dívka k rytmu zrozená" (A Girl Born to Rhythm, her theme song), Jiří Traxler's "Náhoda" (By Chance), and Jaroslav Moravec's slow and haunting "Prosinec a sníh" (December and Snow).

By 1942 she had established herself with Jaroslav Malina's band at the café Vltava for two years of undisputed splendor, but in the last year of the war she was sent to entertain Czech workers in the armament industries. She was definitely not welcome to the postwar Communists, worked as a tractor driver (though continuing to take singing lessons), performed in Poland and elsewhere, and came home in the 1970s to sing in Prague, where she was warmly welcomed by the writer Josef Škvorecký, who kept a keen eye on what was going on in the movies and in jazz.

Bedřich (Fritzek) Weiss, born in 1919 in Prague of a Jewish family, was a talented musician and arranger of jazz tunes, but his public career was short. He began by playing the violin but changed to the trumpet and later the clarinet, fell in with a group of high school students, and, by 1940, was performing with Ludvík; when it became impossible for him to perform in public, he continued to work for Ludvík and Vlach as a skillful arranger. In 1941, his clarinet hidden in his few belongings, he was transported to Terezín, where he continued to write arrangements for Vlach that were smuggled out by a Czech policeman and played by Vlach well into 1944. In Terezín he founded a Weiss Quintett that played in a café established by the camp Freizeitgestaltung (Leisure Time Committee), and he also organized the Ghetto Swingers; he could not know that these last were to perform before a visiting commission of the International Red Cross and together with Martin Roman, a prominent Dutch pianist, in the infamous movie about happy Jewish life at Terezín. That done, the camp commander immediately put the participants in a transport to Auschwitz. Weiss and his aging father came to stand together in front of Dr. Josef Mengele, but the son joined his father voluntarily, and both died together in the gas chambers on April 10, 1944. What remained was his music on a few rare disks and a sensitive ink sketch showing him at the piano, done by the Terezín artist Peter Kien.

My Excursion to Berlin and My Work in a Bookshop

I had better confess that I was a school dropout—for the noblest of reasons and for none whatsoever. Societies and nations were fighting one another all over Europe, and now in Africa too, and I thought it was absurd to sit in class translating Catullus and learning more about J. K. Tyl's plays, written a hundred years earlier for Biedermeier amateurs. One day I simply stayed away from school in stubborn protest against history or rather my dubious place in it. My father was absent once again, my mother wept, but she went to see the honest school principal, who knew that she was Jewish, did not want to burden her with my failures, and later arranged a private Matura *(final examination) for me. I spent my days doing a little Greek and less Latin with two famous professors who, being Jewish, had lost their jobs and were glad to tutor a wayward student. I went on long, slow walks through romantic Prague, over the bridges and back again from the gardens of the Malá Strana. Once I was invited to talk about Prague poetry to a collective of young Zionists, who in a dark apartment on Myslíkova Street prepared for their emigration to Palestine. (Fifty years later, after I had made a brief appearance on a Viennese television program, I was called by H.E. the Israeli ambassador to Austria, who told me he'd been among my earliest audience.) My poetic vacation did not last long because the Prague Work Authority classified me as an unemployed student and ordered me to toil for the Reich. I did not object to the idea of going to Germany, because nobody there would know about my complicated situation. Armed with a valid protectorate identity card, I would blend in with the other foreign workers, I hoped, and perhaps have a better chance to survive on half my identity, as an émigré of sorts, and all on my own.*

We left Prague on a slow train in early September 1941. At the Leipzig main station we were fed sandwiches and coffee by Red Cross nurses, and in a meadow somewhere in Berlin we were unloaded; people from the big factories were waiting there to make their selections. It could have been worse. There was a Danish girl with freckles from a Copenhagen transport, and we made a date (for the next Sunday at 3:00 p.m., at the Hasenheide subway station, of which I had heard vaguely). But she did not appear, and I did not wait long. I found myself in Siemensstadt, in a wooden barracks together with French, Flemish, and Belgian workers, who never slept because they started to play cards as soon as they came back from the production floor. Sometimes, since the first tentative air raids had begun, they gathered in the open to bet a bottle of beer on which plane would go down first, a British or German one.

I was totally unqualified to do anything according to the blueprint.

Admitting to a selective knowledge of German, I was transferred to a big office, where I spent my waking time (not much) sorting bills for spare parts used for something or other and listing them, by hand, on long sheets of paper. I wished I had known more about technical matters because I could have identified the spare parts and, being the master spy from Prague, recognized what kind of machinery (airplanes?) they were used for, information the Allies would have appreciated. But even if I had known the ultimate destiny of these nuts and bolts, how would I have communicated my knowledge to the Royal Air Force? Whether I was tired because of my sleepless nights in the barracks or because I wanted to sabotage Germany's war production, I did not list half the bills and instead carried them, hidden in my shirt, to the toilet, where I tore them to little pieces and flushed them away, energetically.

I simply did not have enough sleep, and a Berlin coworker, clearly an older Social Democrat, told me how to apply for permission to rent a private room. Following his advice and again using my German selectively, I was allowed to move to an abode in the Charlottenburg apartment of a widow with a Polish name and a Prussian obsession with bathroom cleanliness. She had an aging boyfriend at the front, and since she did not trust her spelling, I ended up writing a weekly love letter for her. I was rewarded with ample breakfasts, and the boyfriend may have been surprised by her flights of amorous fancy in perfect German.

Asking for Brötchen (Prussian) rather than Semmeln (Austrian) in the bakery across the street, I was busy digging my little trench, learning the fragile ropes. In the office I shared my lunch with a group of Persians who were equally disoriented, if not more so; we laughed about our daily Zitterspeise (wobbly red Jell-O), and I had to explain to them that contrary to their assumption, most Germans were not called Mahlzeit but used the word at the beginning of meals only to wish each other a good appetite across the table.

One day I had my encounter with the Wehrmacht. I was standing in front of a bookshop, and next to me an elegant lieutenant, with his date, was looking at the books in the windows too. He turned suddenly, and his cavalry spurs got entangled in my pants and tore them wide open. Instead of apologizing, he just looked me up and down, the civilian, clearly a foreign worker in his (damaged) Sunday best, and regaled me with the most vile terms, strangely clashing with his elegance.

There were other encounters. On Wednesdays I usually went to Aschinger's, on the Charlottenburg Chaussee, because it offered a Stammgericht *(no ration coupons necessary) of fresh mussels. One day a young soldier and his girl sat down at my table, and I discovered that it was Günther, whom I had once met back home in a group of Red Falcons (Young Socialists) when I, the wayward bourgeois kid, was looking for the soul of the proletariat. (I found it, literally, in pale Alma, a sixteen-year-old textile worker and fellow member who celebrated the First of May with me in a hospitable wheat field not far from the crowds and the red flags.) Günther recognized me immediately, we both were speechless, and he and his girl quickly left for another table. It was more pleasant to meet Hilde, who had been told of my whereabouts by my Prague friends the Alt brothers, but it was difficult to handle the situation because she liked to drag me to all kinds of cozy places she knew I shouldn't be in, especially a popular tavern in which each couple sat in a big barrel, and though I was not opposed to the idea of a* séparée *(at least its Viennese version, for I had read my Schnitzler), I was afraid that an army or SS patrol would discover me in a tête-à-tête with a buxom Aryan Berlin secretary, not to speak about the dire consequences for her.*

One day in the early fall of 1941 I walked along Charlottenburg Park, and not far from the Russian restaurant—I remember this with precision—I noted a middle-aged couple each wearing a yellow star and the word Jude *on their overcoats. I told myself that it was probably an idea of Goebbels, eager to please his Führer. Next day, however, I received a telegram from my father (he always liked to send telegrams) telling me that my mother's medical situation had worsened—I understood the code—and that I should immediately return to Prague to the apartment, where I was to live again with my mother and grandmother and start with a new job that would protect me from being transported to the Reich. The necessary papers and the* Durchlasschein, *the essential pass, would arrive posthaste. Though I had many doubts about returning to the old situation, which I had wanted to escape, perhaps wrongly, my father insisted that my first duty now was to my mother, and within forty-eight hours I found myself on the Berlin–Prague express. I had my moment of terror when the SS checked the train at the border, but my* Durchlasschein *held up.*

My new boss, it turned out, was a middle-aged Prague German who had sold encyclopedias door to door for André's famous book establishment

and was now opening his own little bookshop, where I was to be the liter-
ate sales assistant behind the counter. I was to keep an eye on Mother and
Grandmother, my father told me, and since the store was close by, I could
be home ten minutes after closing time.

Passing the spot today, midway on Vodičkova Street, where an elegant
sandwich shop, a cosmopolitan baguetterie, *invites the passing multitudes*
to its groaning boards, you would not know how often I had to wash that
shopwindow from top to bottom, together with Josef, the Czech factotum.
In the window you would see books by Hans Carossa and Bruno Brehm,
and when I once exhibited an open map of North Africa in November
1941, showing exactly when General Rommel was beaten by the British
and retreated, the boss's wife, always intent on the politically correct, had a
fit. She ordered me immediately to take the map back into the shop, and
even my argument that customers should have a chance to see the scene of
Rommel's future glorious offensives, did not avail. She did not have an easy
life, the boss's wife; her husband had to join the army, serving not in the
Caucasus or Tripoli but with the army Leitstelle, *directing soldiers to their*
barracks, at the Hybernská railway station, a comfortable fifteen minutes'
walk away. The problem was that since long before the occupation he had
also had a tall Czech girlfriend somewhere in town. He appeared in his
shop only on Saturday afternoon, in a gala uniform and with a potato nose
the color of copper, a Wehrmacht Schwejk to perfection.

We worked under the eyes of his wife, all intent upon surviving, and
she had good reason for concern, because we, the business team or, in the
more epic German terms, die Belegschaft, *consisted of two officially cer-*
tified half Jews, one from Vienna and one local, and three Czechs: Josef,
the jack-of-all-trades, a bookkeeper (who did not seem to have a bathroom
at home because she was constantly primping herself in the one on the
premises), and a Czech teenager apprentice who had never read a book in
her life, not even in her mother tongue. We were not very Aryan or Ger-
manic, to say the least. In the back office Herr Glass from the Wiener-
wald, with steely blue eyes and a Jewish mother, busied himself writing
out, in careful calligraphy with a little ruler and a special pen, bills and
delivery documents. He was a figure from Dickens or the later Viennese
classic Heimito von Doderer. And I, almost ditto, but not blue eyes,
worked in a more dangerous position in front, serving the customers.

It did not take long before I developed my famous ideological X-ray technique to figure out the political views of the clientele. As soon as somebody opened the door, I was sure—judging from the hairdo, the hat, the shoes, or the loden outfit—whether the first question asked would be about Rudolf G. Binding, in which case the customer was conservative to nationalist, or about secondhand books or the Antiquariat, which posed an ominous problem. People who asked for secondhand books were not always satisfied with Adalbert Stifter but sometimes wanted Thomas or Heinrich Mann and, even more dangerous, Alfred Döblin. One had to be hellishly attentive to provide the right kind of volume for the right person.

Sometimes it was easy. Every week or so an elderly man appeared, complete with loden coat and Nazi badge, asked if we had a book by one Franz Kafka, a local Prague writer, smiled contentedly when I answered that his writings were long vergriffen—*that is, out of print—and then disappeared, only to come again. I think we both enjoyed this Kafka-esque game. But sometimes it was more difficult, and when I distrusted the client, I simply brought out old volumes of Ganghofer (Bavarian kitsch) or new novellas by Ina Seidel (Prussian kitsch) until we both were exhausted. Yet among the friends of the Antiquariat were many older intellectuals, invariably distinguished by French berets, who had moved their dramaturgy chairs from Berlin's famous film studio UFA or Munich's Bavaria to the offices of Prague Film at the Barrandov. Since they all came with recommendations from my Czech friend Vladimír, who worked at the big bookshop on Wenceslas Square, I would first examine these eager gentlemen about the early stages of expressionism (about 1912), and only when they passed did I bring up the more interesting stuff from the cellar. Once I consulted my father about one of these patrons of the Antiquariat; when he heard that his name was Hugo Zehder, from Dresden, he told me that Hugo happened to be the patriarch of early Saxon expressionism and beyond suspicion.*

Saturday afternoon was especially busy, for everybody who had a free afternoon, it seemed, suddenly appeared in our narrow premises. Our boss greeted the customers in a parody of old Austrian charm, and we were kept busy moving entire boxes of the current bestseller, a love story entitled André and Ursula, from the storeroom to the shelves. It was also a grand time to sell huge pictures of Prague to visitors from the Reich (always the same, the two corners of Charles Bridge or a view of the castle). Our in-house artist was "Signor" Ballabene, who worked together with his Jewish wife, who helped him every week to bring the canvases to the shop. (Son of an industrialist whose name appears as Vallabene in one of Kafka's novels, he came from the suburb of Karlín.) The old Prague patriciate made its regular appearance. There was Mrs. Bumba, wife of a distinguished laryngologist, and her charming daughter (granddaughter of the famous Slavist professor Spina, a German Christian Socialist minister in the government of the First Republic). But there were also the Reich's Labor Service maidens from the cow barns of the provinces, girls in the uniform of the Bund deutscher Mädchen, *rebellious traces of rouge on their lips, and officers from the training grounds at Milovice, all of whom were reading Mörike.*

One day a blue-eyed girl of thirteen or fourteen appeared. Not in any uniform, she wanted to buy "something philosophical" for her father. She was rather reticent when I asked her earnestly whether her father was of a Kantian or Hegelian persuasion. Ultimately I sold her a new introduction to existentialist philosophy that I thought was timely and well written. She told me only many years later, after I married her after the war and she became the mother of my daughters, that she had lived alone with her father at the time; her Jewish mother had died suddenly because the Jewish physician, the only one allowed to see a non-Aryan patient, came too late.

Among the Saturday regulars was a Luftwaffe sergeant who made himself immediately visible on my ideological radar as an A plus. He came through the door in a slick civilian sort of way, did not click his heels, and in passing murmured something about "Heitler," his way of expressing the Nazi greeting. He usually disappeared between the front shelves of the Antiquariat, which I put in front the better to hide the real stuff, and was clearly displeased with Storm or Keller. Did I not have a rare nineteenth-century comedy entitled Leonce and Lena? *I knew exactly what he wanted, told him to come again the next Saturday, and sold him (for almost nothing) the good Insel edition of the revolutionary Georg Büchner, because he was looking for Büchner's incendiary manifesto* Der hessische Landbote (*The Hessian Country Messenger—"War to the Palaces! Peace to the Huts!"*) *and Bertolt Brecht's* Threepenny Opera, *which we both knew by heart, and not only Macky Messer's song. His name was Gerd, and he always promptly delivered to me the latest BBC news, to which he listened at the Ruzyně airfield, where he served in a radio unit. Gerd came to keep a civilian suit in our apartment, though everything became much more difficult later, and wrote comedies mostly in imitation of George Bernard Shaw. He had been educated in Heidelberg by an older Jewish friend, who, before being transported to the camps, had lived in a little flat above his family's apartment, and I vividly remember Gerd leaning against my father's bookcase, saying, "Give me something to read. I want to write something." But then he could not use his civilian suit and was ordered to fight the Russians in Romania. He spent some time in Soviet captivity and, after his return to Germany, was one of the first young writers to work for the new West German TV; tragically he died in a car accident in 1958. I was happy to meet his daughter Susanne, dramaturg of the Vienna Volkstheater, in the 1960s at the café Mozart, and hear many stories about his life and (unrealized) plans.*

I am recalling these melancholy and picaresque bookshop adventures in some detail because a few Saturday regulars ultimately constituted a circle of friends who prompted me to edit and to type a little samizdat pamphlet of new poetry, illegally distributed to at least a dozen readers or so. We moved, on some Saturdays, from the bookshop to our apartment on Příčná Street, recited our own stuff or Rilke, and thought naively about the future of Bohemia and its sparring nations. The only outsider whose poems I typed was somebody called Franz Peter Fühmann, from a little town in northern Bohemia. I had found his verse in Lyrical Leaflets, *published by the courageous Ellermann firm in Hamburg, and I thought the author, stationed somewhere in Finland and later in Ukraine, preserved a deeply humane and rare sensibility: "everything creative was suspect" (alles Schöpferische war Verdacht), ran one of his lines. I wrote him a fan letter via Hamburg and was very surprised when I promptly received a response in which he revealed himself to be a raging nihilist ready to burn down the world to create a new civilization. Ten years later he was a famous new poet of the German Democratic Republic, and he himself noted the split in his mind, writing, "It was strange. I was, in my subconscious, far ahead of my consciousness. Nazi Germany was at the pinnacle of its triumphs but in my verse the world was constantly breaking apart and turning to coal." I was not surprised to hear in the mid-1980s that he, a disappointed dissident, had drunk himself to death.*

Other poets in my little group included my friend H. W. Kolben, just before he was arrested and sent to a concentration camp; Susanne Brenner, gifted daughter of my Jewish professor of ancient Greek; and myself. I switched from writing poetry in Czech to writing in German only lately because I discovered that my Czech poetry, though grammatically correct, was hopelessly old-fashioned linguistically. No wonder that A., to whom these verses were addressed, never went to the movies with me; even sixty years later, when I visited her, she brought her new husband to our rather unromantic meeting, a consequence of bad poetry.

But there were still people who long after the war gladly remembered our evenings. Among them was ninety-year-old Erich M., who brought to a meeting at the café Paříž circa 1998 a nice collection of memorabilia, including a letter in which we all had thanked him for the poems of his that we had read in his absence. The signatures, still legible, included those of Otakar Prince Lobkovicz and of a young actress who, though her name was Irmgard, signed herself, in view of the future and Hollywood, as "Viola Carroll." I was rather surprised when she called me thirty years later in New York and invited me to attend the premiere of a Richard Strauss opera at the Metropolitan, in the box of her friend, a well-known psychoanalyst.

The trouble was that the Gestapo knew about our poetic evenings—a regular had informed it—and its investigation worked systematically, if slowly. When it finally wanted to call me in, it had to find me in a camp for half Jews to which I had been transported in the meantime. Fortunately it knew only about the meetings, not about my samizdat publication, or it chose to ignore it.

The Fate of Jiří Orten

On August 30, 1941, a young man in Prague who came from the provinces wanted to buy a pack of cigarettes. He crossed Rašín Quai, running along the Vltava River in the district of Smíchov, but found, while the daughter of his landlady waited for him on the other side, that the little *trafika* (cigarette stand) was closed. He turned back, then, when he was in the midst of the traffic lane, heard the vendor holler that he had opened his shop again. The young man turned without hesitation or looking around and was run down by a fast-moving German Red Cross car and dragged many feet. The German driver, upon the entreaties of the girl, put the unconscious man into the car, drove to the hospital, not very far, on Charles Square, where the Czech staff refused to admit him because his papers indicated that he was a Jew. The German driver had disappeared, so a city ambulance had to be called to transport the patient to the nearby Kateřinky Hospital, reserved for Jews. There Jiří Orten, twenty-two years old, a Czech poet admired by many, died without emerging from his coma on September 1, 1941. Had he recovered, he would soon have been required to wear the yellow Jewish star, made obligatory for Jewish citizens in Germany and the protectorate as of September 19, a few days before Heydrich's arrival in Prague.

Jiří Ohrenstein's parents (he chose the poetic name Orten later) both were of Jewish origin and from small villages in central Bohemia before they came to Kutná Hora, once a rich mining town famous for its Gothic architecture. His father, Edvard, a shy and honest man, owned a little textile shop that he had had to buy from his future wife's uncle for a good deal of money. Bertha, Jiří's mother, was a lively woman, liked to tell fairy tales, and enthusiastically participated in amateur theatrical performances, inspiring both her older son, Ota (who after the war returned from British exile to be a famous producer), and the younger, Jiří, to follow her example in one way or another. There are few indications that the family was deeply committed to religious tradition; Jiří wrote a poem about Christmas (difficult to ignore in the shadow of Kutná Hora's magnificent cathedral), and his father was an early and active Social Democrat who at times did some editorial work for the local Socialist paper. Circumstances were modest, and the family was proud of their uncle Josef Rosenzweig, on the mother's side, who completed his legal studies and published two volumes of poetry, calling himself Rosenzweig-Moira to suggest that he felt close to the *Moderní revue,* in which Czech decadents published their verse.

Jiří had a happy childhood, which he later recalled often and in gratitude. He started out, his older brother tells us, as a dedicated reader of *The Three Musketeers* and Jules Verne, but to the astonishment of the family he switched to tennis and skiing and was among the best athletes in the region, traveling a good deal to meets and races and bringing home a sportif vocabulary, strange to hear. And yet, when he was fifteen, he returned to reading and was invited to join a group of working-class kids gathering in secretive meetings in a forest to read poetry to each other. In 1935 he went to a summer camp of the Union of Impecunious and Progressive Students (Socialist, one suspects) in southern Moravia, where he wrote his first verses, and a year later to the union's camp in Slovakia and roamed, on foot, through northern Bohemia. Clearly he was ready to leave home. Taking his cue from his unhappy mother, he decided seriously to study acting at the Prague Conservatory. Breaking off his Kutná Hora school years almost precipitously, he arrived in Prague too early to be admitted and had to spend a year attending an English-language school and working as a file clerk in a credit institute. It was not an unhappy time; Prague, in spite of all the dark clouds, was as lively as ever, he was making many new friends, all committed to poetry and the theater, and he felt that he had made the right decision.

Orten's later years in Prague were overshadowed by the events of Munich and the Second Republic, and the occupation brutally changed his situation. He was able to study for nearly three years at the conservatory and to participate in the affairs of the Student Theater at the Trade Union Center and the Collective Theater of the Young. His first poems, under his own name, appeared in *Haló noviny* and elsewhere, and he was in close touch with the most thoughtful poets of his own generation, Kamil Bednář, Ivan Blatný, and Hanuš Bonn.

Yet the moment came when Orten and his brother and their Jewish friends had to decide what to do, and when many—among them brother Ota and Pavel Tigrid (later of the BBC and Radio Free Europe and, in the 1990s, the Czech Republic's minister of culture)—left for England, Orten resolved to stay, saying that the Czech language was his real home and that he would not leave his love, Věra, a fellow student, who in turn left him for somebody else. The protectorate forced Orten into the solitude of his verse, his diaries, which are magnificent books of meditation, and reading again in the emptiness of his rented rooms, which he constantly changed. He perused two or three books a day when he was not helping out at the Jewish Community Center or clearing the snow from the runways at Ruzyně airfield. Orten was fortunate that he had loyal friends who wanted to protect his work, and the four collections of lyrics that appeared before he died all were published under pseudonyms: *Čítanka Jaro* (1939, A Spring Reader) and *Cesta k mrazu* (1940, A Path to the Frost), under the name of Karel Jílek; *Jeremiášův pláč* (1941, The Tears of Jeremiah) and *Ohnice* (1941, Charlock), by one Jiří Jakub.

Orten was launched by the older poet František Halas, who knew how to be calm in a storm, in a series that featured the first books of lyric poets, and though Czech Fascists knew exactly who Jílek was and attacked him and his Kutná Hora family by name in their newspaper, his friends in the publishing world did not budge. (The spectacle was repeated when the Communists, immediately after 1945, viciously attacked his "bourgeois" individualism.) Václav Černý, editor of *Kritický měsíčník*, continued to print Orten's poems under his real name as long as he could and then went on publishing verse by Jílek or Jakub, whom he placed in the "first rank" among the young poets. "I think of his maturity," Černý wrote about Jílek in 1940, "as one acquired by suffering. And that particular suffering is ever-present, and does not know an ending yet, nor hope, nor an outcome . . . It looks into its own eyes and explores the darkest corners of a bitter world." Later Orten was called an existentialist poet but independent of the French existentialists; his poems, and those of younger friends, surely mark an important moment in Czech poetry, when it turned from surrealist, playful, and collective enchantments with city lights, circuses, and revolutions to the radical interrogation of the self and the question of where and how the lonely individual is to live, or survive.

Orten spent the last months of his life alone, writing, reading, and chronicling his poems in his massive *Notebooks*. He carefully listed, almost in the shape of a poem, what he, as a Jew, was not allowed to do, and he continued to study Rilke, whom on December 12, 1939, he called one of his favorites, together with Francis Jammes, Boris Pasternak, and Fyodor Dostoyevsky. Though his German was rather "modest," he honestly confessed, he translated a few poems by Hesse and Goethe, and more than twenty-five Rilke fragments, as well as two tentative translations of them, can be found in his notes. As time went on, he read more Hesse, Goethe, and Hölderlin than ever. He wrote his own *Elegies* in response to Rilke's *Duino Elegies*, which he certainly read in Paul Eisner's Czech version, from late February to early April 1941—that is, five months before he died. Literary historians would have reason for being eager to know what Jiří Orten and Hanuš Bonn, a young poet employed by the Jewish Community office and translator of some of Rilke's *Duino Elegies*, discussed when they lunched together on June 6, 1941. Orten had always written strophic poems organized by rich rhymes, but after a prelude of free verse in the late winter of 1940, he switched to Rilke's way of writing unrhymed lines—there is a single exception to this—and the question remains whether he did so by merely following Rilke's formal example or because his experiences were too disturbing to express in traditional stanzas, or both.

In delineating his own poetic horizon, Orten does not imitate Rilke's *Duino* poems, and he writes from a radically narrowed lonely site all his own. Rilke wanted to withdraw to his artful tower of Muzot, and his *Duino Elegies* do not hesitate to roam in the cosmic space between the terrible Angels and the geography of his far-flung voyages, appealing to a surfeit of things near the Nile and the Tiber, to antiquity and the modern age. Orten is thrown back to the chamber of his childhood and in vain implores more modest and intimate things to help him and stay with him:

> My paperweights, come back to me again.
> I am so light now, having lost you,
> the smallest wind plucks me from the ground,
> one breath is enough to diffuse me
> into unearthly, unheavenly music,
> only one gesture somewhere behind the mirror is enough
> and I cease to exist, I fall, I dissolve completely.*

Rilke has ambivalent and skeptical feelings about his difficult childhood, as his Third Elegy attests, the one some critics call the psycho-

---

*These and the following verses are translated into English by Lyn Coffin, with the help of Eva Eckert.

analytical one, but Orten never ceases to love his mother and father and in his infinite solitude, where he cannot reach or touch them, wants to feel less pain in a spectral realm on the other side of fate, time, or history:

> Not a withdrawing, no, but I sing the last pleasure
> already behind the memory, on the other side,
> I sing what I was, with fear and terror,
> what we were, whole, more real
> before we fell under the flight of years,
> before consciousness damaged us like this,
> before love plundered our soul,
> before we began to feel that there's no door
> through which one can pass freely
> and step down into the hearts of women and distances,
> that it's necessary not to remember childhood,
> when the flame of sorrow started to burn,
> that in life there is no more world, love,
> stars, breathless space and growth, mother, homeland—
> only in death.

In one of the most compassionate moments of his *Elegies*, Rilke walks through a fairground at the edge of the city and thinks about its rich but hollow promises of happiness and of the false pretense of joyful freedom, the swings, the shooting galleries, the barkers. Orten, visiting the fair of St. Matthew in Prague, searches for something else and feels almost magically drawn to the "trained pony" that is able to count (by turning its head) and answer questions. The trained pony, Orten says in his Sixth Elegy, "gently nodded his head, as if to say that we'd known each other for ages":

> Go ahead, he told me, I know you want to ask a question.
> And so I asked it: Where is there a place for me?
> The pony smiled. He was quiet. He knew how to be quiet!
> Then he got up, he walked over to me
> and slowly said: I am counting something here.

And I know why, and I don't even know how.
But I have to. Do you hear? So do you.
Go nicely home. Learn to be a magician.

The Life of Milena Jesenská

To judge from an increasing number of biographies, anthologies, and learned essays, Milena Jesenská was the most famous Czech woman of the twentieth century, and analogies to Frida Kahlo, though with a few modifications, are not entirely farfetched. The question remains whether her brief affair with Franz Kafka in 1919–20, at a time when she was married and he engaged to Julie Wohryzek, deserves more attention than what she achieved later in life as a political writer and courageous conspirator against the occupying German powers in Prague. Legends abound, including a few feminist ones, and it seems almost impossible to delineate her character, because as her biographer Marta Marková-Kotyková suggests, she changed so often and eradicated all traces of what had gone on before, including husbands, partners, and lovers, famous or not.

Milena was born on August 10, 1896, daughter of a young and impecunious physician who had married a shy rich girl from a good middle-class family; he patriotically described himself as a descendant of Dr. Jan Jesenius, the rector of Prague University who was decapitated with other Protestants in 1621 after the battle of the White Mountain, won by the Catholic powers. Milena belonged to the elite. She entered the Minerva Gymnasium, established to further the academic education of young women (another Minervist was Alice Masaryk, daughter of the sociologist who became president of the First Republic), and while Milena's father made a quick career as a professor of stomatology at the faculty clinics, she had sufficient time (though loyally caring for her ailing mother, who died in 1916) to write for the school paper, to cultivate crushes on her admirable class teacher Albína and a few other young and older men, preferably artists, and to provoke Prague's stolid citizens by promenading with her friends Staša and Jarmila, pretending to be lesbians *à trois* wearing flowing robes, no corsets, and rarely stockings. What was worse, Milena did not care for the ever-important ethnic delineations of Prague life, and infuriating her nationalist father, she began to hang around the café Arco, close to the Hybernská railway station, where young German Jewish intellectuals and writers gathered to gossip about their ideas and manuscripts.

Though Milena did not speak much German, she felt intensely taken with the articulate Ernst Pollak, a bank clerk seriously interested in recent philosophy. (Kafka made only rare appearances at the Arco.) After an abortion she was sent by her father to a psychiatric institution to keep her away from mischief and her Jewish lover. But when she turned twenty-one, her aunts intervened, her father yielded, and she was allowed to marry Pollak, though she had to leave Prague immediately for exile in Vienna, where he obtained another banking position as a foreign-language correspondent.

Her Vienna years with Pollak, from 1918 to 1924, were an almost unmitigated disaster, because he continued his many affairs and spent much time at the cafés Central and Herrenhof with the most important Viennese intellectuals of the moment. Milena was distraught and, rather helplessly confronting the Viennese idiom, looked "like seven volumes of Dostoyevsky," as Franz Blei remarked. But she wanted to assert herself, planned to give Czech lessons, and began to write, in Czech, for Prague newspapers. Her first article, about hungry and cold Vienna, was published on December 30, 1919, in the *Tribuna*; in the 1920s she made regular contributions to *Národní listy* and the liberal *Lidové noviny*. She also wanted to earn her living as a translator, received permission from Franz Kafka, that Prague writer unknown to her compatriots, to translate his prose piece *Der Heizer* (The Stoker, later the first chapter in a novel), which was published in the left-wing periodical *Kmen*. She was not exactly pleased when Kafka, intending a compliment, told her how close her text was to the wording of the original.

After writing long and irresolute letters to each other, Milena and Kafka were happy together in Vienna for a few days between July 29 and August 4, 1920, roaming the woods and basking in the sun, then miserable on August 14, in a shabby little hotel at Gmünd, on the Austrian-Czech border. She had been touched by the tender sympathy

and compassion of his letters, and he, after his calamity with Felice
Bauer and again on the rebound, engaged to another woman, was in-
trigued and repulsed by the corporeality of love. (He had fewer hesitations with prostitutes.) Milena was wondrously alive, like a raging
"fire," Kafka told his friend Max Brod; but he was disgusted by his own
body, not just because he was sick, and felt unable to escape the
abrupt recurrence of happiness and horror. After the hapless tryst at
Gmünd, both Milena, who continued to love Ernst Pollak, and Kafka
knew they were not made for each other, much as it might have seemed
that way earlier, yet it was Milena to whom he handed over his diaries
of the preceding years, clearly a sign of inordinate trust.

In 1924 Milena left her apartment on the Lerchenfelderstrasse in Vienna and Ernst Pollak (who later acquired a doctorate of philosophy and
in his London exile married a woman of high birth), and together with
Ernst's close friend Franz Xaver Count Schaffgotsch, who had returned
from a Russian POW camp, went to a place near Dresden to join a
colony of independent left-wing intellectuals, but not for long. After
leaving the "red Count," she finally returned to Prague and assiduously
worked for the middle-class *Národní listy* and in the editorial offices of a
popular illustrated weekly, mostly writing about fashion as an expression
of style and character, interior architecture, and living progressively.

She moved easily among the avant-garde, married Jaromír Krejcar,
a young architect of bold functionalist ideas, and bore him a daughter,
whom she liked to call Honza, as if she had been a boy. Her life was far
from easy, because she suffered from inflammation of the joints, spent
months in the hospital, and an inevitable operation left her right knee
immobilized and, worse, made her increasingly dependent on pain-
killing drugs. By 1928–29 she was ready to join the Communist Party,
ceased writing for middle-class papers, and began publishing for the
left and in the weekly *Tvorba*, defending the Communist Party line. In
1934 her second husband departed for the Soviet Union, where he
hoped to build some of his modernist projects (he was thoroughly disappointed), but after the Moscow show trials in 1936, Milena herself
could no longer accept what the Soviet political functionaries were
demanding. Krejcar returned from Russia with another woman, and
Milena wanted to start all over again.

By then she had come truly into her own. She was now forty years old, mother of a growing daughter, and physically handicapped because of her intractable knee. She resolved to break with her past, to help other people, and to confront squarely the danger increasingly threatening the Czechoslovak Republic. She continued to attract intelligent men of the left, and in a radical decision, she freed herself from her drug dependence, though not of her habit of dragging her daughter to a daily movie because she could not live without a regular dose of the cinema, and began to write for the liberal weekly *Přítomnost* (The Present) and its friendly editor in chief, Ferdinand Peroutka, whom she had once despised as an enemy of the people. When Peroutka was arrested in the spring of 1939, she immediately stepped into his place, editing the weekly until it had to cease publication. Then, being supported by the young poet Lumír Čivrný, Honza's teacher and Milena's lover, she wrote for the illegal newspaper *V boj* (Into the Fight!), published by the resistance organization of the Czech Army (In Defense of the Nation), run by intrepid officers, and helped distribute it in Prague.

That was not all. Together with Count Joachim von Zedwitz, a German medical student in Prague who owned a sporty small Aerocar and cut an appropriate figure in a leather coat with a little swastika attached, she selflessly helped people escape via the Polish border: Communists, liberals, Trotskyites, Jews, Czechs, Germans. She was arrested by the Gestapo on November 11, 1939, and sent to the concentration camp of Bergen-Belsen in July 1940. Life in the camp, if it could be called such, was made particularly difficult for Milena because many of her Czech fellow prisoners were organized Communists who strongly believed in the future mission of the Soviet Union and who despised her as a hateful "Trotskyite" who had betrayed the movement and written for the liberals. Among these women was Gusta Fučíková, especially inimical to Milena because she suspected her of having had an affair with her martyred husband, later a Communist Party saint. Milena arrived at Bergen-Belsen racked by arthritic pains and was ordered to work in the medical department guarding the records of women infected by venereal disease and particularly endangered by medical experiments. At least she was protected—by an older Viennese Social Democrat in the camp administration—and enjoyed a sudden friendship with Margarete Buber-Neumann, whom the NKVD had handed over to the Gestapo in the days of the Hitler-Stalin pact because she was the widow of a leading German Communist functionary arrested and shot in his Moscow exile.

Milena's state of health deteriorated. She was diagnosed with an inflammation of the kidneys, and after one had been removed, received an inordinate number of blood transfusions, and died on May 17, 1944. She never knew that Count Zedwitz, who himself had been imprisoned for fifteen months, tried with the help of a Berlin lawyer to bring about her release; the Berlin office was destroyed by Allied bombers and the lawyer killed; nothing came of his desperate attempt to help.

In an early essay for the liberal *Přítomnost*, Jesenská seized on the chance to speak openly about the CP, which had quietly disappeared from the public scene after the Czech government had prohibited its activities on October 20, 1938. Undoubtedly she revealed something of her own experience when she wrote that to be a party member always created "difficulties" and "risks" because the party, in spite of or because of its revolutionary claims, had little influence on practical social legislation, usually initiated by the Social Democrats, the CP's prime enemies. In 1933 the Communist Party had abruptly changed its policies, proclaiming that it was necessary above all to fight Fascism together with liberals and Social Democrats, but the change, totally in the service of the Soviet Union, had come too fast, and the "mind of the worker was not so fickle." In changing, the party had lost its inner democracy and thereafter could do nothing but demand "blind faith" and "complete obedience," which did not exactly combine with "independent political thinking." Where thought did not flourish, she added, poems did not flourish either.

In other *Přítomnost* essays, Jesenská constantly and resolutely challenged her countrymen, who were drifting to a new nationalism of the right, with her combative ideas, which closely reflected T. G. Masaryk's legacy. She reported with horror what happened to Jews in Vienna after the Anschluss and could not help noticing that many refugees from Austria and the Sudeten, Jews and non-Jews, were streaming into Prague: "people . . . without documents, on foot, with empty hands. Wandering among us is the reflection of many hundreds of appalling human fates, hundreds of thousands of painful partings, suicides and injustices."

Almost alone among her unwilling fellow citizens, she tried to understand why the republic had lost so many friends among working-class German Socialists, and her arguments came close to those of the philosopher Emanuel Rádl, who believed that the economic crisis hit the Sudeten regions more heavily because of insufficient attention given to them by the central offices in Prague, that while "people in the country were unemployed for three years," as Jesenská wrote, in the Sudeten regions "it was six years." With these refugees in mind, Jesenská pleaded for an international solution to the problem caused by the Munich declarations signed by France and Britain; when confronted with the well-meaning admonitions of a friend that it was her duty to be "first and foremost a Czech" at the present moment, she came, in an essay of May 10, 1939, to the thoughtful conclusion that it was more important to be "a decent person"; being Czech did not mean anything in itself as long as it "was not bound to particular qualities" and the "highest moral standards."

On February 12, 1995, the Medal of the Righteous Among the Nations was posthumously awarded to Milena Jesenská by the Jerusalem Commission, and it was resolved that her name be "forever engraved on the Honor Wall in the garden of the Righteous," at Yad Vashem.

My Friend Hans W. Kolben

In the years of the occupation, people classified as half Jewish had particular difficulties in making new friends because too much had to be explained to "Aryans," and you never knew whether they really wanted to hear about the troubles of your mothers, fathers, or relatives, endangered by new laws or police decrees. We half Jews moved in rat packs, so to speak, and I fell in with the Alt family, who lived in four or five shabby rooms in proletarian Žižkov. There were Mother Alt, two daughters and two sons, and a loyal housekeeper who lived in the kitchen, all adults and all in a fragile situation. They told me that the father of the family, a minor clerk in the economic section of the Soviet Consulate General, had been an atheist not registered in the Jewish Community, and since he had died some years ago, everybody hoped it was now impossible to discover his Jewish origins, and so the family pretended that everything was "normal." Maria, the older daughter, worked in Prague's Social Security Office, Kristina was a dentist's technician in Karlín, and the boys were busy, I assumed, buying and selling old machinery. Madame Alt, rawboned and imperturbable, ran the household with her aging kitchen help, everybody chipped in ration coupons, and on Sundays coffee and cake were waiting. In the summer we walked through the Vltava woods, collecting mushrooms for dinner (the Alts were expert mycologists), and in wintertime we happily hung around in an extra room at the Vikárka, a rather patrician tavern on Castle Hill, famous then and now because some important Czech nineteenth-century authors had quaffed beer there and because later Václav Havel, after his election to the presidency, liked to sit there between office hours.

Only two outsiders were never asked to explain anything to the Alt family, and they were Hans W. Kolben, grandson of a renowned inventor and mighty industrialist, and I. Both of us had reasons to be lighthearted at the Vikárka, because we were ardent admirers of Kristina, the younger daughter, and wrote weekly poems in her praise. My friend's poems were far better than mine, but Kristina was not a young woman easily moved by literary predilections, and as time went on, she invited me to join her on her evening walks up Petřín Hill, where on a bench near the monument of the Romantic poet K. H. Mácha, who knew about love and the month of May and a few other things, she taught me how really to kiss.

Hans was seventeen when the German soldiers came in 1939, and he was twenty when he died of typhoid fever in a concentration camp quarry. His grandfather Emil Kolben had been an assistant to Thomas Alva Edison, in New Jersey, and had later established Prague's Kolben industries, which produced locomotives and heavy machinery and competed with the Škoda works in importance. The Kolbens were of Jewish origin, though Hans was a Lutheran, and they continued to live in their palatial villa with a turret as if nothing were happening. While other Jews were wearing the yellow star, members of the Kolben family went on, in a mysterious way, with their affairs, freely using public transportation and entering cafés and restaurants, without any stars or hesitations. But in the late au-

tumn of 1941 we suddenly knew. Hans was arrested in a street car near the café Slavia because a former fellow student had notified the police that he had discovered a Jew without a star. It turned out that the Kolben family was among those few that, encouraged by the legislative intent of the Czech government, had applied for exemption from anti-Jewish legislation—until Heydrich appeared and declared all government talks about exemptions null and void. Emil Kolben, the famous grandfather, was transported to Terezín, where he died, and his grandson Hans was ultimately sent on from a Prague prison via Terezín to Mauthausen and Kauffering; his younger brother miraculously escaped from the camps and survived.

Hans wrote his poems in the years of his fragile "exemption," when he was about eighteen or nineteen, but they do not show any youthful restlessness or revolutionary impatience. As a Prague poet he remained untouched by the new expressionist idiom and, like Kafka, moved within the classical tradition. If Kafka delighted in Goethe and Stifter, Kolben, I suspect, went back to Goethe and perhaps early Hofmannsthal, ever loyal to the inherited rhyme and the balanced stanza. He was not polemical but pensive; his moment of happiness was an Einst (once) of an earnest childhood in a well-regulated family, and though he had enough imagination to think of hungry and imprisoned people, "their pale opened lips" and their "pushing stream, disfigured forms, gypsum alive," he wanted to discover, above all, who he was in a metaphysical sense. He turned to the Bohemian forests for an answer:

> *And with my fingers now I rediscover*
> *The secret that these dark trees tell each other.*
> *The forest holds a mystery—I feel it.*
> *One day, perhaps, the forest will reveal it.**

Another poem from Kolben's papers, entitled "In das Schmelzen einer Abendstunde [Into the Melting of an Evening Hour]," tries to ignore history, but his vision of the future liberation reveals from what moment of terror the poem emerges:

---

*This and the following poems are translated by Howard Stern (New Haven).

> We know this heaviness will disappear.
> Someday the violins like cherubim
> Will rise on wings of song, and we shall hear
> Their lofty music burst into a clear
> Concert of fire, a jubilation hymn.

Kolben's poem "Bread and Wine" reveals much of his melancholy thought confronting history and humanity and his way of dealing with ancient symbols in a new way, free of the traditional heritage and full of hope:

> Behold, a new seed fell on fertile ground,
> A foreign grass sprang up across the plain.
> And all the lesser grass that stood around
> gave way to mighty waves of solid grain.
>
> And huts began to cluster in the vale,
> and those who lived there never wanted food.
> They lived a simple life, were strong and hale,
> Erect and handsome—for the bread was good.

Yet "simple life" can never endure, and even the human thirst for doing noble deeds turns deeply ambivalent, a blessing and a danger at the same moment:

> And then a second seed fell on the land;
> long slender vines came curling from the dust
> And quickly ripened. In the vineyard stand
> The heavy jars of gleaming purple must.
>
> And those whose former life had been contented
> Grew restless and at once began to long
> For noble deeds. A sudden storm fermented
> Of colors, gods and images, and song.

When I copied Kolben's poems on my old typewriter, he was near death, but I published a few of his verses later, in Vienna in 1947, in

Plan, *where Otto Basil also printed Paul Celan for the first time. I would wish that his last verse would not go unheard:*

> *I hope that people will remember me*
> *As music from a garden, as a dance*
> *Of summer haze, a trembling consonance,*
> *A stifled song of mountains, earth and sea.*

Heydrich at Work in Prague

When Heydrich arrived in Prague on a sunny weekend, he did not waste time on military parades or formal receptions, and his orders, ready long before he addressed his first meeting of the highest functionaries of the occupation regime on October 4, 1941, came hard and fast. He was not inclined to negotiate or to represent, but to change old policies and dictate new ones or, as he informed the Nazi Party chief Martin Bormann, "to sustain a sham-autonomy and, at the same time, to liquidate that autonomy from the inside."

General Eliáš, prime minister of the Czech government since September 9, 1939, was arrested and tried for high treason; factory workers (in contrast with the intelligentsia) were wooed by a new system of rations and new allocations of shoes and cigarettes; and, after another secret meeting with Heydrich's highest functionaries, including Eichmann, on October 10 the first transports of Jews began to leave Prague, initially for Lodz and later for Terezín. This was about the same time that mass deportation of Jews from Germany to the east was beginning.

Heydrich had prepared for the proclamation of martial law and for the defense of its legality within the German system by consulting his ally Otto Thierack, president of the People's Courts in Berlin, before he left for Prague, and he felt free "to deal with unusual incidents," as he said there. During the sixteen weeks of martial law, 486 death sentences were rendered, and 2,242 people sent to concentration camps; most of them, such as General Josef Bílý, a founding member of the DN arrested in 1940, belonged to military or civic resistance organizations that had long been under investigation.

Heydrich carefully orchestrated the executions, as he had done in Germany before, for maximum shock effect. On the first day 6 persons were shot, 20 on the second, 58 on September 30, and the number slowly declined in later days. At least 6 generals, 10 colonels, and 21 other officers were among the executed, but hardly any peasants or workers, and to earn the sympathies of the working people in the factories, Heydrich included among the victims of martial law a number of cattle dealers and butchers, economic "hyenas of the interior front," all of them (169) hanged, not shot. At the same time, about 5,000 more people were arrested, bringing the operations of the non-Communist underground nearly to a halt for the time being; Heydrich had reason to boast that his people had discovered ninety illicit shortwave broadcasting stations. The Communist underground was less involved, for its operations had just begun.

Eliáš had long been under scrutiny by the Gestapo. When he was arrested, he was brought to Gestapo headquarters, interrogated for forty-eight hours, and, on October 1, put to a speedy trial before a People's Court, one of the Gestapo men acting as state prosecutor, a legal irregularity that Heydrich defended on the basis of his new authority. Eliáš, a general in the Czechoslovak state police, had kept in constant touch with the underground, and though the Gestapo did not know half the truth about his contacts with Beneš, it had a long list of accusations ready, all based on its investigation of the Schmoranz people, a small but highly efficient resistance group in the government press office, and on the disclosures of Otakar Klapka, former lord mayor of Prague, who, a diabetic, was dragged from the concentration camp to Prague. Eliáš was sentenced to death, the Czech government held an impassioned meeting to discuss whether it should resign immediately in protest (it did not), and President Hácha asked twice that Eliáš's life be spared. After a week Hácha was told that the execution would be postponed because Eliáš was needed in further investigations of the resistance. Eliáš was finally executed on June 19, 1942, but that was after Heydrich had been killed.

Heydrich had resolved to split the resistance by favoring working people over the intelligentsia; in his policies he followed the example of the Arbeitsfront in the Reich, combined with a good deal of pragmatism and, curiously, a dash of Othmar Spann's ideas of "nonpolitical class groups." (A few disciples of that Viennese philosopher among the old guard Sudeten Kameradschaftsbund [League of Comrades] had already been sent to concentration camps.) In Prague, Heydrich made use of what he found—that is, the National Central Trade Union Agency—and ordered its functionaries to announce on the shop floors that great changes were imminent. On October 24 he invited union delegates, their own Václav Stočes presiding, to a pep talk at Hradčany Castle. Subsequently he increased some of the rations to the German level, distributed two hundred thousand shoes in the factories, insisted on the establishment of canteens to serve free lunches (thick soups) to people working long hours, and instituted a program of workers' holidays in former luxury hotels at Luhačovice Spa and elsewhere. (Until 1944 eighty thousand workers went, but there were at least a few instances of refusals.) By April 1942 a reform of the social system was ready: pensions for old people and invalids were raised by 20 percent, and those for widows by a third. Václav Král, who wrote a three-volume study of the 1939–45 economic situation from a Stalinist point of view, had a hard time accounting for the compliant attitudes of the working class and shifted his attention instead to the misdeeds of the high bourgeosie.

Anti-Semitic legislation had already begun in the Second Republic when Jews were removed from the civil service in January 1939, and it continued under Neurath, with his decree of June 21 extending the validity of the Nuremberg Laws to the protectorate. Jews had to wear the yellow star as of September 19, 1941, three weeks after Heydrich had ordered this in the Reich, and when he came to Prague, systematic deportations commenced, the first transports going to Lodz (and farther, to Chelmno, where exhaust gas was used to kill people) between October 5 and November 3. For a few weeks Prague's Jewish Community and its Gestapo supervisors discussed a number of possibilities for establishing a ghetto either in Prague itself or in small towns—Stará Boleslav, Kyjov, Český Brod, or Boskovice, in Moravia—but Heydrich's men distinctly preferred Terezín. This eighteenth-century garrison town, built by the emperor Joseph II in the 1780s and, as Theresienstadt, named for his mother, the empress Maria Theresa, had many fortifications and barracks. The Jewish Community had no choice but to give in. On November 24 a first transport from Prague, a group of 342 able-bodied men, was sent there as an Aufbaukommando, and on December 4 another 1,000 men followed. Within a week the first transports of families, soon to be separated, arrived.

As of October 1, about 88,100 Jews lived in the protectorate (approximately half of them in Prague), yet Heydrich's SS transported to Theresienstadt 141,000 people, including Jews from Germany, Austria, Holland, and Denmark. Conditions in the small town, or rather in the eleven or twelve old military barracks, their damp casemates, and a few houses, were unspeakable; nourishment was insufficient, and disease rampant. While 88,000 people successively were transported farther east to the gas chambers, 33,500 died in the camp itself. (As H. G. Adler believes, only a little more than one-tenth of all people sent to Terezín before November 1, 1944, were rescued.)

In contrast with Neurath, Heydrich had definite plans for Prague's German university, which should function on the Slavic periphery, as he saw it, and contribute to the germanization of eastern and southeastern Europe by developing ethnic studies in history, social anthropology, law, and the science of race. Heydrich's man for overseeing this work was Hans Joachim Beyer, a forty-three-year-old SS Hauptsturmführer and docent, who had been earlier sent by the Reichssicherheitshauptamt (Chief Security Office of the Reich), run by Heydrich, to teach in Danzig and Posen. In February 1942 Beyer came to Prague and, in the absence of a strong university rector and against the views of the Ministry of Education in Berlin, tried to remove some of the older professors, even when they were active in the Nazi Party, in order to position younger people from the SS. Though he did not entirely succeed, after the death of Heydrich he appropriated Heydrich's idea of a foundation under which all relevant scholarly research would be carried on by four groups. The one for *Volkswissenschaft* (folk research) was chaired by him, and with the full support of Heydrich's successor he acquired an old palace on the Malá Strana to house the Slavic libraries from the Czech university, as well as many books from libraries in Warsaw and Minsk. Fortunately not much came of these intrigues and reorganizations; an order for the arrest for Beyer was issued only on July 1, 1946, and he later taught at Flensburg, in northern West Germany.

In his media policies, Heydrich resolutely favored "activists" who in newspapers, broadcasts, and books demanded the close integration of the Czech nation into the German Reich. Among this motley group of journalists was Emanuel Vajtauer (b. 1892), who, after finishing his studies of philosophy and psychology, had joined the anarchists and the ultra-left faction of Czechoslovakia's young Communist Party and gone to the United States, where he was imprisoned and then extradited (1921) because of his radical activities. He wrote a spate of books, including *Lidská duše* (*Human Soul*; 1922) and *Ellis Island* (1928), and later was editor of the *České slovo* (Czech Word). (In 1945 he escaped from Czechoslovakia, never to be seen again.) Vladimír Krychtálek (b. 1903, in Brno), who never finished his studies at the technical university, in the mid-1930s worked for *Lidové noviny*, went on a study tour of China and the Soviet Union, switched to the agrarian press, becoming editor in chief of *Venkov* (The Country), and was appointed president of the National Union of Journalists. During the German occupation he demanded that family members of political émigrés be imprisoned in a special camp (they were). (After 1945 Krychtálek in turn was tried by a court of retribution and hanged in 1947.) Karel Lažnovský came from a family of miners, by 1925 was active in the Communist Party, and in the 1930s worked for various national liberal papers. In 1940–41 he was editor in chief of *České slovo* and wrote his *Rozmluvy s dějinami* (Conversations with History, 1940), reinterpreting the Czech past according to the demands of the German occupying forces.

These "activists" were invited to come to Germany, where Goebbels himself welcomed them, but their propaganda articles about the idea of the Reich—whether they referred to Duke Wenceslas paying medieval tribute to the German emperor or to Nazi Germany as a revolutionary force—did not impress the Czech public, and their newspapers lost readers. As a group the activists constantly tried to pressure Hácha's government to issue declarations in favor of the occupation regime, provoked individual ministers by impertinent interviews, and loudly demanded that they be supported in their fight against the broadcasts from London. The government was not particularly eager to deal with them, and when, on September 18, 1941, Eliáš invited the activists for a conversation and a light repast, events took a dramatic turn: within days four of the activists came down with symptoms of a strange flu. When Karel Lažnovský died on October 10, the attending physician believed he had succumbed to a rare form of typhus. Heydrich, at any rate, declared that he was murdered; Lažnovský was buried in state, and at his grave the superactivist Emanuel Moravec declared they would continue his fight until their final triumph.

Moravec himself, favored by Heydrich personally, was a different kettle of fish, because he had been widely known for more than a decade as a legionnaire, colonel of the general staff, military writer close to the offices of presidents Masaryk and Beneš, and, in the desperate days of Munich, an upright patriot demanding that the Czechoslovak Republic be defended at all costs. Paradoxically, it was the trauma of the Munich decisions that drove him into the arms of the Germans.

Departures

One afternoon in late September 1941 my mother told me she had gone to Josefov to the offices of the Jewish Community (I wonder whether she had been there ever before), stood in line, and received her yellow stars, made of cloth, with black lines and the word Jude *in the middle. At home, Mother took needle and thread, which she handled so well, and sewed the stars to two blouses and a dress, as the decree required. Immediately the star made it impossible for her to move freely through the city, since all parks, gardens, and many streets were forbidden to Jews, but she found a way to ignore the decree at least occasionally and pretended with my help that we were regular citizens among others. My mother owned an elegant handbag, square, black, and shiny, a little Hollywoodish à la Claudette Colbert, and if she held it at a certain angle, pressed against her breast, the yellow star could not be seen at all, and when we walked together, mother and son, nobody suspected anything. So we could walk slowly through the parks—preferably distant Vinohrady parks, where* there would be no neighbors—on the few sunny days, enjoying the fresh air and the warm light, but we did not dare sit down with the old people on the benches.

Once, I remember, we challenged the decree at a special event. It was New Year's Eve of the evil year 1942, and my father suggested that we all attend the night performance at his cinema on Příkopy. He gave us tickets, and we sat in the balcony, close to a corner in case we had to make a fast exit, and watched a funny comedy. My mother enjoyed herself, relaxing her grip on the famous black purse, but when the lights went on at the end, she pressed it dutifully against her dress again—and just in time, because a couple leaving began to stare at us ominously; my father told me the man was K., an old theater colleague of his, who knew exactly our family situation from way back. So the new year did not start well. We were afraid, at least for three days and nights, that K. would call the police, but he was an honest man and did not. That was my mother's last opportunity to see a movie, for we did not dare repeat such an excursion. Even walks through the parks became rare.

After the transports started, acquaintances and friends disappeared without a word or with only a few, and those who were still around fell silent and shrugged their shoulders in hopeless confusion when asked about somebody who had gone. Encounters to say goodbye were limited, but I remember that one day my colleague in the bookshop Mr. Glass, half Jewish as was I, invited me to say adieu to Eva L., who had received her transport order to Terezín. We all knew her melancholy and complicated story. Eva was the daughter of a well-known Prague journalist and writer who had escaped to England in time, but she had refused to go because she was in love with a young Austrian who promised to take care of her. They tried to escape together, but it was too late. Eva was briefly imprisoned, and he was sent to Dachau; after she had been released, she tried again to leave, but nothing worked. Now she invited us to her little place for a last evening before she had to go to the transport center.

My colleague acted as host, as it turned out, and two other young men and I sat and sipped glasses of white wine until he announced that Eva had invited us each to make love to her before she left. It was not a gangbang (whatever that word means and which I learned only fifty years later) but a strangely decorous affair, and so it happened that I was asked to en-

ter the small bedroom, where I found Eva, after my predecessor had left, her body warm and clad in a chemise dating from better times. She was a little older than I, her ash blond hair cut short. She embraced me right away, and though I responded as I should have (I assumed), I still felt or thought I felt that I disappointed her, because I wanted to be as tender as I could while she expected a gust of passion, wordless and strong. Then I left the bedroom, we drank another glass, my successor had his moment, and finally Eva came out of her room, clasped us all one after the other, and we left. We never saw her again. It is believed that she died in Bergen-Belsen in the last year of the war.

A few months later my father told me I should take leave of Paul Kisch, brother of the more famous Egon Erwin Kisch of the old Prague family resident at the ancient house at Melantrichova Street, and I trudged there rather unwillingly. Literary history, or rather Prague rumor, had it that Paul, in stark contrast with his brother, had always been a German nationalist, albeit with some liberal inclinations, and had written a dissertation on the nineteenth-century German playwright Friedrich Hebbel, who had spoken of the Slavs as "servant nations." Everybody knew that old anecdote circulating among Prague, Vienna, and Berlin intellectuals about Paul's discovering in the fall of 1918 that his radical brother commanded the red troops occupying many government buildings in Vienna: he stormed into Egonek's office, saw him sitting there in his glorious, if improvised, Bolshevik uniform, and told him in no uncertain terms, "Just you wait, I'll tell Mama!" But here it was the fall of 1943, and when I entered the room, I saw Paul, now an old man, immobile on a sofa, in the outfit of his German dueling student fraternity of 1910, with gloves, plumes, and saber, a stony figure from another time, if not another planet. We did not talk much, I wished him well, stutteringly, for his journey was to begin the next morning, and when I closed the door again, I suspected that he had proudly wanted to show me, a young student, something of Prague's forgotten past, possibly those black, red, and golden glories of the German liberal nationalists who had fought together with their Czech allies during the first weeks of the 1848 Revolution.

I still thought of that strange evening when my father told me in the spring of 1948 that he had seen Egonek, now an internationally famous Communist author, downtown and had jokingly asked him what his com-

rades would do if they lost the impending elections. Egonek answered that in that case red machine guns would be positioned all over Wenceslas Square. Egonek and his allies won the elections, but he died on New Year's Eve that year, just in time not to be dragged, along with other Jews high up in the Communist hierarchy and with heroes from the Spanish Civil War, by his own comrades to the show trials in Prague, where such figures were accused of participating in Zionist and imperialist conspiration against Socialist society. His brother had died, as I read nearly sixty years later in the Terezín Memorial Book, *on October 12, 1944, in the gas chambers at Auschwitz.*

The Case of Emanuel Moravec and a New Government

Emanuel Moravec was born in 1893 to the family of a modest Prague merchant whose people came from Kutná Hora. (His mother may have had German ancestry, or so he later claimed.) The boy went to a Smíchov high school and later to a technical-vocational institute, putting him at a certain disadvantage, since Czech educated classes usually sent their children to Latin and Greek humanist gymnasiums, and then worked as an inconspicuous clerk in two Prague firms. On the first day of World War I he was mobilized, trained in Salzburg as a machine gunner, and sent to the Carpathian front, where together with many other Czechs he surrendered to the Russians and was dispatched to a patriotic POW camp in distant Samarkand. This was where he met his first wife, who happened to be closely related to Lenin's successor Aleksey Rykov, who was assassinated in 1938. Moravec hoped to join a Czech unit to fight the Austrians, but the czarist government was slow, and like his comrade Radola Gajda, he was happy to enlist in the Serb Division of Volunteers, which sent him off to fight the (Slavic) Bulgarians allied with Germany. He fought them at the Bulgarian village of Amzač, and in September 1916, with his nerves paralyzed and in shell shock, he was transported to a hospital, where he stayed for six months; later he went to Kiev to join the Czechoslovak Legions, established by Czech and Slovak soldiers formerly of the Austrian Army but now ready to fight for the Allies and an independent Czechoslovakia. He met T. G. Masaryk, whom he greatly admired, and was promptly sent to Romania for further training. After his return he fell from his horse, broke his collarbone, and began to write on military matters; his first effort was a technical article on fortifications published in the army newspaper in the summer of 1918, and hundreds more followed. Moravec was promoted to captain in the fall of 1918 at Omsk, and General M. R. Štefánik, minister of war in the Czechoslovak government, who on an inspection trip to Siberia noted his high qualifications for army intelligence, put him in charge of an island near the shores of Vladivostok, where the legionnaires quarantined their brethren-in-arms who had turned to bolshevism. Moravec and his young family were repatriated on board American ships and reached Trieste in August 1920 and Prague soon thereafter. Officers of the legion were offered a chance to continue in the regular Czechoslovak Army, and Captain Moravec, army intelligence, was immediately sent to easternmost Užhorod, where the army confronted the inimical Hungarians.

After so many adventures, the continuities and discontinuities of a military career followed: a stint at the Prague War College, a command at Michalovce in eastern Slovakia, and then a return to Prague to teach at the War College and at Prague's Technical University. By now he had a second (Slovak) wife. His superior officers attested that Moravec was "thoughtful" and "well read," and by the early 1930s his articles on geopolitical and strategic issues were being published in the most important liberal newspapers and periodicals, including the *Democratický střed* (Democratic Center), run by Dr. Hubert Ripka (who was later close to Edvard Beneš). Moravec also wrote for the *Lidové noviny* and Ferdinand Peroutka's *Přítomnost* (The Present).

Moravec had edited a slim volume of President Masaryk's speeches to soldiers, and on May 5, 1933, Masaryk, meeting him again, asked him to write a book, broadly conceived, about the republic's military situation, strategic and psychological. Moravec, never laconic, wrote two volumes, *Vojáci a doba* (Soldiers in Our Time, 1934) and *Obrana státu* (In Defense of the State, 1935); many people believed that these works amply confirmed that the author had become the president's spokesman on military matters.

A picture of the Brod family, c. 1912

A wedding photograph, 1920

ABOVE LEFT My father, the poet, on the balcony of the Theater of the Estates, c. 1914

ABOVE RIGHT My mother on a Sunday excursion, c. 1921

My mother, c. 1936

ABOVE LEFT On Příkopy Boulevard, 1941

ABOVE RIGHT My Ladin grandma

The Ladin children, c. 1898

My friend H. W. Kolben
(from the Kolben family archive)

German troops arriving in Prague,
March 15, 1939
(Czech News Agency, Photo Service)

Hitler looking down on Prague,
March 16, 1939
(Czech News Agency, Photo Service)

Konstantin Freiherr von Neurath (left)
and Emil Hácha in conference, April
1939 (Czech News Agency, Photo Service)

Ascending to power: Reinhard Heydrich (left) and K. H. Frank, September 1941 (Czech News Agency, Photo Service)

June 18, 1942: German SS and a Czech fire brigade trying to drown the Czechoslovak parachutists hidden in the crypt of St. Borromaeus Church in the New Town (Czech News Agency, Photo Service)

A barricade waiting, early May 1945 (Czech News Agency, Photo Service)

Prague Germans expelled from their apartments, early May 1945 (Czech News Agency, Photo Service)

SWING ORCHESTER
LEADER: MARTIN ROMAN

Brass: Reed: Rhytm:
Kohn,   Weiss,   Libenský,
Gokkes,   Vodňanský, Nettl,
Vogel,   Donde,   Goldschmidt,
Taussig,   Schumann,

A rare poster announcing a performance in Terezín by the swing orchestra of Martin Roman, which featured Fritzek Weiss on clarinet. Weiss was killed with his father in the Auschwitz gas chambers on April 10, 1944. (Adalbert-Stifter-Verein, Munich, Library Archives)

President Václav Havel (left) awarding the Medal of Merit to me, October 28, 2000 (The President's Press Office, Prague)

Moravec's views on foreign policy complicated matters, however. Increasingly, he began to doubt Beneš's traditional reliance on France and asked, especially after Italy's aggressive war in Abyssinia and the growing German danger, whether it would not be advisable to seek support from Italy, Poland, Hungary, and Russia. Personally he liked a democracy of the "strong hand" more than interminable conflict among many political parties, and when, in 1937, the writer Jaroslav Durych, sympathizing with General Franco in Spain, attacked the liberal Karel Čapek for being too much a "civilian," Moravec sided with Durych, all the while, however, insisting on the resolute defense of Czechoslovakia against the German threat.

In the days of the final mobilization to oppose Hitler and then of the Munich Conference, he was extraordinarily resolved to prevent his country's capitulation; at one point he left his command post in southern Moravia, drove in his little private car to Prague, and, in his field uniform and all, stormed into the president's office to exhort Beneš to fight (only to be thrown out by General Jan Syrový, chief of staff). After Beneš signed the capitulation of the army, a group of officers elected Colonel Moravec to speak to the president again—but to no avail. On November 14, 1938, Colonel Moravec was "furloughed" along with many other officers suddenly unemployed, felt betrayed and desperate, and thought about emigrating as a military adviser to one of the small Central American republics.

It did not happen because sometimes the Germans had a well-developed sense of who would be useful to their cause. In mid-October 1938, before the Prague general staff decided that he had to stop publishing, Moravec in his last republican article had declared that Czechoslovakia, even if deprived of Bohemia and its border regions, needed its army because the dangers of war continued and the army would prevent the republic from turning into a scene of bloody conflict. Without the border regions, he acknowledged, Czechoslovakia would be a much smaller power, but without the army "it would amount to nothing." In his desperation he began to write a book and finished it that summer, by which time the Germans had decided to deal with him in a way he did not expect at all. It likely began with a visit from a military expert affiliated with the Office of the Reichsprotektor; in any case he was invited to Germany and, when he returned, to make a broadcast about it, as he faithfully did . . . in favor of the occupation power.

Moravec himself said that his book *V úloze mouřenína* (In the Role of the Moor, 1939), consisted of "far-ranging and disorderly considerations," but there are reasons why it was read by so many people, including German military observers (there were five printings within two years). In the title Moravec alluded to a well-known verse by the German poet Friedrich Schiller speaking of a good servant who was let go unceremoniously after he had loyally fulfilled all his duties, but the book was at least partly a geopolitical essay that had wide implications and many statistics on Czechoslovakia's army divisions, airplanes, and the production of iron and steel and partly the enraged confession of a soldier deeply offended by the capitulation of the republic. Moravec revived some of his older ideas, including that of a generational conflict that ranged across all Europe, pitting against one another the twenty-year-olds, "those inexperienced dreamers"; "experienced and productive people in their forties (approximately his own age-group); and deplorable, "calculating and cautious" sexagenarians who unfortunately could not muster the courage to defend the republic come what may.

Moravec showed unwavering respect for Masaryk, who had always recommended studying historical change, and invariably disparaged Beneš, who he thought had failed to develop policies in response to the changing situation in the early 1930s and could not ward off Poland's and Hungary's territorial demands, ultimately presented in synchrony with those of Germany. Moravec offered a precise and readable blow-by-blow report of developments from 1935, when France lost its military hegemony in Europe, to the Anschluss and then Munich in 1938, and showed a good deal of his surprisingly old-fashioned feelings about "the ancient kingdom of Bohemia," now irreversibly lost: "the nation raged, the soldiers fell silent . . . in desperate pain." His scholarly and critical biographer Jiří Pernes suggests that his book was not yet a document of perverse collaboration but rather a text that showed him searching for a measure of how the Czech nation might accept the fact that Germany was its "fate" without sacrificing its dignity. Yet Moravec was infected by illiberal ideas, as in his railing against the triple egoism responsible for the tragedy of the republic, by which he meant "the system of the Western plutocracies that considered Czechoslovakia a subservient colony," the overaged politicians of the traditional political parties, and "the Jews," who were unsoldierly and had their own reasons to misuse Czech patriotism.

Moravec was certainly the most professorial and theoretical among the activists, but that changed abruptly when Heydrich came to Prague and discovered the true ambitions of this onetime soldier. Against President Hácha's protests, Heydrich insisted that Moravec be included in the third protectorate government as minister of education and popular culture.

Heydrich was not in a hurry to consolidate the government, which had been effectively dysfunctional since Eliáš's arrest, and he was using the interregnum to further his own aims by relying on the trade unions, the activist journalists, and the shock effects of executions and mass arrests. President Hácha was deeply affected by the arrest on September 24, 1941, of his chief of office and minister without portfolio Jiří Havelka, a loyal liberal, and it is clear that Heydrich used the Havelka case to pressure the ailing Hácha into dishonorable political compromises. Havelka was put under house arrest, and thereafter Hácha's speeches were written by Josef Kliment, an ambitious believer in the *Reichsidee*, who served in the president's office unopposed. Only on January 19, 1942, was the new government introduced and confirmed by the Office of the Reichsprotektor; it had been planned by K. H. Frank. It was a curious amalgam of experts long devoted to the Czechoslovak Republic, older right-of-center bureaucrats, a German from the Reichsprotektor's Office (for the first time), and Moravec.

Jaroslav Krejčí, an expert in constitutional law, had been minister of justice in the Second Republic and had become prime minister after General Eliáš's arrest; he now continued in that function and convinced Richard Bienert to accept the position of minister of the interior. Bienert had entered the Bohemian police administration as early as 1916, actively worked for Masaryk and Beneš's secret organization toward the end of World War I, been head of the Prague police in 1920–25, and later chaired the regional administration of Bohemia; K. H. Frank did not trust him, and he had been briefly arrested when the war against Poland started. Adolf Hrubý, minister of agriculture, who as a youth had been a Bolshevik legionnaire, had made his political career in local agrarian organizations; elected to the Czechoslovak Parliament in 1935, he was the first chairman of National Solidarity, showed considerable skill in handling the Fascists but ran into some trouble with the German authorities and Hácha, only to emerge again now, as Heydrich began to woo the peasants.

Josef Kalfus, who had joined the Czechoslovak tax services as a young man, was first appointed minister of finance as early as 1936, then reappointed by both General Syrový and Beran, after Munich. He had been instrumental in securing financing for the army and showed considerable audacity by quickly privatizing a number of government accounts during the night of March 14–15, 1939, thus saving them from German seizure. Jindřich Kamenický, a railway man all his life, had been minister of post and transport in the brief pre-Munich government of September 1938, had valiantly solved problems caused by the general (if useless) mobilization of the army, and by 1939 was director general of the railways, immediately offering employment to hundreds of students when the universities were closed in November 1939.

Two new members of the government were Heydrich's personal choices: the German economist Walter Bertsch, who was to die in a Brno prison, long after 1945, and Emanuel Moravec, who soon assumed the role of government spokesman and established an organization in imitation of the Hitlerjugend to reeducate Czech youth. He shot himself in a German military truck when the Czech citizens of Prague rose against their oppressors in May 1945.

Thalia Divided

Occupiers and occupied confronted each other not just in the struggle for administrative power waged between the protectorate government and the Office of the Reichsprotektor, or on the subterranean battlefields where resistance groups fought the Gestapo. In their own way, public cultural institutions were intensely involved; among them were

the Prague theaters, which had been open to the public since the eighteenth century and now performed for audiences more strictly divided
than ever by both language and ideology.

The Czech theater in Prague under the German occupation moved
between an intense commitment of their audiences to support their
national institutions and the policies of the occupation regime to remove its enemies and at the very least to prevent open demonstrations
against it. Theatrical life was made possible by an economy in which
people had more money to spend on theater and movie tickets than on
other discretionary purchases; big and small houses were sold out
every evening in Prague, as in the provinces; and it may reveal something about the situation that people usually discussed issues of cen-
sorship (outwitted, of course) and repertory rather than of finances.
The question whether the occupation regime was more interested in
controlling Prague's movie industry than its theaters has not been discussed in Czech patriotic literature, but the answer is evident: Berlin
cared more about the technology and mass appeal of the movie industry than about the theater.

The German supervisors of Prague's theatrical life—sometimes August Ritter von Hoop (in Czech parlance the Kangaroo, because his
name was pronounced "Hopp!" or "jump!"), his boss at the Office of
Reichsprotektor, Wolfram von Wolmar (generally called Osram von
Tungsram), and later Emanuel Moravec, who made it a particular
habit to interfere—opened and closed theaters at will. Right at the
start, in March 1939, the Reichsprotektor took over the Neues
Deutsches Theater, which had gone bankrupt in the Munich days and
had become a ward of the Czech state, and declared it to be the
Deutsches Opernhaus, offering operas and operettas mostly performed by traveling ensembles. The occupying powers also returned
the old Theater of the Estates, which in 1920 had been taken over by
a group of restive Czech actors, to the German domain to serve as the
Deutsches Schauspielhaus, and they retained the Kleine Bühne, a
theater famous for its stagings of avant-garde plays from the Weimar
period and earlier. They called it the Chamber Playhouse, and its audi-
torium was reduced to 260 seats.

The Czechs in turn quickly refurbished the old Varieté hall in Karlín within weeks to use as a Prozatimní Divadlo (Interim Theater); it is still going strong today, with imported musicals. Again, as with many novels and movies, the fundamental response to the pressure of the German occupation was a new historicism that turned to the treasures of Czechoslovakia's national tradition. Onstage that meant popular nineteenth-century plays by V. K. Klicpera, K. Sabina, and J. K. Tyl or occasional performances of texts of the popular heritage, Christmas plays or staged recitations of poetry. Many more German and Austrian plays in translation were performed than ever before, including some by Kleist, Goethe's *Urfaust* and *Tasso*, Grillparzer, and a good deal of Gerhart Hauptmann's more important plays, including *Kollege Crampton* and the satirical *Der Biberpelz* (The Beaver Pelt). Very little Schiller was put on; he was perhaps too loftily rhetorical, considering the circumstances. Meanwhile Czech performances of Shakespeare and Molière were curtailed, and as the war went on, Polish, French, British, and Russian plays were not allowed to be staged, except for a rare performance of the nineteenth-century Russian realist A. N. Ostrovsky in the provinces; instead attention turned again to the Scandinavians and, above all, to Ibsen. One discovery that outlived the German occupation was the work of Carlo Goldoni, which offered many excellent roles, especially comic ones, and remarkable opportunities for producers to reinvent the commedia dell'arte. When in the 1950s Bohuslav Martinů wrote a comic opera on Goldoni's *La locandiera*, he was working in the tradition of the protectorate theater.

Earlier avant-garde work was kept alive by E. F. Burian in his little theater at the modernist Mozarteum building on Jungmannova Street, but he was badly in need of a bigger space to experiment with his collective recitals, Voice Band, and for his productions combining words, lights, music, and film. He began with his D 34 (Theater 34) but moved to the bigger Poříčí, where he and two assistants were arrested on March 12, 1941, and sent to the concentration camps. Burian was eager to have his own Czech repertory, and when texts were missing, he had modern Czech prose stories dramatized with great success, such as Božena Benešová's "Věra Lukášová," the fragile story of a young girl (1936), or Viktor Dyk's *Krysař* (Pied Piper, 1940), in which the title figure rather closely resembled Hitler. He was particularly fond of recitals of romantic and patriotic verse—e.g., Mácha's "May" recited in the baroque garden of the ancient Waldstein Palace—and of František Halas and Jaroslav Seifert's new poetry in celebration of Božena Němcová, who established the traditions of modern Czech prose. Politically, Burian was of the left in a complicated way: he supported the Communist Party but turned against the Soviet condemnation of the avant-gardist Vsevolod Meyerhold in 1937, only to reverse course when he was back from the camps after the war, renouncing his own avant-garde past, writing a play justifying the Communist regime's death sentences against a liberal woman member of Parliament and a dissident intellectual of the left (just hanged). He took over the Theater of the Army and died in 1959.

Burian's *Manon Lescaut*, written by the poet Vítězslav Nezval following Abbé Prévost's eighteenth-century novel, was one of his most important productions and one of the most joyous moments of the protectorate theater, a happy union of language, stage, and acting that premiered on May 7, 1940, and was sold out every time it was played; people went to see it again and again. Though the play was romantic entertainment close to comedy, later critics rightly insisted that it was "a battle for the Czech language won in terrible times." Burian had planned elaborate music for the play, but during rehearsals he changed his mind because he grasped that Nezval's language was wondrously musical in itself. Nezval followed Prévost loyally, with the young, attractive, and irresponsible heroine (played by Marie Burešová) and de Grieux (Vladimír Šmeral) painfully in love, ready to forgive, easily duped, and blindly passionate; the prose gives way, again and again, to elaborate ballads, poems, and chants, including a final song about the Mississippi quite reminiscent of "Ol' Man River." For years young people on evening walks through Prague recited Nezval's verse "ach Manon Manon hříšnice [Oh Manon Manon sinning]," as if the lines were magic incantations. I know, I was there.

The fortunes of Prague's Czech City Theaters, run by an association and subsidized by the city government, were complicated by political and institutional problems during the occupation. The City Theaters comprised the ornate Vinohradské divadlo (Vinohrady Theater), often competing in excellence with the National Theater and the

small Komorní divadlo (Chamber Players), on Hybernská Street, relying mostly on contemporary plays, high and low. When the Gestapo
closed Burian's avant-garde Poříčí Theater in March 1941, German
and Czech authorities insisted that the City Theaters take it over, and
in June it was reopened with a production of Gozzi's *Princess Turandot*.
Unfortunately this was followed by Eberhard Möller's virulently anti-
Semitic *Rothschild siegt bei Waterloo* (Rothschild Wins at Waterloo).
Five months later the Vinohrady Theater was closed without warning.
It turned out that the Office of the Reichsprotektor planned to use it
as a Grosses Deutsches Varieté, mostly for its own military officers in
Prague; it offered the Vinohrady building to the director of the Berlin
Variety Show, though he did not want to come to Prague and de-
manded the impossible, including a new superbuilding on Wenceslas
Square. Subsequently the Vinohrady Theater was, in a grand gesture
by Emanuel Moravec, returned to the Czechs, who discovered that
much of its interior had been nearly destroyed by a German team that
had shot a few films there.

Of all the Czech figures in the theater of Prague during the protectorate, František Zavřel, civil servant, novelist, and playwright, was the
most dubious and, possibly, pitiable. He was not a militant Fascist, like
General Gajda, nor did he become a political collaborator, driven by
visions of the Czech lands being rescued by the Third Reich, like
Emanuel Moravec, but, rather, an old-fashioned, conservative nationalist. Unfortunately he believed that liberals and leftists in the republic
had conspired against his literary talents, and seeing himself as a Faust
among little people loyal to Masaryk and Beneš, in the years of
occupation he vented his rage against his adversaries in epigrams and
leaflets that he distributed himself. Zavřel had been born in 1885 in a
small village of the Vysočina hills along the Czech-Moravian border,
son of a teacher; educated at the small-town gymnasium at Chrudim
and at the Prague Faculty of Law, he served in the Ministry of Commerce but was more or less forced to resign his position in 1931, after an anti-Beneš novel he had written was impounded by the police.
He worked as a lawyer and traveled a good deal in Italy (he cared
more for Renaissance than Fascist Rome) and France (he admired
Napoleon). His first play, on a Czech historical theme, was performed

in 1920, and others followed, but he developed a distinct feeling that his advance as a playwright was being blocked by powerful liberal enemies. By 1940 he was able to complain to Moravec and the German occupiers, with the predictable result that his plays were performed at the National Theater during the protectorate but to half-empty houses. In 1942 he wrote memoirs that resolutely confirmed his will to fight on but suggested that he would not continue writing plays.

Zavřel's nationalism was to a high degree a complete anachronism, and his memoirs also revealed how much he belonged to the mid-nineteenth century rather than to his own time. His grandfather had revered F. L. Rieger (1818–1903), patriotic chief of the Old Czech Party, and young Zavřel fully identified with his father, who preferred the conservative Karel Kramář (who would have liked to have seen the czar on a Czech royal throne) to the liberal Masaryk, whom he condescendingly called the Great Moralizer. In *Fortinbras* (1930), he deplored what he thought was a Czech lack of fortitude, watched Mussolini from afar, ignored Hitler, and had his protagonist remark on a trip to Berlin that the faces of the Germans were not those of 1918 but, rather, showed a remarkable "return of the old Prussia"—dangerous to the Czechs living in corruption and lassitude. His alter ego, Petr Dan, is certainly not pro-German; on a trip to Brno in 1930, he sadly notes that the capital of Moravia is still very German in appearance and escapes to nearby Austerlitz to indulge in his untrammeled cult of Napoleon.

Emanuel Moravec was demonstrably wrong when he remarked in a tense conversation (1940) with František Götz, dramaturg of the National Theater, that Zavřel's play about Wallenstein was "the only play corresponding in its idea to the real relationship of the Czech lands" to the Reich. Zavřel celebrated his idea of *polobozi* (half gods) in five plays about Caesar, Christ, Jan Hus, Wallenstein, and Napoleon as reflections of his ego rather than as manifestations of the German Führer. Wallenstein, dreaming of the crown of the medieval Reich on the head of his (dead) son, is a half-mad dreamer rather than an exemplary political figure relevant to Central European power politics of the 1940s. Zavřel was an insatiable egotist, pulled the wrong strings to have his plays performed, and was found in November 1947 on a bench on Letná Hill, homeless, hungry, and sick. He died a month later in a Prague hospital.

It is strange to consider that, in protectorate Prague, the Austrian Richard Billinger (1893–1965) was among the playwrights whose works were most often performed in Czech as well as in German. Billinger's political attitude was ambivalent; in two mercifully short poems he assured the Führer of his loyalty to the Reich and let himself be invited occasionally to official celebrations of the regime, yet he did not become a Nazi Party member, was imprisoned for three months after a critic had denounced him as a homosexual, and he was hated by the ideologists, including Goebbels and Rosenberg. His scenic world of mostly Bavarian blood and soil was less upright and more decadent than the party critics would have wished, and his principal characters had a Dionysian streak that contrasted oddly with the blue-eyed fortitude of typical Nazi heroes. When Veit Harlan selected Billinger's play *Der Gigant* (The Giant, 1937) as the basis for his odious film *Die goldene Stadt* (The Golden City), he had to write the script in an anti-Slavic way that was absent in the original, which concentrated on a strong father and impassioned daughter. Billinger had a strong and original theatrical instinct, pitting a naturalist materiality against an expressionist vision; it is possible that German and Czech audiences enjoyed his plays for totally different reasons.

Die Hexe von Passau (The Witch of Passau, 1935), produced at the Ständetheater in Prague on October 10, 1940, and at the Czech National Theater on June 20, 1941, goes back to the late Middle Ages to show how the burning of a Bavarian woman accused of being a witch triggers an armed revolt of peasants who have been long oppressed by church authorities eager for taxes and tithes. Valentina Ingold, daughter of a blacksmith and peasant leader, likes to perform in religious plays that the archbishop dislikes, especially one about Mary Magdalen. She is denounced as a witch because she charms people, and she is sentenced to the pyre, though the church authorities hesitate to burn her because they fear the restive peasants. Young Jörg, rich son of a miller and in love with Valentina, offers a way out by proposing to marry her, but Valentina, after a brief moment of hesitation, refuses his hand, and she declines a similar favor offered by Count Klingenberg, an army officer, who has fallen in love with her. She is burned, and Count Klingenberg joins the rebelling peasants ready to strike.

In spite of this late medieval claptrap, Billinger worked with modern stage techniques (theater on theater when Valentina performs), and the Prague critics unreservedly praised Marga Klas as Valentina, in the German performance, and Olga Scheinpflugová, Karel Čapek's widow, in the Czech version. In *Der neue Tag*, the reviewer thought the play showed the resistance of the folkish (*völkisch*) idea to ancient Roman law, but Czech audiences, less interested in abstractions, may have enjoyed watching the suppressed peasants revolt.

It was almost inevitable that the Interim Theater, on October 17, 1942, put on Heinrich Zerkaulen's *Der Reiter* (The Rider), another historical play about German witch-hunts, with a protagonist who revolts against the oppressive forces of the church and the law. Czech audiences did not fully understand that the *Reiter* resembled an exemplary Hitler Youth leader, though they recognized that the portrait of "mad" Emperor Rudolf, who, residing at Prague Castle, pardons the witches, was done with a good deal of understanding.

By an order of September 6, 1939, Goebbels had put the direction of Prague's German Theater in the hands of Oskar Wallek, a fifty-year-old actor-director who had been born in Brno (as Walletschek) and worked in the Moravian and Bohemian provinces. An early member of the Nazi Party, he was in 1934 the director of Munich's Gärtnerplatz Theater. In spite of Wallek's Moravian origins, the German Theater in the Prague of 1939–44 had a strongly colonial character, imposed from above to entertain and educate the natives, as well as the many German soldiers and functionaries stationed in the city. And it disregarded most local talent or expectations, even though the stage workers, often Czech, had been taken over from the old German theater, closed in 1938. Wallek, whose work was fully subsidized directly from the Office of the Reichsprotektor, was able to gather his principal actors from all over the Reich, and they were sometimes of the first rank: Maria Schanda from Berlin, Edith Herdeegen from Bonn, Marga Klas from Cologne, Albert Johannes from Dresden, O. E. Hasse from Hamburg, and, by 1940, Inge Schürmann of Cologne, who became a star at the Vienna Burgtheater after the war.

Wallek was unable, of course, to fill the three houses at his disposal—the Ständetheater, the Opera House, and the Chamber Play-house—so he systematically organized lavish guest performances by German and Italian troupes, including the Berliner Schauspielhaus, the Wiener Josefstadt, the Vienna and the Florence operas, and Milan's La Scala. Among the guests was the actor and producer Fritz Ré-mond, who reminded his audiences that there existed, at least in his art, a world totally free of the Nazis; an important Frankfurt theater still carries his name, proudly and deservedly, today.

In the fall of 1941 Goebbels ordered that the opera company in Duisburg, whose building had been bombed out by Allied air raids, was to move to Prague, and on November 28 it began its performances with Wagner's *Lohengrin*. It was fully and independently funded, under its own adminstration, and Wallek was told to concentrate on his own repertory. His preferences ran to the serious and classical, and he liked to focus on schoolbook productions of Kleist's *Prinz von Homburg* (Prince of Homburg), Schiller's *Kabale und Liebe* (Intrigues and Love), and *Die Braut von Messina* (Bride of Messina), Lessing's *Minna von Barnhelm*, a good deal of Grillparzer, including his *Medea*, and an occasional Italian comedy by Cesare Meano, a writer who was close to the Roman Fascists. Goethe was mostly absent, and Wallek left comedies of Austrian, German, and Hungarian provenance to his assistants, who had to satisfy the cravings of a wartime audience for lighter fare, such as Anton Hamik's *Der verkaufte Grossvater* (Granddaddy for Sale), Martin Costa's *Hofrat Geiger* (after the war made into an Austrian movie), and the musical play *Ein bezauberndes Fräulein* (A Charming Fräulein) by the composer Ralph Benatzky. When Wallek scheduled Schiller's somber *Die Braut von Messina* during a Christmas holiday, hardly anybody showed up, but the comedy *Diamanten aus Wien* (Diamonds from Vienna) had to be repeated more than forty times to never-ending applause and sold-out houses.

By 1943 Wallek had been promoted to SS *Standartenführer*, and he duly staged Curt Langenbeck, Gerhard Menzel, and Erwin Guido Kolbenheyer, representing the regime, but he also produced *Nausikaa*, a play by young Eckart Peterich, whose *Venetianische Sonette* (Venetian Sonnets) was, in samizdat copies, read among the German soldiers on the Italian front (1944), a first signal of a non-Nazi literature to come after the war. Wallek also staged three plays by the Prague novelist and playwright Franz Hauptmann (1895–1970), a lawyer and bank manager who after the war worked as a dramaturg in Leipzig and an editor in Mainz. Hauptmann's early historical plays had been staged by the German Theater in Prague in the 1930s; the plays staged during the war—*Die Entscheidung* (The Decision), a drama about Napoleon, the village comedy *Der goldene Helm* (The Golden Helmet), and a play about the Borgias, *Das Verhängnis* (The Calamity)—were respectfully welcomed but showed more erudition than dramatic force. In the first, Hauptmann ingeniously employed a three-level stage (perhaps a modification of a Shakespearean scene) but filled it with little more than wordy speeches and historical costumes.

On September 1, 1944, by orders of Goebbels, who had declared that "total war" now required a concentration of all fighting energies, all theaters throughout the Reich, including the Czech and German stages in Prague, were closed. So it happened that the German Theater in Prague ended its activities, rather unheroically, with summer performances of the operetta *Der Vogelhändler* (The Bird Seller) and *Granddaddy for Sale*. Wallek himself withdrew to Coburg, in Germany, was briefly held by the Allies, but reemerged as early as the fall of 1945, under the eyes of the French occupation forces, as producer at the Tyrolean Landestheater in Innsbruck; he was appointed intendant of the Upper Austrian Landestheater in Linz in 1953–56 before he retired to Germany again.

The Theater at Terezín

In protectorate Prague, theatrical life went in separate German and Czech ways more than ever before. But the Terezín prisoners, under Gestapo control and in the permanent shadow of annihilation, showed incredible courage and strength of imagination. In spite of disease, hunger, and continuing transports to the gas chambers, theater in many languages, including Yiddish, was played in garrets and cellars, new texts were written, and they restored the unison of creativity characteristic of Prague in the mid-1930s and earlier.

In the Terezín Amt für Freizeitgestaltung (FZG, Office for Free-Time Activities) many Jewish intellectuals and artists worked together to arrange lectures and readings, staged plays and musical performances. Older Jews from the cities, whether Prague, Berlin, or Vienna, continued to speak German while younger people from Prague and country towns preferred Czech; still others were perfectly bilingual. But language was not of primary concern, and important groups formed rather on religious, political, and philosophical grounds. There were Czech Jews, celebrating the traditions of Masaryk's liberal First Republic; Jews who hewed to the traditions of German idealism and classical literature; Christians both Roman Catholic and Lutheran (about 10 percent of the population); Communists, meeting secretly; Zionists of religious and/or Socialist persuasion, especially among the younger Jews, cultivating more Yiddish than Hebrew; and Hungarian, Danish, and Dutch Jews, who often participated in musical activities.

Yet not everybody believed in the achievements of Terezín cultural life, and H. G. Adler, an erudite musicologist and the first analytical sociologist in the Terezín community, warned against the possible illusions, or self-delusions, created by the stars of the Freizeitgestaltung and suggested that Terezín's cultured activities played into the hands of the Gestapo, which wanted to present the Jewish concentration camp to international opinion as a kind of spa. Many others, as the historian Livia Rothkirchen has shown, believed in culture as an "elixir of life" and went on working in their own ways until they were transported to the gas chambers. Unfortunately self-delusion and the "elixir of life" were not inevitably opposed to each other, considering the time and place. In the fall of 1944, for example, Terezín's SS commanders demanded that theatrical performances, including Jacques Offenbach's *Tales of Hoffmann*, be put on to impress visiting international observers.

It would be difficult to insist on a neat differentiation among literary and musical genres in the narrow spaces of the Terezín garrets and cellars. Between the end of 1941 and the fatal mass transports of 1944, simple meetings of friends developed into more organized lectures, readings, and actual performances on improvised stages. The Miloš Salus group, including Milena Illová and Anna Auředníčková, arranged many readings of older and modern Czech verse, works of K. H. Mácha, S. K. Neumann, František Halas, and Jiří Wolker, as well as Čapek's translations of Rimbaud and other recent French poets. A German group gathered around Philipp Manes, from Berlin, with organized readings of classical writers and the poetry written in Terezín by Otto Brod (brother of Max), Georg Kafka, Peter Kien, and H. W. Kolben. The Freizeitgestaltung introduced a rich program of more than twenty-two hundred lectures offered by more than 520 highly qualified speakers, each of whom received thirty grams of margarine for each performance. Dr. Leo Baeck, Berlin rabbi and renowned philosopher, gave a cycle of lectures on "From Plato to Kant" that attracted nearly 700 listeners to an ice-cold garret. Also from Berlin was the feminist and rabbi Regina Jonas; in Terezín she was promptly deprived of her license as rabbi by the resident rabbinical committee, but she was permitted to continue as a lecturer on Jewish social questions. The many groups arranged more than one hundred lectures on the theory and practice of drama; actual dramatic readings, especially of Goethe's *Faust* and Lessing's *Nathan the Wise*, attracted many listeners. Among the lecturers were Gustav Schorsch from Prague and Carl Meinhold from Berlin, who were among the first to develop plans for full-fledged theatrical performances.

The repertory of Czech plays performed at Terezín did not substantially differ from that of the Prague Czech theater in the late 1930s and early 1940s, and at times it continued to reflect the ideas and achievements of Prague's avant-garde; plays by fellow prisoners—e.g., Zdeněk Jelínek's *Komedie o pasti* (A Comedy About a Trap), which was close to cabaret in style—were particularly welcomed by the audience. Gustav Schorsch, Jiří Orten's friend and colleague from the Prague Conservatory and the founder of the small experimental stage D 99 in Topič's popular bookstore, taught many theater seminars in Terezín, worked with children, and directed Gogol's *Ženitba* (*Marriage*) in February 1944; his inventive staging of this play was repeated twenty-two times and long remembered by survivors. He also staged Peter Kien's *Loutky* (Puppets, translated from the German), about daily life in the camp, and had many unfortunately unrealized plans to perform plays by Rolland, Griboyedov, and Calderón.

The actress Vlasta Schönová, who had worked with a group of young writers and actors at the Prague Jewish Orphanage, staged Cocteau's *The Human Voice*, Jiří Wolker's *Hrob* (The Grave), Josef and Karel Čapek's *Lásky hra osudná* (Love's Fatal Game), which was repeated twenty-one times in 1941, and František Langer's popular *Velbloud uchem jehly* (A Camel Through the Needle's Ear). Other groups, including one led by Ota Růžička, offered Chekhov's one-act plays and Molière's *George Dandin* and, following the avant-garde traditions of E. F. Burian, staged Czech ballads and *Esther*, a play in the Czech baroque folk tradition, as late as April 1944. It was František Zelenka (1904–44), one of Prague's most innovative avant-garde architects and scenic designers, who had worked with Voskovec and Werich in their Liberated Theater, who created the scenery and costumes for Terezín's most important theatrical events, whether Czech or German, including the costumes for *Esther*—magic out of nothing.

The German repertory at Terezín was more middle-class and conservative than its Czech counterpart. The truth was that younger and gifted German and Austrian producers and actors had better and more prolonged chances to escape earlier, mostly to the United States, so their colleagues from Berlin and Vienna who were transported to Terezín belonged to a little older generation; Kurt Gerron, who had worked with the young Brecht, arrived with a later transport from Holland. Among these German and Austrian producers and actors were Carl Meinhold, who once had run at least four Berlin theaters, and Erich Oesterreicher and Ben Spanier, who managed in Terezín to produce G. B. Shaw, Ferenc Molnár's entertaining *Spiel im Schloss*, Hugo von Hofmannsthal's somber verse drama *Der Tod und der Tod*, and plays by fellow prisoners Otto Brod and Georg Kafka.

In the summer and fall of 1943, theatrical entertainment was offered to the children in Terezín. Vlasta Schönová's dramatization of the famous children's book, by Jan Karafiát, *Broučci* (Fireflies) was repeated thirty-three times, more often than any serious play for adult audiences; little puppet theaters were playing for children; and Prague's distinguished Loutkové divadlo (Puppet Theater) had its season, with all the puppets, scenery, costumes, and lighting created by the well-known sculptor Rudolf Saudek.

Cabaret performances, starting as early as 1941, were popular among all audiences, but the Czech and German, or rather Viennese, groups went their own ways, following different cultural traditions and expectations. Karel Švenk, who was called the Terezín Aristophanes, had a left-wing past, so it is no surprise that in his cabaret revue *At' žije život* (To Life!), which was repeated forty-four times, he mostly worked in the Communist *agitka* style, with short polemical scenes, often more anticapitalist than anti-Nazi, punctuated by songs of invincible optimism ("On the ruins of the ghetto we shall laugh"). And in his play *Poslední cyklista* (The Last Cyclist), Bořivoj Abeles, the hero, a Jew, by chance ignites a space rocket and sends the (Nazi) government of the Mad to outer space. (The play was only rehearsed publicly, not staged, because the Council of Elders feared that the camp command would intervene.) Another Czech cabaret group initiated by Josef Lustig and František Kowanitz was, even more than Švenk, inspired by the Liberated Theater of Voskovec and Werich. They used Jaroslav Ježek's music with new texts and tackled everyday problems in Terezín, including those of the internal camp administration, with wit and precision. Members of these Czech and Viennese cabaret groups differed in age and training, the Czechs being disciples of the avant-garde, and the Germans and Austrians, among them Hans Hofer and Leo Strauss, being professionals of the older generation, often mocking Viennese traditions but mostly presenting highlights from the sweet operettas of yesteryear. A performance of the new operetta *Das Ghettomädel* (The Ghetto Girl) was rightly rejected by many.

Music was astonishingly alive in Terezín, and in many ways and shapes. Rafael Schächter, who had worked in Prague, organized moving concert performances of Smetana's *The Bartered Bride* (November 28, 1942) and *The Kiss* (July 20, 1944), and he staged Pergolesi's *La serva padrona* (The Maid Turned Mistress). Other groups gave theatrically simplified but beautifully cast performances of *Aïda*, *Rigoletto*, and *Carmen* (sets by Zelenka) and Vilém Blodek's more modern *V studni* (In the Well), which was the last performance before the fall transports of 1944. Hans Krása's opera *Brundibár*, in which the good children, in unison with their dog, a cat, and a sparrow, ultimately triumph over the evil organ-grinder Brundibár, was originally rehearsed and performed at Prague's Jewish Orphanage in the winter of 1942–43, and after the composer had been transported to Terezín and the score had been rescued by the director of the Children's Choir, was staged at Terezín on September 21, 1943; it then had fifty-four more performances, possibly with a few adaptations of the score.

Viktor Ullmann's opera *Der Kaiser von Atlantis, oder der Tod dankt ab* (The Emperor of Atlantis, or Death Abdicates), with a libretto by Peter Kien (who may have remembered Karel Čapek's *The White Plague*), was systematically rehearsed at Terezín but never performed because the mass transports to Auschwitz made it impossible. This composition, scored for five singers and a fifteen-piece orchestra, was less melodious than *Brundibár* and more stridently modern in its elements of jazz and with its allusions to Josef Suk and, ironically, the Nazi anthem. After the score was thought to be lost for a considerable time, it turned up in H. G. Adler's collection of Terezín documents.

A theater of Jewish ideas developed, perhaps rather uneasily, side by side with the avant-garde Czechs and the German and Austrian Jews cultivating their own cultural traditions, even in radically changed circumstances. Egon Redlich's one-actress play *Velký stín* (The Great Shadow), written in imitation of Jean Cocteau's *The Human Voice*, in which a baptized Czech woman of Jewish origin rethinks her life after her arrival at Terezín, raised insistent questions about assimilation; Redlich himself noted in his diary that the audience did not like it, but he had wanted to deal with the religious rather than the national aspect of the issue. A Jiddische Bühne presented excerpts from J. L. Peretz's *Di goldene kejt* (The Golden Chain), a play, written in 1909, in which a wise rabbi wants to end evil by prolonging the Sabbath, as well as dramatic monologues of Sholem Aleichem's *Tevye der Milkhiger*, a modest precursor of *Fiddler on the Roof*, in which Viktor Ullmann provided variations on Jewish folk melodies. On October 10, 1943, an affiliated group presented *Jüdische Lieder und Verse*, with texts gathered by Irene Dodalová and the piano accompaniment by Gideon Klein; scenic little presentations of traditional Jewish stories were offered to the children by Walter Freud, possibly in imitation of the Purim *shpiels*, on Queen Esther and Chanukkah. Franz Kafka, who had been enchanted by a visiting troupe of Yiddish actors in Prague in 1912, would have happily approved.

The Death of Heydrich

On July 18, 1940, the (provisional) Czechoslovak government-in-exile was recognized by Britain, while the United States promised to consider seriously whether to do so. (In the summer of 1941, after the German invasion of the U.S.S.R., the Soviets accorded Beneš's government formal recognition, and the United States followed in September.) Churchill, meanwhile, favored the Czechoslovaks, at least more than his predecessors did, but Beneš confronted grave problems. The production of war matériel in the protectorate had increased by at least 20 percent; peasants delivered the required agricultural products, which allowed the Germans to create much-needed reserves; and Beneš's soldiers, of the former intelligence service, complained that the resistance at home was not committed enough to direct action against the occupiers.

František Moravec, now London chief of Czechoslovak intelligence, asserted later in his memoirs that Beneš himself was responsible for the plan to ambush and to kill Heydrich, but it was not an idea reflective of Beneš's political habits, which were usually characterized by memorandums, discussions, and negotiations. Yet in the early fall of 1941 Beneš, who had become nearly obsessed with the necessity to renew the integrity of the Czechoslovak Republic, and feeling under increasing pressure from the Allies, tried to show that Czechs and Slovaks were ready to contribute to the war more actively. He was proud of the precise and important information provided by his Prague resistance groups to Allied intelligence, but after Heydrich's coming to Prague, communications between Czechoslovakia and London were nearly cut off. It seemed necessary to renew contacts and to train groups of Czech and Slovak parachutists who would drop into Bohemia with radio materials and new orders. Among the 160 parachutists trained by British special operations there would be two men who would take an oath to find Heydrich and to kill him.

The special training provided by the British was thorough, but Czech intelligence agents in England did not know much about living conditions in the protectorate or about the techniques of the Gestapo, which placed informers in the underground and organized its own "resistance" groups to attract people ready to fight. Beneš was impatient, hoping that October 28, the symbolically significant day of Czechoslovak independence, would be right for a spectacular action that could be interpreted as a spontaneous signal of national resolve. But training schedules and meteorological conditions had to be respected. The initial drops were disastrous, for the first parachutist landed in the Austrian Alps rather than in Bohemia, and another one, though landing at the right spot, had to look for help from an underground organization that had been infiltrated by the Gestapo; he was arrested and later executed at Plötzensee Prison.

In early October 1941 František Moravec decided that Josef Gabčík, a Slovak NCO, and Karel Svoboda were the two men who would undertake the action against Heydrich, but Svoboda had an accident and was immediately replaced by Jan Kubiš, a friend of Gabčík's. Gabčík and Kubiš were brought to London from a secret training camp in the English countryside, informed about their task, and later invited to meet Beneš, who had tears in his eyes, Moravec wrote, when he bade them goodbye. On December 28 the final orders came. A Halifax long-range bomber was ready on an airstrip near London, and the Canadian pilot decided that he would transport not only the group Anthropoid (Gabčík and Kubiš) but also the groups Silver A and Silver B, consisting of trained radio operators charged with reviving contact with the resistance groups and, above all, Paul Thümmel, an outstanding German agent working for the Czechs. All in all there were sixteen men and a good deal of weapons, ammunitions, and radios. At 10:00 p.m. the Halifax was in the air; it flew over Calais, Darmstadt, and Bayreuth, the pilot skillfully avoiding German planes. In Bohemia, however, he lost his orientation in the clouds, and the Anthropoids had to jump anyway, followed by two parachutes heavy with technical gear.

From that day the two soldiers had until late May 1942, or five months, to prepare for the killing of Heydrich. Neither Heinrich Mann, who wrote a novel about the Reichsprotektor, nor Douglas Sirk, who made a Hollywood movie about him, could fully express the extraordinary combination of incredible courage, fatal mistakes, tragedy, and bloody grotesque that are part of the story, which was unraveled a generation later by Miroslav Ivanov, G. S. Graber, Günther Deschner, Hellmut G. Haasis, and a host of other historians.

The Halifax bomber, roaring over the wintry Bohemian landscape, by mistake dropped Kubiš and Gabčík near the village of Nehvizdy, eighteen miles east of Prague, and left the two totally disoriented. The ground was frozen hard, and Gabčík hurt his left foot on landing; for days he was unable to walk unaided. The two, who did not destroy their parachutes, dragged themselves to a nearby stone quarry, leaving footprints in the snow, only to be discovered there by a local game-keeper and a miller who had heard the airplane; these two, without asking any questions, helped the soldiers establish contact with a group of patriotic members of the Sokol (the traditional Czech gym-nasts' association) at Lysá, on the Elbe River northeast of Prague. They in turn organized medical help, fabricated certificates to show that both young men were suffering from digestive ailments, and arranged for them to go by rail to Prague on January 8.

In the capital, Gabčík and Kubiš were readily hidden, sometimes together, sometimes separately, in many modest family apartments, in Žižkov, Dejvice, and elsewhere, never dwelling too long in one place and untiringly roaming the city (including Hradčany Castle) to recon-noiter the most convenient spot to carry out their orders. Their host families, the Moravecs, Fafeks, and Ogouns, later mercilessly exe-cuted, were Sokols; or former members of the Masaryk League Against Tuberculosis, a civic association committed to medical enlightenment, who continued their meetings; or Czech Brethren active in their church. Spring came, and the most stringent military orders did not prevent Gabčík and Liběna Fafková from falling in love and cele-brating their formal engagement on Sunday, May 24, in her family's apartment.

The two soldiers did not know anything about earlier discussions in London before they were dispatched to the Continent, but František Moravec writes in his memoirs that he had warned Beneš that German revenge for the murder of Heydrich would be terrible, possibly endan-gering the remnants of Prague's organized resistance to the occupation. Beneš, impatient for action, had replied that he considered himself the commander in chief, and given the international situation, sacrifices were inevitable and necessary. Gabčík and Kubiš had been instructed not to establish contact with the resistance, owing to the possibility of

Gestapo infiltration, but they had no other choice than to accept underground support in order to survive and to do what they had to do.

In the Prague underground, suspicion ran high that the two had come with special orders concerning Heydrich. Whether the Anthropoids talked or not, local members of the resistance feared total annihilation and did not wish to see the London orders executed. (Later analysts believe that at least twenty people in Prague knew or correctly surmised what Gabčík and Kubiš had in mind.) But radio communication with London was not functioning, and it was only after one Alfred Bartoš, one of the three parachutist radio operators in Silver A, sent out together with Kubiš and Gabčík, turned up from hiding with a radio transmitter that a protest could be sent to London on May 4 saying "the assassination . . . would not only endanger the lives of prisoners and hostages, it would also cost thousands of other lives, plunge the nation into unprecedented subjugation, and at the same time sweep away the last vestiges of any organization among us." A similar warning was transmitted by another group on May 12.

In a meeting with representatives of the underground on May 23, Kubiš and Gabčík ran into almost unanimous opposition. Gabčík said he wanted to act immediately on his own, but he was reprimanded by Adolf Opálka, the parachutist with the highest military rank, who had been dropped long before the Anthropoids. He was under orders, Opálka said, not to go it alone. In the meeting in the Ogouns' apartment, it became evident once again that the underground and London had parted ways, as far as the Anthropoids were concerned.

At Easter time, Heydrich and his family had moved to a villa at Panenské Břežany, formerly owned by a Jewish family, from which the Reichsprotektor was regularly driven in an open car and without a bodyguard to his Hradčany offices. A Czech carpenter employed to take care of the antique furniture at the castle had a chance to see Heydrich's schedule and reported to the underground that the Reichsprotektor was scheduled to leave Prague on May 27 for an appointment in Berlin and perhaps Paris; the Anthropoids, joined in the meantime by the parachutist Josef Valčík, immediately knew that they could not postpone action any longer.

On the morning of May 27, 1942, they took their positions at the Holešovice suburban hairpin curve, at which Heydrich's car had to slow down. At 10:30 a.m. Valčík signaled with a little mirror that the car was approaching (fortunately the day was not overcast), and when the dark green Mercedes, driven by SS Scharführer Johannes Klein, slowed down, hemmed in, on one side, by a tram car of the No. 3 line, Gabčík opened his coat and tried to use his Sten gun, which, however, did not function. Heydrich ordered his driver to stop, instead of rushing on, rose from his seat, and took aim at Gabčík with his own pistol, but it did not work either. Kubiš, from the other side, promptly threw a special Mills grenade, which hit the right rear end of the car and wounded Heydrich gravely. Chaos ensued. All the windows of the nearby tram car were shattered by the explosion, and the passengers ran for cover. Gabčík took his (ladies') bicycle, parked under a tree, and pedaled off, while Heydrich's corpulent driver tried to halt Kubiš, who shot him in the knee and disappeared over the Vltava bridge nearby. A passing Czech baker who saw Heydrich's uniform refused to take him into his delivery van, but he was finally put on a small truck loaded with parquets and floor wax that reached Bulovka Hospital, not far from the hairpin curve, only thirty minutes later. Heydrich could have been saved by British penicillin, but in spite of many transfusions, sepsis from his wounds advanced inexorably as he drifted in and out of coma; he died on June 4, eight days later.

The attempt on Heydrich's life triggered an avalanche of terror. By noon on May 27 Hitler had been informed of the attack and had called K. H. Frank to demand that ten thousand Czechs be immediately executed and to offer a reward of one million reichsmarks for useful information. The Czech government added another million. Hitler first asked Frank to assume the duties of the Reichsprotektor, but within a day he changed his mind and promoted Kurt Daluege, chief of the Ordnungspolizei, to take over, keeping Frank, once again, second-in-command. Daluege believed that the ambush had been the work of the local underground, but Frank knew better, and the protectorate government preferred to accept his view. He immediately declared a state of emergency, halting all traffic in and out of Prague, and during the night of May 28, twenty-one thousand uniformed SS and Wehrmacht

officers searched the city from house to house, without any tangible re-
sults. Kubiš was well hidden by his host family, and Gabčík, who had
dyed his hair, went off with his beloved Liběna on a spring walk
through the city. Executions of hostages commenced.

On June 7 funeral celebrations for Heydrich were held in Prague,
and on June 9 in Berlin, with Teutonic pomp. Police and Gestapo investigations still had yielded no clues, and Hitler directed his rage
against the mining villages of Lidice, because it was allegedly a base of
foreign action, and Ležáky, where a British transmitter had been
found. At Lidice, to become famous the world over, all the male vil-
lagers were shot, the women dragged to the concentration camp of
Ravensbrück, north of Berlin, the children dispersed "for further education," most of them to the gas chambers of Chelmno; of ninety-
eight, only six were found after the war. The village was destroyed.

On June 16 events took a different turn. Karel Čurda, a parachutist
in Opálka's group, fearing for his life and desirous of earning the
rewards, informed the Czech police and the Gestapo of his orders; he
directed their attention toward the Moravecs, one of the families
that had sheltered the plotters. The Moravecs' young son broke down
and revealed that all the parachutists were hiding in the Church of
St. Cyrillus and St. Methodius on Resslova Street in Prague. On June
18 the SS tried to storm the church but only after a prolonged exchange of fire. Three of the parachutists died, including Kubiš, who
killed himself after being gravely wounded, and the four others withdrew to the crypt, where they hid in the ancient niches carved out
for coffins. There they survived an attack by tear gas (affecting the
attackers as well) and an attempt to drown them (with the help of
a Czech fire brigade) until an old stone partition was broken down,
opening the way to the crypt. Grenades were thrown, shots fired,
and all four died, most of them by their own hand. When Kurt
Daluege was tried after the war, he informed the court that in the
wave of terror after Heydrich's death, 1,331 people, including 201
women, had been executed, but he said nothing about the 3,000 Jews
who were sent at that time from Terezín to Auschwitz. The traitor
Karel Čurda was tried in 1947 and after a rather brief trial was sentenced to be hanged.

My Mother Leaves

During the night following the attack on Heydrich, the German occupy-
ing forces were still without a clue, though they had found the bicycle on
which one of the attackers escaped, and they organized a manhunt of gi-
ant proportions. By midnight or so an SS patrol had entered the house,
where we—Grandmother, my mother, and I—lived on Příčná Street,
near Charles Square, ringing bells and knocking on doors with their rifle
butts. When I opened our door, one soldier remained in the corridor and
several others came in running; they tore the covers from the beds and
made my grandmother and my mother, in their nightgowns, stand with
their faces to the wall, while I, a little apart, had to raise my hands. They
opened all the doors, looked into nooks and crannies and under the beds,
and left again, making a good deal of noise with their boots and weapons,
and repeated their useless search next door. My grandmother, who accord-
ing to family lore had once declared that things would not turn out
too badly because Germany was a cultivated nation, began to shiver;
my mother put a dressing gown on her shoulders and went to the kitchen
to make some tea. Nobody could think of sleeping; the night was dark
and noisy, with the sound of truck brakes and shouted military commands
reverberating. It occurred to me that we could have hidden anybody out-
side on our balcony, since the soldiers never looked there, but I was not
sure that the neighbors across the street would not have informed the po-
lice if they had seen a shadow among the flowerpots—for fear of their own
lives.

In Le Rouge et le Noir (The Red and the Black), *Book 2, chapter 1,*
Stendhal tells us that a citizen alarmed by the intrigues of the political
parties would do best to hide out "in a fourth-floor apartment off the
Champs-Élysées" if he wanted security and peace, but Jewish citizens of
Prague in the time of Heydrich and Frank would have been ill advised to
follow such a suggestion. Chances were better in the countryside; the me-
dieval city was too narrow, its people (especially the concierges) were too
greedy, and while Czechs were not racists, there were the old tensions be-
tween Jews, some speaking German, and Czech nationalists. Jiří Weil's
renowned novel Život s hvězdou (Life with a Star), *tells the story of a for-*
mer Prague bank clerk, Josef Roubíček, a Jew who has lost everything, sur-

vives for some time doing a menial job at the Jewish cemetery (at least he
and his friends plant a few vegetables among the graves and have something to eat), thinks long and hard before he dares to pretend to kill himself by drowning (his personal papers are conveniently found in a bag at
the river's edge) and then to hide for the duration of the war in a small
room in the little suburban house of his friend and neighbor Materna, a
workingman and active Socialist whose leaflets he corrected in the past
without really sharing their ideas. Actually, in Prague, 227 Jews who hid
or who survived with false papers (the so-called ponorky [submarines])
emerged in the days of liberation; in Berlin they were 1,321 in number,
and in Vienna nearly 800.

A few months before being sent away, my mother and grandmother
had to leave their apartment and move to Josefov, one of the old districts
where Prague Jews were concentrated before being transported to
Terezín. My mother was not surprised, and instead of moving in with
strangers and causing much discomfort, a convenient solution was
found: Mother and Grandmother moved in with Aunt Irma, who had
run her chic dressmaker's salon out of her apartment and now, after she
had had to close shop, had ample space to offer. At least the three
women were together, Uncle Karel and his family having long gone to
the east somewhere and Uncle Leo living in England, though nobody
knew where. They did not have a telephone or a radio, but I was told the
three ladies had their morning entertainment because they discovered
my father living across the square in a cellar apartment, with a young
actress from the provinces, of course, calling herself, hopefully, Diana
York. Aunt Irma closely observed, from the heights of the fifth-floor windows and with the help of the family opera glasses, what was going on
and provided a running commentary for her mother and sister. Papa
emerged every morning from the cellar apartment, rather disheveled
(Irma's commentary) and with an empty bandaska (metal bottle) went
to get fresh milk for Diana's breakfast; of course, he had German ration
cards (Irma). My mother added that in her time Papa had not done anything for the household, needless to say, and now he was fetching the
milk!

It did not last long. A few weeks after my grandmother and Aunt Irma
had left, my mother received her transport orders and began to pack her

*little valise. I took off a few hours from the bookshop (the boss's wife grum-
bled), and found my mother ready and dressed in her sporty costume, the
yellow star, woolen stockings, and the heavy shoes she always wore for her
Silesian and Austrian excursions in the hills. We waited for tram No. 14
to take us to the assembly point, the main hall of the Prague Trade Fair;
fortunately there were two tram cars, since Jews were allowed to use only
second cars. Yet there was a problem: the doors opened, and we climbed in
and stood in the middle space, where I put down the valise, but a middle-
class Czech fellow citizen protested, shouting that Jews were not allowed
in the middle of the second car but, according to police order, only in the
back of it. He went on screaming, red in the face, so I took the valise and
guided Mother through the crowded car to the back, where a space
opened for us in silence, all eyes averted, because people were ashamed
and afraid. The tram crossed the Vltava bridge and stopped in front of
the hall, we wended our way to the crowded entrance, and the young Jews
charged with keeping order there waved us through, the mother with
the star and the son without it. Evidently the situation was not new to
them.*

*In the great hall, nearly as big as a soccer field, people were squatting
and sitting on their luggage, forming little circles of families and friends,
while orderlies (with white armbands, I think) flitted about in theatrical
and useless importance. I found a place to put down the valise, and my
mother sat down on it, like everybody else. In the course of the years I have
tried many times to recall what she said and what I said then and there,
but I do not remember much, if anything: the dark brown color of the
sturdy valise, my mother's hair streaked with a little gray, a few children
running around, and some old people, all alone.*

*I think my mother admonished me not to neglect my future studies—
we both assumed that the occupation would end soon, somehow, and I
would go on to the university—and we also talked about Aunt Irma and
Grandmother's being at Terezín, so she would not be by herself. We embraced, she kissed me, and I threaded my way to the exit, accompanied by
jokes from the orderlies who checked my papers, which were not marked
by J for Jew, and told me to stay put, since I would soon be in a transport
anyway. I stepped out on the ordinary street, cars and trams running by,
people going home from their offices. Two men stopped me right away. It*

was my father and Michal Mareš, a Czech anarchist writer who had accompanied a friend to the hall. They asked me what was happening inside, and I told them what I knew. They had been circling the block for some time, and they wanted to stay. But I had to return to the shop. My boss's wife gave me hell because I was late, and I do not think Mareš and my father were still at the hall when the transport left for the railway station in the early dawn. Besides, my mother would not have been particularly happy to see my father then, once again the bystander, waving to her from afar.

CHAPTER IV

THE END OF THE PROTECTORATE

K. H. Frank: Up from the Provinces

Karl Hermann Frank, born on January 28, 1898, at Karlsbad and hanged by the neck at Pankrác Prison in Prague on May 22, 1945, was a provincial party functionary who succeeded after Heydrich's death in outmaneuvering his competitors and asserting his dictatorial independence until in the last weeks of his rule in Prague, Hitler transferred nominal power to the army and to Field Marshal Ferdinand Schörner. Frank had an irregular and incomplete education, and even his friends called him rough and egotistic, if cunning when it was a matter of his career. It is clear that his second marriage, to Lola Blaschke, M.D., a cultivated woman of Prague's educated German middle class, contributed to his rise among the splendidly prominent. When Frank encountered the elegant Heydrich, himself an upstart, though of a different kind, he decided to take belated riding lessons, but photographs show him not on horseback but rather, in evident imitation of Hitler, standing in an open black Mercedes. He was not a man of far-reaching strategic concepts (except for his idea of locating the Czechs, after a German victory, to the east), and in contrast with Heydrich, he showed a marked propensity to assume command on the spot, as he did at the burning of Lidice or during the operation Auerhahn in the winter of 1944 directed against anti-Nazi partisans in the Beskid Mountains. Yet he also demonstrated considerable pragmatism, for example, when in 1945 he had the idea of negotiating with the Americans to salvage the situation as the Soviet Army advanced from the east and the Western Allied forces from Italy.

Frank's father, Heinrich, an elementary school teacher, active member of the Turnverein, and admirer of Bismarck, in baptism gave his son the names Karl Hermann to confirm his allegiance to K. H. Wolf, a radical Pan-German member of the Vienna Parliament; the paternal aversion to Austria, the church, and the Czechs defined the son's horizon forever. He was an unruly boy (a friend, in a fight, shot out one of his eyes with a sling, and his glass eye gave him that immovable look), and after breaking off his legal studies at Prague University, he accepted subaltern jobs in industrial concerns in Vítkovice, in Moravia, then returned to his hometown to work for a private railroad. He became increasingly active on the fringes of the nationalist parties and in the Wandervogel, a youth organization originally known for its opposition to the petty bourgeois world of its fathers. By 1923 he decided that he wanted to learn the publishing and book business, moved to Saxony to apprentice himself to the Wandervogel publisher and bookseller Matthes, then served in its Leipzig branch, and, after three years, was back in his home region to open an "Egerland house of books and art" at Elbogen. This was a resounding financial failure that burdened him for years with creditors' legal claims. In 1925 he married Anna Müller, a local typist, who bore him two sons and readily helped in the bookshop, but she was unable to fulfill all of Frank's ambitious ideas about marriage and success. In 1931, at the height of the Great Depression, he moved once again to open a bookshop in the center of splendid Karlsbad, but his financial misfortunes continued, and he later ascribed blame for the world economic crisis to Czech machinations. He spent most of his time with the Turnverein and various Sudeten groups jockeying for organized power in the region and in the Czechoslovak Parliament.

Hitler's ascent to power in Germany immediately strengthened the aspirations of these nationalist groups in the Sudetenland, but it did not necessarily create a unified strategy among them in their conflict with the Czechoslovak Republic. The radical DNSAP (German National Socialist Workers' Party), closest to its sister party in the Reich; the well-organized DNP (German National Party); and the Kameradschaftsbund, mostly academics who firmly believed in the idea of the corporative state, competed with one another, and only in the fall of 1933 was a kind of unified organization established. On the suggestion of Mariano San Nicolò, the South Tyrolean nationalist rector of Prague's German university, it was led by Konrad Henlein, the rather nondescript chairman of the Turnverein, and was called, in a military way, Sudetendeutsche Heimatfront (SHF, Sudeten German Homeland Front). It seems that K. H. Frank was the first to build up an efficient local group for the SHF at Karlsbad. His bookshop had gone bankrupt, and he switched to a modestly paid secretarial job at a local party office, taking care of all propaganda matters and concentrating on a strictly political career.

In 1935 the new movement, now called Sudetendeutsche Partei, was still riven by conflicts between "autonomists," including Henlein and some members of the Kameradschaftsbund, who rejected the Führer principle (by 1940 some of them had been sent to concentration camps), and the Pan-Germans, looking toward the Reich and Fascism. Frank built his career on being independent of the Kameradschaftsbund people around Henlein, with his inherited sympathies for the older generation of nationalists. In 1935 the SP prided itself on having a thousand local groups, and when elections came in May, it pulled in 1.25 million of the German votes, or 15.2 percent of all Czechoslovak voters, becoming the strongest political party in the republic and dealing a crushing blow both to the German activists and to the liberal republic itself. In 1937 Henlein named Frank (who had become chairman of the SP parliamentarians in Prague) his deputy and submitted in his letter of November 19 to Hitler's policies, and after the Anschluss of Austria fully accepted Hitler's authority. After Munich, it was Frank who accompanied Hitler in the motorcade from Böhmisch Leipa to Prague and with him entered the castle of the Bohemian kings on Hradčany Hill.

Yet right after the occupation Frank was the number two man again, once Neurath was appointed Reichsprotektor. Hitler long insisted on appointing *Reichsprotektoren* because he held fast to a medieval, or colonial, idea of the German Reich as the *Schutzmacht*, or protective power for the region, entrusting the function to representatives of the ancient Reich itself (not to the Sudeten), and Frank was at a hierarchical disadvantage. Yet he had other cards to play: in the fall of 1938 Hitler had promoted him to *SS-Gruppenführer,* and he had begun his ascent in the SS; soon he was a *Brigadeführer,* and Himmler appointed him, on April 28, 1939, chief of all police forces in the protectorate, including the SD, the Gestapo, and all SS formations. Frank never hesitated to make use of his authority even at the risk of creating administrative frictions. Contemporary observers noted that Neurath and Frank did not entertain the highest opinions of each other; to Neurath, Frank was an uncouth provincial, and to Frank, Neurath was merely a mild-mannered diplomat whom Hitler had appointed in Prague only to assuage the British.

Yet in important political matters, Neurath and Frank collaborated, much to Heydrich's astonishment. A Memorandum about the Future of the Protectorate and the Czech People, perhaps first sketched in their separate offices yet consolidated in a unified document, was presented to Hitler in late August or early September 1940, in a triumphant moment after the defeat of France. At that juncture, the memorandum argued, war production was essential, but Frank elaborated far-reaching plans for the assimilation, or rather *Umvolkung* (national transformation) of many Czechs. High schools, and later even elementary schools, were eventually to be closed; all Czechs were to go through German schools, and the Czech language was to be reduced to a local dialect. Frank divided the Czechs into three groups: those who had profited from the republic, along with the older intelligentsia, who were not to be assimilated; those of an older generation who had had their doubts about the new republican ways of 1918, to be considered for possible assimilation; and peasants, workers, and people who had not been guided enough by the German authorities but who could be malleable. Only "racially" valuable Czechs were to be assimilated as Germans, while others, depoliticized and neutralized, were to be resettled somewhere in eastern Europe or submitted to a *Sonderbehandlung,* the usual term indicating physical annihilation.

It is more than probable that Frank, via Himmler, successfully undermined Neurath's position, but he must have been surprised when, upon being ordered on September 24, 1941, to report to Hitler's headquarters at Rastenburg, in East Prussia, he learned that Neurath was to be succeeded, at least for the time being, by Heydrich, who was quickly promoted to *SS-Oberst-Gruppenführer,* while Frank was relegated again to aiding him in his new position. Frank was surely aware that he had lost opportunities for independent action: Neurath had come from a different administrative system, but Heydrich, the most powerful general in the Reich security apparatus after Himmler, belonged to the same police and SS hierarchy. Heydrich was well informed about the situation in Czechoslovakia through the SD and Gestapo, and while Frank later strengthened his personal position by convincing Heydrich to recall to Prague General Rudolf Toussaint, Frank's ally in the days of Munich, as Wehrmacht representative there, Heydrich was always careful to keep Frank on his right side, when publicity photographs were made, and the two invariably proceeded in unison when it was a matter of reducing or undercutting the "autonomy" of the Czech government.

On May 27, 1942, Frank was among the first to arrive at the Holešovice spot where Heydrich was ambushed, and Hitler told him on the telephone that afternoon to take over Heydrich's duties for as long as the acting Reichsprotektor was incapacitated. Heydrich's death on June 4 should have freed Frank from being the permanent deputy; he certainly went on as if he were undisputed ruler of the protectorate, signing decrees of execution, initiating and supervising the widely flung efforts to discover Heydrich's enemies sent from abroad and their local allies; he was also present at the identification of the victims whom the SS killed in June 1941 at the Orthodox Church and at the burning of Lidice. He had argued against Hitler's orders to execute ten thousand Czechs on the spot, rightly fearing repercussions among both industrial and agricultural workers, but he was confronted again with Hitler's belief that a Reichsprotektor from outside the protectorate should be named. In his order of August 28, 1942, Hitler chose a double solution: he elevated Frank to the position of German minister for Bohemia and Moravia, charging him with all the administrative duties that earlier Reichsprotektoren had to carry, but he also insisted on the appointment of a new Reichsprotektor to represent him in Prague. Frank had a difficult time with this new official, Police General Kurt Daluege, but Daluege was sick and on August 23, 1943, asked Hitler to send him on medical furlough for two years; Dr. Wilhelm Frick, formerly Prussia's minister of the interior and an old Nazi Party member, who succeeded him, was not particularly interested in the job, by now mostly ceremonial, and preferred to live in Bavaria, far from the conflicts about Bohemia, not to mention all the other issues that competing German bureaucracies fought over.

It is not entirely paradoxical that Frank was instrumental in putting an end to the activities of the Vlajka people in Prague and elsewhere in the protectorate, however well they served Germany as paid and unpaid informers. They had tried twice, with totally insufficient means and preparations, to interfere with the business of the protectorate government: once on August 8, 1940, in the Old Town of Prague, trying to storm the general secretariat of the Národní souručenství, and, in a second desperate attempt on January 25, 1941, trying to take over Prague's government buildings (only 8 percent of the membership responded to the mobilization call). What was left of the Vlajka people fought among themselves, constantly attacked activist journalists, especially the former Communist Party members among them, and Emanuel Moravec, now a member of the government, since he had once been a Freemason and also close to Masaryk. Moravec had been friendly to them for some time, mostly to entice the Vlajka Youth Organization and its chairman, Dr. František Teuner, to join his own Kuratorium (Committee) for the Education of Czech Youth, where he offered well-paid employment. But after renewed attacks he complained to Frank, who told Jan Rys, the Vlajka leader, on April 18, 1942, that all assaults on Moravec had to end and that the Vlajka activities would have to cease as of April 21, 1942.

After Heydrich's death, Rys turned again to the SD and to Frank, but by then the Germans had run out of patience. Sent to Germany to work in industrial jobs were 350 active members of the Vlajka, among them Rys's girlfriend, who was ordered to Munich, and on December 12, 1942, Rys and František Burda, chief of the Vlajka newspaper, who mostly distinguished himself by blackmailing Jewish businesses, were sent as honorary prisoners to the concentration camp in Dachau. There they were intensely disliked by the other Czech prisoners. (In

1945 Rys was freed by the Americans who liberated Dachau; he was sent to Capri to recuperate but asked to be repatriated to Prague to defend himself and his Vlajka friends against all accusations; he was tried, together with Burda, sentenced to death on June 27, 1946, and hanged. Count Thun-Hohenstein, who would have been foreign minister in a Vlajka government, was sentenced to life but later escaped from a working detail to Germany and Canada, where he married and peacefully died in 1994.)

The confederacy of conservative German officers who in 1943 and 1944 plotted against Hitler would have finished Frank's rise, but their haphazardly organized plan to murder the Führer did not go well. After several failed attempts, on July 20, 1944, Claus von Stauffenberg placed a British time bomb under Hitler's conference table in his Rastenburg headquarters, but a general unknowingly pushed the packet away from Hitler; when it exploded, four officers were killed or mortally wounded, but Hitler emerged alive, though bruised and with his eardrums damaged. Stauffenberg had left shortly after planting the bomb and, convinced that Hitler was dead once the bomb went off, had the code signal Walküre (Valkyrie) immediately sent to the main Wehrmacht offices in occupied Europe to communicate the order that all party functionaries and SS commanders should be arrested. Hitler, however, immediately telephoned Goebbels in Berlin, and he in turn mobilized loyal troops to march to the Wehrmacht headquarters on the Bendlerstrasse to arrest the other members of the conspiracy. (Five were shot right away, and about two hundred arrested and executed later.)

In Prague, events took an almost grotesque turn. General Ferdinand Schaal of the Wehrmacht arrested Frank's deputy, Dr. Robert Gies; Frank was absent from his desk, and when Schaal telephoned Frank, Gies could be heard shouting that he had been arrested by the Wehrmacht. Frank had heard confused rumors from Berlin, did not want to take any chances, and immediately left Czernin Palace in a small armed convoy, taking the southern road to Benešov, where strong SS tank garrisons were stationed and where he withdrew to Konopiště Castle, former seat of the imperial Austrian heir to the throne. Unfortunate Schaal heard about the collapse of the conspiracy in the meantime, apologized first to Gies and then by phone, and citing his obedience to the orders of his superiors, to Frank himself, who had returned to Prague. Frank had the Gestapo take Schaal into custody, and he and three staff officers were quickly executed, on Frank's orders, at the Villa Jenerálka in the Šárka Valley, near Prague.

Yet there were local repercussions. Among the Wehrmacht conspirators arrested was Friedrich Karl Klausing, who happened to be a son of Friedrich Klausing, rector of the German university, a member of the Nazi Party since 1933 and of the SA. Hearing of his son's arrest, the elder Klausing went to Frank and declared that he wished to atone for his son's crime by immediately going to fight at the Russian front. But a so-called court of honor, convened by the Sudeten SA, declared that only the father's voluntary death would clear the name of the family. Klausing wrote a last letter to the Führer, Frank, the fatherland, and his family and, still not understanding his son, shot himself in his Prague office on August 6, 1944, two days before his son was executed in the Plötzensee prison. His wife had to leave the rector's official residence, but Frank generously offered her a four-room apartment, which she declined, only to be given six rooms, doubtlessly taken from a Jewish family.

In the autumn and winter of 1944–45, Frank faced the task of opposing Martin Bormann, secretary general of the Nazi Party, who constantly intervened in Bohemian affairs, which included by then the work of accommodating in Prague and in the protectorate the tens of thousands of German refugees fleeing Allied bombs and the advancing Soviet Army and of taking action against both parachutists dropped by British planes and Slovak, Czech, and Soviet partisans fighting against the Germans in the Moravian Beskids, the Vysočina hills at the Moravian-Bohemian borders, and the Bohemian Brdy Mountains. Discipline in Czech factories was low, and sabotage of the railroads increased. On February 14, 1945, Prague was bombed because of a navigation error of American pilots (causing the deaths of five hundred civilians), and then in the spring Allied crews aimed with greater precision, attacking factories, refineries, and communications in Prague, Kolín, Ostrava, and Brno. On April 29 they nearly destroyed the immense Škoda Armament Works in Plzeň.

In the late winter and early spring of 1945 citizens of the protectorate, of whatever language and origin, listened to the most improbable rumors and kept their ears glued to the evening news, Czech, German, Swiss, or Allied, and wondered when the hour of the great change would arrive. After the bloody battle of Stalingrad in the winter of 1942–43, in which the Wehrmacht had lost at least two hundred thousand soldiers, Stalin's armies had begun to push the Germans out of the Soviet Union, and by April 1944 the Germans had had to relinquish Ukraine. Allied troops had landed in Sicily in the summer of 1943 to drive to the Italian north, Mussolini had been arrested by his own countrymen on July 23, 1943, and Rome welcomed the Allies on June 6, 1944. General Patton's tanks broke through the German lines near Avranches, and Paris was liberated by the Allies and General de Gaulle's Free French on August 25, 1944. Romania, Bulgaria, and Hungary switched sides and joined the anti-Nazi coalition; Aachen, the first German city in the west, was taken by American troops in October 1944; Breslau, in the German east, had been encircled, though not taken, by Soviet troops by February 1945; and the Soviet armies continued their drive toward Berlin.

On April 3, Frank for the last time visited the Führer in his subterranean Berlin bunker, where he heard Hitler reject all potential political solutions because he still believed that Field Marshal Ferdinand Schörner, whom he was to declare in his last will and testament to be his successor as commander in chief of the German Army, would win the day in military battle. Frank was shocked by Hitler's sick and disheveled appearance, but he went on pursuing his own political and more pragmatic plans, believing he had won over Foreign Minister Ribbentrop. In the last week of April he convened a motley group of Czech and German government functionaries and industrialists at Czernin Palace to form a "mixed delegation" that would negotiate with the Americans to see if the protectorate could be peacefully transferred to American hands, with Czechs and Germans guaranteed equal rights, in return for a slowdown in the Soviet advance. The delegation consisted of Bienert, now head of the Czech government, who in 1918 had been Masaryk's trusted confederate; Adolf Hrubý, minister of agriculture; two Czech industrialists and their German colleague

Bernhard Adolf; retired General Vladimír Klecanda, formerly Czecho-slovak military attaché in Switzerland; and the Austrian Dr. Hermann Raschhofer, professor of international law and Frank's legal adviser.

Their special plane left on April 25 in the early morning and landed in Neubiberg in Bavaria, still in German hands. But Field Marshal Al-bert Kesselring had little advice to offer, saying he did not even know where the front line was. Two members of the delegation immediately returned to Prague, while Hrubý and the two Czech industrialists pro-ceeded to SS HQ at Bad Tölz to negotiate the possible exchange of prominent prisoners. (There were none, and the three men went back to Bohemia.) General Klecanda and Dr. Raschhofer, meanwhile, hop-ing to see the archbishop of Milan in preparation for a papal interces-sion, had to stop at Bolzano, by now in U.S. hands, and tried in vain to cross over to Switzerland. Ultimately, Raschhofer wisely decided to seek refuge with his parents at Salzburg while adventurous Klecanda returned on foot and by auto stop, hitchhiking to Prague, where he re-ported to Frank that the mission had totally failed.

On May 6, Prague erupted in open revolt against the Nazis, and the Czech National Council sent a delegate to Frank to negotiate the pos-sibilities of an armistice. Frank was trapped on Hradčany Hill but managed to move to the Wehrmacht headquarters of General Tous-saint, in suburban Dejvice, to prepare for his departure from Bohemia. In the early morning of May 9 he left in the direction of Rokycany and Plzeň, southwest of Prague, as did twenty-five thousand German sol-diers, who were made to relinquish their weapons at the city line, and German civilians. His four cars—Frank in the second; his wife, three children, and a governess in the third—did not get very far; his pres-ence was noted by Czech gendarmes who telephoned their colleagues farther down the line, and at Rokycany, already in U.S. Army hands, Frank's car was stopped in front of the local abattoir.

Frank did not resist when he was formally arrested by one Consta-ble Ranc and transferred by the U.S. Army to Plzeň and then Wies-baden for further interrogation. He had seen his family for the last time. Eventually the Allies decided that he was to be handed over to Czechoslovakia's authorities, who put him on trial in Prague. He was sentenced on March 22, 1946, and executed two months later. Patton's army transferred his wife, a medical doctor, to an American prison and later handed her over to Soviet authorities, who jailed her at the Lubyanka Prison in Moscow and then, under the watchful and protective eyes of a Soviet general, sent her to Siberia. She worked there for ten years, until German prisoners were repatriated. She found her three children after a long search in the Federal Republic, and it is said that, carrying papers in her maiden name, she visited Prague again after the Velvet Revolution.

The Girl with the Velvet Band

It was not the best of times to fall in love with a young German woman, and even after sixty and more years, I recall that it happened suddenly. And I remember, or rather I do not wish to remember, how strong my feelings were when we met, in the midst of the war, for endless walks through Prague's gardens and streets. I saw her first walking up and down in front of a little theater—it was the Kleine Bühne, *established by my father a generation before—waiting for the box office to open. It must have been spring, to judge from my memory of her appearance and the soft air, or so it seems to me. Nazi theoreticians of race would have classified her immediately as Dinaric, or rather Alpine, I thought, with her dark brown hair and eyes, her face sunburned rather than pale, and her long limbs in continuous motion. She was clad in a simple blouse and a severe skirt that showed right away she was German rather than Czech, though a narrow black velvet band on her short hair was curiously refined, if in a provincial way. I know I am not exaggerating when I say that her candid face and the black velvet band left their mark on me forever. After staring a little impolitely, I passed her by, because I did not see the slightest possibility of buying another ticket and addressing her, out of the blue, among the German crowds during intermission, later.*

If I were writing a novel, I might say that I caught my breath, but I did not do so because it seemed so inevitable when she entered the bookstore the following Saturday afternoon, again in a blouse and skirt, though a different ensemble, and with the velvet band in her hair. She looked around for a while and then asked me, the busy clerk, whether we carried inexpensive editions of older authors. I was ready to bring up from the cellar Goethe's complete collected works in forty volumes and add my own poetry for her too. But not to leave her was at the moment the most important thing in the world, so I asked courteously if she had a particular century in mind, or perhaps the Romantics? She said that she was looking for Eichendorff's novella Aus dem Leben eines Taugenichts *to read on a little trip she was planning. She was certainly speaking not Prague German, which is easily recognized by its closeness to Czech phonetics, but an idiom from the Bohemian mountains of the north, with its broad vowels, and I suddenly realized that if she had come in the uniform of the* Bund deutscher Mädchen, *the black triangle on the sleeve would have clearly said "Sudetenland." I did not feel the cold sweat I should have felt. I pretended to look for an Eichendorff, though I knew we had none, and told her that I could perhaps get one later in the afternoon if she really needed it before her trip. My idea did not seem entirely outlandish to her, and she simply said she would be on the seven twenty-five evening train leaving from the main station for Brandeis, in the hills of eastern Bohemia. And she left the shop.*

It was four, and the shop would close at six. I had time enough to run home, snatch the Eichendorff from my father's library, cross Wenceslas Square to the main station, find the train, and look for the girl with the velvet band. There she was, standing at the open window of a little train bound for the eastern hills. She reached down to take the slim book and asked how much she owed me. I answered that it was a gift to her for her weekend trip. She was not at all flirtatious as she told me about her plans to spend Sunday walking through the woods, which she missed so much in Prague. I had my own thoughts about a young German woman tramping alone through the Czech Jizerské hory. Then the whistle sounded, the train left, and I stood there clearly feeling that something important had happened but I did not know what, something wonderful but, considering the circumstances, bitter and impossible. When she returned the next Saturday afternoon to the bookshop to thank me for the book again, we began walking through the city, and I was overwhelmed by a quiet confusion and the wish that our walks would never end.

In another century or on another planet we would, I hoped, have held hands from the beginning or looked into each other's eyes deeply, but the moment of history was against us. For nearly two years she was my steady date without ever being my date. The first three weeks were the most terrible of all because I was afraid to tell her that I was a half Jew according to the laws of the land (hers and mine). But when I did so and looked into the distance, she was astonishingly calm. She told me that in her school a girl had had similar difficulties before being expelled and that she had suspected something because I did not wear a uniform and did not speak about joining the army soon. Strangely enough, that was all, and when I later talked to her about my mother and about Terezín and Auschwitz, she accepted me with a kind of unspoken, guileless, serious serenity that would have seemed to be indifference if she had not revealed that, in her own way, she was willing to sympathize with me. Once she went to Vienna for a week, saw Wilhelm Kienzl's Der Evangelimann at the opera there, and in a letter to me quoted a line from the chorus, "Blessed are those who suffer persecution," underlining the quotation so firmly on the thin paper that she partly tore it where she pressed the pen too hard. Even after half a century I am moved by the memory of the torn green paper.

My difficulties began with her given name, which sounded awfully Wagnerian and, considering her appearance, absolutely inappropriate. So I simply changed Waltraut, the woman at home on the battlefield, by making a little consonant adjustment, to Waldtraut, the woman to the forests born. She could not hear the change when I spoke her name, but it seemed more poetic and just. Otherwise, I did not know much about my lovely Sudeten enemy. She was a medical student who also held a part-time job as an assistant at the Institute of Physiology and was busy many mornings setting up the experiments with which her professor illustrated his introductory lectures. I usually walked down from our apartment to the Albertov district, where the medical schools and hospitals were— twenty minutes then, but more than half an hour when I do it now—and in front of the institute I would whistle something from Bizet's Carmen or the chorus from Puccini's La Bohème, Act II. In her little room above the main entrance, she would open the window when she was ready and then come down, unpretentious and without the slightest trace of makeup, and we would go for our walk, mostly to nearby Vyšehrad hill or through the gardens of the Malá Strana (or die Kleinseite, as she put it) and up to Hradčany Castle or the wooded Petřín. W., of course, did not know any-

*thing about the Czech tradition that young people placed bunches of vio-
lets on the monument there to K. H. Mácha, poet of love and spring. I
think we instinctively avoided downtown because we did not want to be
seen by too many acquaintances, German or Czech, who would have
wondered about such an odd couple. When a Czech friend once saw me
with W. going down Národní třída, toward the river, he called me next
day and suggested that it would be perhaps more patriotic not to be seen
walking with so obviously German a girl. We never went to the Ständetheater or the Národní divadlo for obvious reasons, but we hung around
outlying cafés or occasionally had an elegant dinner at a chic place on
Michalská Street frequented by upper-class Czechs or Germans at separate tables, and, considering the slim budget of my patriotic friends, totally extraterritorial (you also had to pay for the ration coupons). We were
there on the night of Mussolini's arrest, and I invited W. to choose her
dishes from the leather-bound menu, we had something flambé, and the
waiter, in impeccable tails, did his best.*

*Slowly, in bits and pieces, W. told me more about herself and the situ-
ation of her family, and it was not a happy story. It turned out that in
Masaryk's republic her father had been a school inspector, but he had
been removed from his position by the new Sudeten regime after the Munich Conference, because it was decided that as a believing Catholic he
was unfit to continue. So he had to find himself an office job in private industry, and it was unfortunately far from where the family lived on the
Schneeberg, close to the border with Saxony. His wife, W.'s mother, suffered from a strange and recurrent paralysis and had to be taken care of by
a friendly neighbor when he was away. It turned out that W. was a regular churchgoer; she belonged to a group that gathered around Father
Paulus, the official student chaplain, and attended his stern spoken mass
regularly. It would have never occurred to her to rush on Sundays to the
eleven o'clock mass at St. Jacob, in the Old Town, as did many Prague aes-
thetes, including myself, throughout the war because a magnificent orchestra and chorus there performed Mozart and Dvořák. On holidays she
often disappeared to Leitmeritz (Litoměřice) to listen to the famous ser-
mons delivered by Pater Bitterlich, the resident bishop's vicar-general,
who had been her teacher in school. (I visited Pater Bitterlich in 1946 in
a parish in Vienna, where he had found refuge, and he showed me a*

school photograph of W.) Yet she was not—to my regret, since it deprived me of a possible argument of self-defense—a Catholic who had concluded that under the present circumstances Christian beliefs were a political act. Father Paulus had decided this, though, and he joined the army to escape arrest and the concentration camps. W. went on believing without asking radical questions about the disorder here on earth. At least we had something to talk about, so we did not discuss just the Romantics, Goethe, the history of Prague (the more distant the better), and Rilke, patron saint of our walks.

There were occasions and excursions when we behaved like ordinary people, as if we were not skating on thin ice and were not in danger from any random uniformed patrol who might by chance check our unequal identity papers. Once I took it into my head to accompany W. to Leitmeritz. This old bishopric was just beyond the demarcation line separating the Sudetengau, now belonging to the Reich, from the protectorate and only three miles from Terezín, where my mother had died. W. wanted to bicycle there all the way from Prague, and though I was able to convince my friend Kari to let me have his bicycle—I did not tell him why I wanted it—W. was far stronger and better trained than I, and I had to give up halfway, panting hopelessly in a ditch, totally defeated by her athletic performance. We agreed at least that I would look for her in the cathedral or, if I did not find her there, wait for her at the border checkpoint on the Czech side.

The trick was that, for a "fee" of twenty cigarettes, one could deposit one's identity card at the checkpoint, the Czech border police would turn a blind eye to further procedures, and one could cross over, no questions asked. I left the cigarettes and my identity card and crossed over into the Reich. But I did not find her in church and went to have a glass of beer at an inn on the market square: a young man of military age but not in uniform and visible, I thought, for miles. I returned, walking, not running, to the demarcation line, where W. was waiting for me, radiant in the sun, her stockings rolled down to her ankles, and the bike, which she had borrowed at the Institute of Physiology, next to her in the grass. Fortunately she too wanted to return by train; we loaded the bikes and arrived in Prague before darkness came. This was July 20, 1944, as the radio reminded us next morning, the day of the failed putsch of the generals against Hitler, and I did not dare think about what might have happened to me if a military or SS patrol had found me in Leitmeritz without an identity card and three miles from Terezín. I would have had a hard time explaining that I (the half Jew) was just waiting for a young German woman visiting the bishop's vicar-general.

W. was perhaps more audacious than I, or not burdened by my political anxieties. I told her one day that a group of friends had hidden their skis and other winter gear with a peasant family in the Beskid Mountains, after first sacrificing one pair of skis and old woolen gloves to the German authorities, who collected them for the army fighting in Russia. It was she who suggested that we go skiing for a few days after Christmas to the Beskids, on the Polish-Slovak border, and off we went on a cheap train through all of Bohemia and Moravia to the northeast. She was a far better skier than I, of course, and as soon as we started our ascent to the Radhošt', dominating the Beskid Mountains, she was far ahead of me, and I had great difficulty keeping up with her. The mountain hut at the Radhošt' was occupied by a bunch of Hitler Jugend, but they left in the afternoon, and the Moravian landlady, uninterested in ethnicity, language, race, or the political situation, gave us a little room, clean and with two beds, each in a different corner. W. withdrew to the toilet (unromantically noisy behind a thin wooden partition) to change while I slipped into my best pajamas, and she returned in an old-fashioned flannel nightgown straight to her bed in the far corner. She bade me goodnight from there but I went on my knees (I meant it) and asked her to take me into her bed for a little while (I would be quiet, I promised), and yet I was glad when she told me that I knew myself that it was impossible. I agreed. We extinguished the light and slept that night, and the following three, each on our separate bed as if it could not be otherwise.

I remember a summer Sunday when we walked through the hills on the shores of the Vltava south of Prague. It started to rain, and there was, far and wide, not a roof in sight. We crawled for cover into the thick underbrush under the fir trees and bedded down in a green cave. I do not hesitate to use that ancient image, because the forest provided its natural presence, but whatever the image of the green cave might once have suggested, we did not touch each other, though we were separated only by an inch or so when I bent down to create a human umbrella. It was strange—and not strange at all. We were increasingly close to each other, and when because her little room at the institute had running cold water but nothing else, she asked me if she could take an occasional hot bath in our apartment, she appeared with a piece of soap and a towel like a schoolgirl (while I had prepared a choice of soaps and perfumes). We behaved with perfect civility as if our practical agreement was nothing special at all. When she was finished and came out of the bathroom, her face was shining, a little fragrance emanated from her dress, and I made a cup of tea, to behave like a gentleman of the cosmopolitan world (or so I thought). When I returned to that apartment after sixty years and took a shower there, I could not help thinking of her bony young body, which I never saw, in the steaming tub.

The Allies were preparing to land on the Normandy beaches, I knew that I would be going to the camps for half Jews soon, and our conversation more often than before strayed from poetry to the disparity between (her) belief in perfect transcendental truth and the injustices here on earth. She was often melancholy; after being ordered to work as a nurse assistant in the Prague hospital for Czech women prisoners, she was shaken, and something happened in her mind that she had difficulty describing. One afternoon she telephoned and for the first time told me that she needed me. I ran down to the Albertov. She came out immediately without waiting for my whistled signal, clad in a shabby dressing gown, her eyes red from weeping, and told me that a friend of hers, an airman serving at the Russian front, was missing. I, instead of telling her that fortunately the Soviets knew how to fight, tried to console her, betraying all my beliefs. She was a human being, weeping on my shoulder.

She said she wanted to go home immediately, and we trudged to the station. I decided to accompany her as far as the demarcation line. She lay down on the wooden bench in an empty compartment, and I knelt beside her, putting my face on her breast, silent but keenly feeling the rattling of the train. If I were a novelist, I would say that I saw sitting on the telephone lines flitting by nearly fifty thousand dark huge birds with fiery eyes staring at me, the Jewish prisoners from Prague once riding the same train to Bohušovice station before walking the mile or two to Terezín, or at least that I saw my mother quietly sitting in a corner of the compartment. But I did not see anything. We were alone there, W. weeping because of the death of an enemy of mine, and I trying to forget that she was German. I do not know how I got out of the train at Bohušovice, but it was the last time I saw her, ever. I went to the camps, and she died in the Allied air raid on Prague on February 14, 1945, killed in Charles Square by a bomb dropped not far from the old Benedictine monastery, founded in 1347, which was nearly destroyed. After the end of the war most Sudeten Germans were expelled from the country, and when her father received the expulsion order to leave his house, he killed his wife, by now totally paralyzed by muscular dystrophy, set fire to the house, and died in the flames.

Prague Movies During the Occupation

Historians have long agreed that National Socialism efficiently combined obsolete ideas, like its nineteenth-century racial theory, with the most recent technology, as in the production and distribution of movies or in building airplanes and highways. As far as movies were concerned, Hitler, at least until 1939, was an eager, if not pathological, movie addict who watched a movie (often American) every evening and left the control of the film industry to his minister of culture and propaganda, Joseph Goebbels, who was keenly aware of the political importance of movies in manipulating power. As early as April 26, 1933, Goebbels addressed the staff of the Berlin office and studios of the giant German UFA film company, announcing the *Gleichschaltung* (political takeover) by the National Socialist film authority and confirmed his measures affecting the organization of all German culture by law on September 29. Goebbels was convinced that Germany had lost World War I because in 1917–18 the sullen and hungry nation did not have the will to keep on fighting, and he was resolved not to let that happen again. From then until the end of the Third Reich almost half of all Nazi films were comedies, and only 14 percent outright propaganda. By the 1940s, in the midst of the war, Goebbels wanted to continue German film productions, but since Allied air raids were destroying the Berlin studios, he commandeered the Barrandov film studios in Prague, which had modern equipment and well-versed technical crews.

Bohemia and Moravia had always compared well with England and Italy in the number and size of their cinemas, and this was true even after the Munich Conference. During the years of German occupation the number of Prague movie houses and the number of both Czechs and Germans buying tickets increased markedly. Patriotic suggestions that Czech audiences, on principle, boycotted German movies must be taken with a grain of salt, since German musicals especially, with tap dancing and the Hungarian Marika Rökk, were quite popular.* Whether interest in the cinematic arts was paramount may be a different question; many consumer goods were unattainable, apartments were unheated, the city was dark, police checked on people in cafés and restaurants, public dancing was not allowed most of the time, and so it was said that in the evening people went either to the movies or straight to bed.

In the development of the Prague film industry, the Havel family was by far the most active force, and inevitably they clashed with the German occupiers—with the Reichsprotektor politically and, economically, with UFA and with the Cautio Treuhand, the agency charged by the German government with buying or expropriating independent production firms in and outside Germany. Václav Havel, the future president's father, scion of a patrician and conservative family, had long had far-reaching ideas about modern living, and he had been active in the student organization of the early First Republic and the Czech YMCA. In 1923 he went on a trip to the United States, traveling from New York to San Francisco and Hollywood, learning about recent trends in investment, real estate, and film, and he returned to embark on a hands-on construction job that changed the architectural boundaries of Prague. In 1924 he began building a Garden City of prefabricated houses on the Barrandov bluffs overlooking the Vltava River a few comfortable miles south of the city center. (The bluffs were so called after the nineteenth-century French paleontologist Joachim Barrande, who explored their sedimentary rocks.) These houses were

*The protectorate had 1,101 cinemas in 1939, 1,181 in 1942, and 1,195 in 1943. In Prague alone, the number of movie houses increased (from 108 in 1939 to 111 in 1944), and audiences doubled, exactly as in Germany too, at least until 1944, when intense Allied air raids destroyed many movie houses.

bought up by many members of Prague's new financial and artistic elite. In 1927 the Garden City was crowned with a modern café and restaurant on top of the Barrandov terraces, an acknowledged copy of the famous Cliff House in San Francisco, which Havel had seen on his trip. The Garden City became a center of chic Prague life, whether up in the Trilobit Bar, added a little later, where R. A. Dvorský and his band played their elegant tunes, or down at the foot of the cliff, where a swimming pool was built and all the starlets could be seen.

In 1931–33 the Havels built the Barrandov Film Studios as a center for new productions, which until then had been mounted in large beer gardens or corners of suburbia. The first Barrandov movie, a Czech thriller, was completed in late January 1933, a week before Hitler came to power in Berlin. The activities of the atelier were directed by Václav's brother Miloš, who had been active in the film business since the early 1920s, imported the first U.S. western to Prague cinemas, and organized the AB film corporation. He was also the owner of the Lucerna film group and co-owner of the palatial Lucerna cinema in downtown Prague. In 1939 he was first in the line of fire when the Germans tried to take over.

Czech Fascists agreed with the German occupiers that the cinema was of prime importance in the handling of power, and only twenty-four hours after the Wehrmacht marched into Prague, they tried to take over the entire film industry, including all the big movie houses and the distribution companies. General Gajda, their leader, undeterred by the meager turnout that responded to his appeal to meet at the Coal Market in order speedily to patch together a new government, went ahead with his detailed plans to take over the Barrandov Studios, and he delegated Josef Kraus, a production assistant, and two other Fascists to rush to their physical premises that very morning of March 16, 1939. Kraus immediately dismissed the administrative director and demanded that Walter Schorsch and Jiří Weiss, two company directors of Jewish origin, leave the premises. The staff and technical personnel protested, whereupon Gajda sent out another group, consisting of Dr. Zdeněk Zástěra, an old-time member of the Fascist organization, the film director Václav Binovec, and the painter Jan Tulla, to join Kraus in breaking the resistance. In the meantime Miloš Havel was notified by telephone about what was going on, and he talked to Zástěra, whom he asked to abandon his illegal attempt to interfere with his business. The Fascists, vicious but unsure of what they were doing, left, with the exception of Binovec, who stayed for the afternoon meeting of the board of directors, but in vain, since the board declared it would not discuss matters with him. Miloš Havel still had sufficient authority to deal with these Fascist amateurs, but confronting the Germans was a different matter.

Barely a month later Neurath's office appointed a Saarländer named Hermann Glessgen (who had applied for Nazi Party membership only in January) special commissioner for all matters concerning cinematography in the protectorate. In a programmatic memorandum, he stated that film was an expression of Czech culture that was highly cherished by the nation but that a yearly production of nearly fifty movies was far too much; German interest dictated that Czech production be reduced and guided (the verb was *steuern*) to make room for German movies. The most practical way to accomplish this would be to concentrate all companies in the hands of Germans, who would own a majority of the shares. For more than a year brave Miloš Havel was put under relentless pressure by Glessgen and his allies, including the Gestapo, which arrested him briefly and ransacked his office at the Barrandov, and by the Cautio Treuhand, run by Max Winkler, who had considerable experience in legal expropriations. Glessgen argued that AB was a Jewish enterprise because Havel's Jewish friend Osvald Kosek, who owned some of Prague's most important movie houses, had been a director, but Havel pointed out that as of March 16 the name of Kosek (who had left for the United States) had been deleted from the list of board members. Glessgen answered that the defining dates of the laws would simply be changed, but Havel continued to resist. Frank and President Hácha intervened in the discussion of whether AB's capital was to be increased or not, and ultimately lawyers for the Cautio Treuhand and for Havel signed an agreement dated April 26, 1940.

The document stipulated that Havel would transfer 51 percent of AB's stock to the Cautio Treuhand, which would pay him 6,885,000 Czech crowns in successive installments, guarantee the possibility of producing at least five Czech films yearly at the Barrandov studios, give him a free hand as far as his Lucerna film group was concerned, and grant further credits if he should run up high production costs. Havel immediately established a board of dramaturgs for Lucerna consisting of some of the most important Czech writers in order to protect them from conscription for the Reich.

The situation was fluid, to say the least, because Winkler was busy concentrating all of Germany's film companies, which now included UFA, Tobis, Terra, Bavaria, and Wien-Film, under one political and economic roof. Though the new corporation was still called UFA, it was not the old firm anymore but a superorganization, stretching far out into the occupied territories and employing, in Berlin alone, more than five thousand people. In November 1941 a new German board of directors for the AB group, including the small Hostivař studios in the suburbs of Prague, decided that the company would forthwith be called Prag-Film. New halls were built and outfitted with projectors, and film laboratories in Paris and at Rome's Cinecittà, pilfered by the Germans after the fall of Mussolini in 1943, were moved to Prague. By 1944, after Allied air raids had destroyed the film studios in Berlin, Goebbels visited Prague in November and solemnly declared that it was the future metropolis of German film. Simultaneously, writers and actors were regularly meeting in the Czech underground to discuss a new Socialist law to regulate the future nationalization of the Czech film industry after the defeat of the Reich.

Czechs had made films with Germans or Austrians, or different language versions of the same script, during the late 1920s and early 1930s, and for them too, a UFA contract was often considered an important first step toward Hollywood. The cute comedienne Anny Ondra (or Ondráková), born in Poland, and her (first) husband, the actor and director Karel Lamač, began working together in Prague in the early 1920s and, after she had made a spate of British movies, including an Alfred Hitchcock thriller, established their own production company in Berlin in 1930, only to part ways when she married the German boxing champion Max Schmeling. (After the war Schmeling became a regional Coca-Cola representative.) The situation changed radically when the young Czech actress Lída Baarová, who had started in Prague in 1931, signed up with UFA in 1934, made a few movies in Berlin with heartthrob Gustav Fröhlich (they were lovers on- and off-screen), and so enchanted Goebbels that he wanted to divorce his wife, Magda, and give up his party position in exchange for an ambassadorship to Tokyo, if only he could marry the Czech diva. The affair almost made German history. Hitler resolutely intervened, Goebbels submitted to his Führer, stayed with Magda and his brood, and Baarová was promptly extradited from the Reich to her homeland. In Prague she was able to make a few movies, which are in fact her best, since she was protected by Miloš Havel, but under German pressure she had to leave for Italy, where she played minor roles at Cinecittà before again returning home late in the war.

Petr Bednařík's admirable archival researches have demonstrated that Germany's occupation authorities had their own trouble with some of their trustees and special commissioners. In Prague this was especially the case regarding the film business. Unlike the theater world, the film industry, with its complicated and often conflicting organizations and offices, the allure of the famous stars, high salaries, easy credit, and incessant partying at the Lucerna Bar, attracted all kinds of people, to judge from what the hard-drinking witnesses said, and not all of them kept above corruption and the flourishing black market. Hermann Glessgen, who came from the Catholic Volkspartei, was a prototypical carpetbagger who had made himself impossible in his previous life as a teacher and journalist by not paying his bills, had gone on to Prague, where he continued his way of life on a much grander scale: he obtained four fur coats for the star Adina Mandlová, not to speak of his own suits and other acquisitions that he charged but never paid for. After the important contract with Miloš Havel had been negotiated, his superiors immediately dropped Glessgen; after prolonged judicial procedures, he was sentenced by a Berlin court to six months in prison and was never seen in the film business again.

His colleague Karl Schulz, first German trustee of the Barrandov Studios, had been in the industry since the 1920s and came to Prague via the Bavaria AG. In 1942 Schulz was investigated because of his black-market activities, buying rationed goods, including cognac, food, and textiles, from Czech employees and selling them at lower prices to people he needed to favor in Berlin; he made up the difference from funds of Prag-Film. He was sentenced by a Berlin court to nine months in prison, together with his buddy Max Winkler of the Cautio Treuhand, who emerged after the war as the owner of the Kultur-und-Wirtschaftsfilm AG in Düsseldorf.

The Prague moviegoer, especially of the younger generation, did not have reason to complain about the international repertory of movies available, however, and American films were shown in Prague, as in Berlin and elsewhere in the Reich, at least until December 1941 and Pearl Harbor. In the mid-1930s American imports had dominated the Czech market (54 percent in 1938), and only in the Second Republic did German productions advance to first place, American ones fall to second (37 percent), and Czech to third place (17 percent), where they had been several years earlier. In the Second Republic nationalist and anti-Semitic sentiments emerged in force, and as early as October 1938 Prague cinemas had to be renamed if they sounded too international rather than Czech: Hollywood turned into Máj (May), Alfa to Aleš (the name of a famous Czech painter), Fénix to Blaník (a hill famous in Czech myth), Adria to Adrie, and Apollo, with a patriotic twist of sorts, to Amerika. The recent and most modern downtown cinema, originally called Broadway, first changed to Na Příkopě, because of its location, but later the Germans insisted on calling it Victoria. After Munich, films with the actor Hugo Haas, of Jewish origin, were not shown anymore; they included Karel Čapek's anti-Fascist *The White Plague* (*Bílá nemoc*), but people watched the pacifist *No Greater Glory* and *Gunga Din*, at first prohibited and then released to popular acclaim. At Christmas 1938 *Alexander's Ragtime Band* made its festive appearance, and later Leslie Howard (in spite of or precisely because he had been born in Budapest) was praised as Professor Higgins in *Pygmalion*.

Czech film production was particularly strong in the most difficult years of the republic—forty-nine films in 1937 and forty-one in both 1938 and 1939—but thereafter film production rapidly dwindled to only ten in 1942 and eleven in 1944. The single film made in Prague in 1945 was not shown until after the war.

After Heydrich's arrival in Prague it was nearly impossible to speak about "national autonomy" or even "autonomy of national culture," and producers, scriptwriters, and actors had a tough time defending Czech interests unless they expressed the arguments of German nationalism except turned around. Some of the various ways chosen by Czech film-makers to defend their country's independence were more successful than others; it is possible to argue that the movies of pure entertainment (in Fascist Italy, comedies about the upper-class world were called white telephone movies) did far better, with their wit, irony, and elegance, in fighting at least by implication against a world of aggression, than did most of the historical and peasant kitsch films about Czech life in the past.

The most popular movie made in the protectorate was a biopic about the musician František Kmoch, who in the decades before World War I made Czech folk songs, as performed by his own orchestra, well known all over Central and Eastern Europe. (In Austria at the same time, the director Willy Forst made a number of films celebrating the gifts of popular Viennese musicians, so different from those of the Prussians). *To byl český muzikant: František Kmoch* (He Was a Czech Musician) was produced by the small Elekta-Film group at the Hostivař studio, and when it was released on February 9, 1940, it broke all attendance records. The screenplay, stitched together by three writers, tells of the young teacher Kmoch, who, much to the regret of his school's principal, prefers his music to his pedagogical duties; he is suspended, moves to the small town of Kolín, charms local audiences with the performances of his orchestra, and soon travels far and wide (even to czarist Nizhniy Novgorod, barely hinted at in the movie). Vladimír Slavínský was an experienced director, but this was not the best of his movies. While the first half was dramatic enough, with Kmoch leaving not only the school but the principal's daughter, the second was far less so, consisting of a sequence of musical performances and Kmoch's triumphant return to his admiring parents, wife, and three daughters—a middle-class apotheosis, not a celebration of wayward genius.

To tell the truth, the critics were not overwhelmed by the artistic merits of the movie, though they sympathized with the reasons for its success. Otto Rádl, in the *Kinorevue*, declared that all the film's merits were in its music, not in superior acting. In the conservative *Venkov*, A. M. Brousil suggested that some of the actors behaved like amateurs (with the possible exception of Jana Ebertová as the principal's daughter), and the *Národní listy* (National News) gave bad marks to the famous Ella Nollová, playing Kmoch's weepy mother, but praised Zita Kabátová, playing Kmoch's wife, and Jaroslav Vojta (of the National Theater) as Kmoch's father. Of course, everybody agreed that it was a nice movie to see, to hum the old melodies, and to leave the cinema with the right sentiments in one's heart. Prague audiences certainly felt that way: three major movie houses ran the film concurrently for months, and 337,000 tickets were sold in the city alone. The National Acting Award for the year 1940 promptly went to Jaroslav Vojta, even though the screenplay required him to tell the audience what to think and feel about Kmoch, and not to Otomar Korbelář, playing Kmoch himself, whose performance was considered a bit anemic.

The elegant comedy *Dívka v modrém* (The Girl in Blue), has kept much of its unusual charm because it was created by a group of totally different individual professionals working together in a productive ensemble. *Dívka v modrém* was produced at Miloš Havel's AB-Barrandov Studios for Lucerna Film, and released on January 26, 1940, to respectable reviews and considerable popular success. (It is still shown today on Czech television on early Saturday afternoons, in the "Films for Contemporaries" series, the average age of the viewers being eighty or so.) It is a kind of Pygmalion story or, rather, a story about an old picture coming to life. It starts at a Bohemian castle whose antique furnishings are being sold at auction, but nobody wants to bid on the seventeenth-century picture of a young woman because rumor has it that it is cursed. The lawyer who supervises the auction, Dr. Karas, agrees to take the picture home, cannot help admiring the woman, and one night kisses the picture, whereupon she steps out of the frame, alive and enchanting, and, speaking impeccable Old Czech, introduces herself as Contessa Blanka of Blankenburg and declares that she does not want to return to the picture. The lawyer, who is falling in love with her, has a 318-year-old problem on his hands, and he bravely tells people that Blanka is his cousin from abroad because she attracts the attention of so many admirers, including one who appears in appropriate historical costume and woos her, playing an antique mandolin. Happily, Blanka does not go too far; she confesses to being a student, Vlasta, who had been asked by the lawyer's friends to play an elaborate joke on him, and the couple hastens to marry, much to the regret of a young widow who had set her eyes on the once-eligible bachelor.

Most critics seemed to have been surprised that Czech film producers, with their penchant for either serious, low-class, or tragic work, were capable of turning out a "charming little play," light, airy, and even elegant. A. M. Brousil admitted in *Venkov* that the picture had taste, including the constructivist interiors by Jan Zázvorka and Jan Roth's camera work, with its preference for half-lights to stark contrasts of white and black. The critics, caught in their own moment, did not comprehend that much of the film was an ingenious parody of the prevalent historicism of most popular costume dramas. Audiences had a chance to confront the past, however heroic or patriotically virtuous, from an ironic distance, and the critic who suggested in the *Kinorevue* that the haunting, jazzy theme song "Dívka v modrém" (composed by S. E. Nováček with a text by K. M. Walló) should have been more old-fashioned, was surely on the wrong track, considering that the song has become an indestructible evergreen. All the cast members had an opportunity to show their best talents and not work against them: Oldřich Nový, playing the lawyer, born to the dinner jacket and with a self-irony close to Maurice Chevalier's; Lída Baarová, more convincing as dark-eyed Blanka than as a student of Czech philology; sophisticated Nataša Gollová, as the disappointed young widow; as housekeeper, the unchanging Antonie Nedošinská; and Jindřich Láznička, quietly comic, as the lawyer's secretary.

But Oldřich Nový, who had often visited prewar Paris and had loved its tradition of light, intimate comedy with a few chansons interspersed, did not have Vlasta Burian's mass appeal. Burian, not only in his own theater but in eight movies released during the years of the protectorate, indisputably reigned as the king of comedy. He came from a Prague plebeian suburb and the popular variety show, and his friends speculated that his color blindness was more than balanced by a fine ear for language sounds, his gift for imitating inappropriate idioms, and his uncanny capability to mimic everyday Czechs. He had made his first movie as early as 1923, together with the team of Anny Ondra and Lamač, but he never really changed. Over the years he reliably and grotesquely created immediately recognizable Czech characters, whether a male nurse (in *U pokladny stál* [He Stood at the Box Office], 1939), a street singer (*Ulice zpívá* [The Street Sings], 1939), a minor bureaucrat (*Katakomby* [Catacombs], 1940), or the guy who did not buy his railway ticket in time (*Přednosta stanice* [Station Master], 1941). An entertainer of millions but a loner and paradoxically saturnine in private, he was not particularly liked by his colleagues, who were offended by his ostentatious lifestyle (a white car, a big villa, a passion for tennis, and a hunting lodge), and after May 1945 he had to pay dearly.

Politically the most dubious movie of the protectorate years was František Čáp's *Jan Cimbura*, made at the Barrandov Studios for Lucerna Film and released in Prague on November 21, 1941, just in time for the Christmas business. The screenplay was based on a novel by J. Š. Baar, a Catholic priest and prolific writer of village stories; how closely, or not, the movie followed the novel was later a matter of prolonged discussion. In the movie, two friends return after long military service to their village in southern Bohemia, and while Josef comes to marry Marjánka, who is to inherit a farm, the poor and landless Jan Cimbura has to work hard as a hired hand. Still, Jan impresses everybody (except the other village lads) by his honesty, intelligence, and prowess. When his friend is dying, Jan Cimbura promises him that he will take care of Marjánka and the children, and later, after he has rescued them from a burning forest, Marjánka and Jan happily marry, to the joy of the village. The film also includes the story of a disreputable Jewish innkeeper who employs a buxom dark-haired waitress and lends money at exorbitant rates to the unsuspecting peasant sons. The enraged village women band together, mistreat the girl, set fire to the inn, and force the Jew to leave the village.

It would be nearly superfluous to argue against this blood-and-soil kind of movie, sticking closely as it does to the traditional clichés of both Czech and German film: the peasants in their elaborate Sunday outfits and their wives clean and starched (never mind the stable), Jan Cimbura smelling the spring earth before he starts plowing, mighty clouds on the horizon. The ideological element emerges clearly when Cimbura, on a walk through Prague, admires Hradčany Castle, the interior of its cathedral, and Charles Bridge as patriotic monuments of Czech history, though in fact they are also symbols of a shared Bohemian history created by the Luxembourg, Polish, and Habsburg dynasties and their architects. Unfortunately the march of the Czech peasant women against the Jewish inn much resembles the revolt of the Württemberg citizens against Jud Süss, in Veit Harlan's German movie of the same name, which was shown in Prague a year before *Jan Cimbura*, in late November 1940; the camera dwells rather lovingly on the faces of the peasant women when they whip the waitress, skirts up, with sting nettles and destroy the inn.

Directly after the liberation of Prague in 1945, František Čáp was called to the Investigative Commission of Film Workers and a year later to the National Security Commission, whose members wanted to learn more about this "pogrom scene" in *Jan Cimbura*. It is possibly to the credit of Czech intentions that they investigated the circumstances right away rather than wait for years, as a German court did in the case of Veit Harlan and his *Jud Süss*. (However, both Čáp and Harlan were exonerated.) Čáp defended himself by combining two arguments: that the scene was part of Baar's novel and that it was inserted into the movie only at the insistence of a German Barrandov "trustee." Surprisingly, two Czech witnesses, one of them a professional literary historian, declared that the pogrom scene was indeed taken from the novel. But while it is true that Baar believed that Jews differ "in blood, language and religion," he definitely did not advocate violence against them. In the novel, Solomon Steiner's shop and inn originally have many Italian and German customers who are working on the railroad; once their job is finished, Steiner (played in the movie by František Roland, employing the tritest Jewish clichés) loses customers because the Czech peasants, guarded by their angelic wives, won't patronize him, and when he decides to leave, they give him transport to the railway station, where he takes the train to open his business somewhere else. The waitress (in the movie, Stanislava Strobachová, of the Na-

tional Theater), who shows lots of stocking, has already left long before, because the Czech peasant lads in the novel are immune to her
charms and the village wives have no reason to rough her up.

Public discussion of *Jan Cimbura* continued in the generally left-
wing weekly *Kulturni politika* (Cultural Policies), which in late December 1945 published an open letter from Jiří Weiss, who had returned to
Prague from his London exile to make movies again, to the surrealist
poet and Communist Vítězslav Nezval, who ran film affairs in the re-
constituted republic. Weiss wrote that he had promised himself never
to write about his Barrandov colleagues but added that he had to make
an exception because he had just attended a performance of *Jan Cimbura* at a small movie house on Wenceslas Square, with other
Czechoslovak soldiers of Jewish origin also in the audience, and was
confronted both with the first anti-Semitic scene in a Czech movie and
with anti-Jewish remarks from the audience members after the movie
was over. He could not but ask himself how it was possible that the
producer of *Cimbura* was being allowed to make films again after having made this anti-Semitic film at a time "when the German beasts
killed my mother in Auschwitz" and Jews had to wear the yellow star.
Weiss did not apologize for the strong words he used about Čáp, and
he was fully supported by Jaroslav Žák, a writer of popular novels and
movies; in the continuing discussion at least two letters were published from readers who asserted they knew the countryside and the
dubious role of Jewish business there.

Čáp left Prague after the Communist putsch, made a dozen movies
in West Germany, among them *Die Geierwally*, a proverbial *Schnulze*
(peasant kitsch), moved to Yugoslavia to do a spate of films for Tito,
and died in Portorož in 1979. Jiří Weiss left his native country for the
second time in 1968, taught at Hunter College in New York, made another movie about Czechoslovakia under the German occupation (a
West German–French coproduction), and died, ninety-one years old,
in 2004 in Santa Barbara, California. It is strange, to say the least, that
Jan Cimbura is marketed today and recommended to fans as coming
from the "Golden Treasury of Czech Cinematography," with the accompanying text totally silent about its anti-Semitic scenes.

The last film produced in the protectorate was Václav Krška's *Řeka čaruje* (The Enchantments of the River), which was shown only after the liberation, first in thirty movie houses countrywide and then in Prague itself, on January 25, 1946. It corresponds, in the history of Czech moviemaking, to the German film *Unter den Brücken* (*Under the Bridges*), produced in the last months of the Third Reich and shown only after its demise. The Enchantments of the River aptly shows that Krška's commitment to his native southern Bohemia does not ever deteriorate into a blood-and-soil spectacle, because it keeps the landscape, above all, its rivers (the Otava and Sázava flowing into one), attuned to individual fate and not to that of history or a nation.

Krška began as a novelist, far from Prague, and learned a good deal from his lifelong mentor, Fráňa Šrámek, the poet of life and sensuous anarchy, and if in the film he turns to any ideology at all, it is a lyrical populism favoring the people on the riverbanks, vagabonds, fishermen, farmhands, and millers, over bourgeois city residents. The river keeps flowing and rejuvenates, almost mystically, and you cannot err if you stay close to its living waters. A fairy-tale change definitely occurs in the life of the aging commercial counselor Kohák, who one day runs away from his dreary home, his domineering wife, and an existence without meaning to the southern Bohemian river of his youth and becomes a sort of tramp. At least one reviewer, the surrealist poet František Listopad, ironically wrote in the *Mládá fronta* (Young Front), that Krška's piece was a "movie for elderly gentlemen." But Krška was not a realist, and factuality was the least of his concerns; one of the few symbolists to make a film during the protectorate, he liked to experiment with unusual camera angles, combining different shots in recurrent superimpositions, and in true lyrical manner, he worked with the voice of the river audible only to the happy few. Krška's later masterpiece was his *Měsíc nad řekou* (The Moon Above the River, 1953), a film version of Fráňa Šrámek's play of the same title, with Dana Medřická in the role of a young woman who wants to make her own choices in life (possibly the first feminist in Czech movies). It was not surprising that by the later 1950s Krška had run into serious trouble with Communist critics, who accused him of "individualism" and other sins. He was an artist all his own and died in 1969, when the younger generation was beginning to battle the hard-liners.

———

It would be misleading to chronicle Czech film production in the years of the German occupation without considering what happened after May 1945 and the liberation of Prague, when revolutionary retribution in dealing with collaborators, informers, Fascists, and despoilers of national honor affected possibly more than a million citizens. Those in the limelight were among the first to be arrested, and at least one of them wrote in her memoirs that it was better to be safe in prison than to be lynched by a mob in the streets. Lída Baarová returned in 1944 from Rome to Prague, where Hans Albers advised her to go to Bavaria, but when she did so in the spring of 1945, she was promptly arrested by American counterintelligence officers, imprisoned in Munich, and repatriated to Prague, where she was in danger of being accused of high treason. Her mother died of a heart attack while being interrogated, and her younger sister, Zorka Janů, a talented actress herself, committed suicide by jumping out of a window. Lída Baarová's later life resembles a melancholy movie. In 1947 she was released from prison, where she had spent most of her time typing menus for the police dining rooms, and after adventurous complications left Prague with her new husband, Jan, for Austria. She settled in Salzburg, divorced and remarried, again made a number of movies in Italy— Fellini's *I Vitelloni*—and Spain, and returned to Prague, the first of a few fleeting visits, in April 1990. She died, quietly and alone, in Salzburg in 2000, and only a handful of people attended the reburial of her ashes in Prague, a few months later.

Adina Mandlová, the unruly daughter of a provincial railway inspector, was always attracted by high living among the prominent and rich. From 1932 to 1943 she made forty-five Czech films, together with Hugo Haas and Oldřich Nový, as well as one innocuous German comedy with the comic Heinz Rühmann, and received the National Film Award of 1943. She played the vamp on-screen and off, involved herself too closely with the German Barrandov trustees, quite aside from her Czech lovers, and was hauled off to prison in May 1945 and accused of being the mistress of K. H. Frank himself. After her release, she married a war pilot with a British passport, moved to England, and made a few attempts to return to stage and screen, but when she was invited to Prague in 1966 to perform in *Hello, Dolly!*, she did not fin-ish studying for her role. She returned to Prague to die when she was eighty-one, and her witty and honest memoirs were published there in 1990.

Nataša Gollová was the most intelligent among the young film stars of Czechoslovakia in the 1930s and 1940s, especially in her roles as flapper, garçonne, or sophisticated teenager. She was the granddaugh-ter of the most eminent Czech historian at Charles University and long hesitated whether to devote herself to the stage, modern dance, or the movies. She studied in Paris, fell in love with Tristan Tzara, who regu-larly visited her in Prague, and later with Dr. Wilhelm Söhnel, one of the German Barrandov trustees, who was from northern Moravia and had studied in Prague. In May 1945 she volunteered to go as a nurse to liberated Terezín, where typhoid fever raged, and became infected herself. She was not charged during the time of retribution, and though Czech citizenship was briefly returned to Söhnel (who later represented the UFA corporation in Vienna), Nataša Gollová was ex-iled to provincial theaters and an occasional movie and television part. She died in 1988, seventy-six years old, in a home for the poor.

Vlasta Burian was arrested in May 1945 and held until September, when the prosecutor, having examined the charges against him, ruled that he did not merit trial before a People's Court. It was the begin-ning, not the end, of legal procedures in which the secret police re-peatedly intervened. And while spared a trial before a People's Court, Burian was tried by a penal commission in 1946 and a special penal commission in 1947, which declared that his previous acquittal was null and void and sentenced him to public censure, a fine of half a mil-lion crowns, and three months in prison because his social relations with Germans "were more than were necessary." That he had per-formed in an anti-Semitic skit directed against Jan Masaryk was not mentioned. He was allowed to perform sporadically after 1953, died more or less in disgrace in 1962, and was rehabilitated only in 1994.

On June 30, 1945, Václav Kopecký, the Communist minister of culture, attacked Miloš Havel publicly, and in October a special com-mission ruled that he would not be allowed to work in the movies any-more. He was to be sentenced by a court of retribution, but procedures against him were stopped in December 1947. Later he escaped to Austria; he was arrested on Austrian soil by a Soviet patrol and returned to Prague, where he was sentenced to two years and an additional period of forced labor. In 1952 he succeeded in escaping to the Federal Republic, where he went into business in Munich and established a popular restaurant serving Czech cuisine; it was much liked by actors, intellectuals, and people from Radio Free Europe. Though he had won a case against the old Treuhand, his partner cheated him of his profits, and when he died in early 1968, he left all of 171 deutschmarks, 15 pfennigs (about $40.75) to his brother. His ashes were quietly transferred to Prague to the family tomb at the Vinohrady cemetery in early April of that year, and a photograph there shows his nephew, the future president of the Czech Republic, in sunglasses and with long hair, among the sparse crowd.

Communications from Terezín

We did not know much about what happened in Terezín to my grandmother, Aunt Irma, and my mother. Rumors in Prague abounded. Some people received preprinted postcards from there and camps farther east, and parcels were sent in the hope that they would arrive. It was difficult to guess what was true and what not, and many expected that communications would function better once a Terezín routine was established, or they pinned their hopes on the special detachment of Czech state police that was ordered to support the small SS contingent there. The historian Miroslav Kárný has analyzed the wartime performance of such Czech gendarmes, who were quite well paid, and believes that 3 percent of them, persecuted by German authorities during the war, were arrested because they helped Terezín inmates; this number does not include sixteen who were briefly held because they had helped themselves to tobacco, sardines, or perfume when they checked the luggage of an arriving transport (the term was šlojs [sluice]). Fourteen gendarmes were sentenced to long prison terms for helping Jews in one way or other, were sent to the concentration camps of Ravensbrück, Mauthausen, or the Terezín Small Fort, and while most of them returned after May 1945, two of them, Vilém Vlach and J. A. Černý, perished in the Small Fort.

I did not know exactly how my father operated, always a mystery, but it was very expensive to receive and send letters through the good offices of a gendarme. During a few months in 1942 and 1943 at least fragmentary communications arrived, and we returned notes to my mother. I enclosed a poem occasionally. My seventy-five-year-old grandmother, who had left Prague on June 20, 1942, in transport Aae, of which 928 people did not return and 73 survived, died within a few weeks or so, and I do not remember whether I heard then or later that "she simply turned to the wall and fell silent," but we felt that she did not, at least, suffer for a prolonged time. My mother had been in the transport of July 23, 1942, AAt, of which 947 died and 52 survived, and we did not know for a long time how she fared, but my father was in touch with a good Czech gendarme (never mind the fee) who told him that mother had stomach trouble and needed special pills. It was not easy to get a Swiss pharmacological product (Ciba, I remember) on the black market, nor did we know whether the pills reached her. One day my father was informed that my mother had died because of bleeding ulcers that could not be treated. Only much later did I receive a document from the Prague Jewish Community stating that she had died on June 26, 1943, at the age of fifty-one.

Four years later I was to hear more about my mother in Terezín, and in a most unlikely place, an office of the Prague Ministry of Culture. I had been invited to give a lecture on Franz Kafka in Vienna, but I needed an exit visa to leave the Czech Republic for occupied Vienna. I was told I had to start with the Ministry of Culture and then proceed to the Soviet Kommandatura, and when I was shown into a small office at the Ministry of Culture, now totally Communist, I did not have much hope. Kafka was not considered a culture hero by the comrades, and the stern lady with a party badge on her blouse was not fond of Kafka either, it seemed. But then, when she saw my name on the petition, she was suddenly a changed person and told me she had shared a spot on the straw with my mother for months, had read all my notes and my few poems, and how happy my mother had been when she received an occasional letter from home. I got the stamp right away, the bumashka (document) of the Soviets turned out to be a mere formality once the Czech comrades approved my trip, and so it happened that I was able to give my lecture, the first one about Kafka in hungry postwar Vienna, in the summer of 1947. I later found out that my mother's earthly remains had been burned, the ashes kept in paper cartons, and after some time thrown into the river Ohře, which flows near Terezín. I always imagine that they were swept away into the mighty Elbe and carried by its waters to the free amplitude of the North Sea.

In the Camps and in Prison

On a late September day in 1944 I received a Gestapo order to join a transport of half Jews, and since a few groups had earlier been sent to a camp near Benešov, twenty miles or so south of Prague, I assumed I would go there too. My departure from the bookshop was a fast affair; a week before I was to leave, a young Czech man from Vienna materialized to take over my job and I had to instruct him what to do; when two Gestapo men appeared, leather coats and all, I was sent to the back room while Josef pretended to sweep the floor in order to listen in to what they had to say to our obsequious madame. (They talked about me, Josef warned me.) I was foolish enough to believe they had simply come to check on me. But the situation was more complicated, and I was mistaken in my belief that I would go to nearby Benešov, where, everybody seemed to know, the famous tenor Jára Pospíšil occasionally entertained his fellow prisoners (1943) with his popular songs from the operetta stage.

In early October, we gathered in a little villa on Hradčany Hill and, mostly young and middle-aged men speaking Czech and German, spent the first hours of our captivity hanging around and discussing the latest from Benešov. Once a Gestapo officer, Commandant Hans Günther, appeared for an hour coolly to survey the scene. We were happy to discover that down in the bowels of the heating system a young Jew who worked there in the evening regularly left for home and was willing for a little tip to telephone our families and let them know how we had fared so far. It seems that literary people are naturally attracted to each other: my first buddy was a son of Professor Friedrich Slotty, famous for his explorations of Greek syntax and Etruscan, formerly at Jena University, member of the Prague Linguistic Circle, then chased from Prague's Charles University but, after the war, one of the most distinguished philologists in the German Democratic Republic.

Early the next morning our train left from Hybernská railway station, and it was clear after thirty minutes that we were not going to southern Bohemia but moving in a northeast direction. Our "wise men," a self-appointed committee of knowledgeable engineers, declared that it was not impossible that our train was going to Auschwitz. We spent a frightful time watching the names of the little stations going by until the wise men said that the danger had passed: we were heading toward Breslau, in Silesia. Short of the city, however, the train suddenly stopped; we staggered out in the middle of nowhere and found ourselves on a great plain, pale and empty from horizon to horizon. Later we were told that we were close to a place called Klein-Stein, where we had to build a camp before we could sleep under a roof. In the light of dawn the next day we discovered nearby a circle of flat tents peopled by Kirghiz tribesmen and their families who had left the Soviet Union as German Hiwis, or Hilfswillige (labor help), and were now engaged in building an airfield for the Luftwaffe, as we were to do, though less willingly than our new Kirghiz friends.

That renowned German organization was fortunately missing; everything was a little haphazard, and after we had erected the walls of our wooden barracks and built our palandy (boxes of wood and hay on top of each other to serve as beds), we roamed for a day or so across the plain. I discovered a lonely old church and, nearby, a kind of inn, or rather Luftwaffe bordello; the many blond ladies were quite willing to serve fresh beer and much else besides, if I only had reichsmarks, which I did not. I did not see any guards, and our wise men, changing into camp leaders, told us that it was better to work here than in Auschwitz or elsewhere. I learned rule number one—namely, that it was foolish to line up for the evening soup too early, because the good stuff (noodles, etc.) was at the bottom of the large pot. We all worked in a quarry where we were kept busy breaking large stones into small ones. From time to time a Kirghiz colleague appeared with a slow horse and a cart into which we shoveled the stones until he commanded, "Davolna [enough]", and we rested again on our hammers and shovels. It was all rather boring, and I teamed up with Ivan, who happened to be a former Prague schoolmate of mine, to keep our brains alive, and since he had, for reasons unknown, studied Arabic, he introduced me to the complicated system of Arabic noun plurals, until the Kirghiz izvoščik returned, ready to shout his refrain of davolna! (Ivan became a dentist in Toronto after the war.)

I wish I had continued my Arabic studies longer, but one early morning an ordinary German policeman in a green uniform appeared in front of my palanda and in the presence of one of our wise men formally arrested me, saying that I was to be transported back to Prague because I was under investigation by the Gestapo there. He let me pack my bag, but then he took out his professional handcuffs, clamped one around my hand and put the other cuff to his bicycle, which he pushed ahead, I trudging alongside, and so we made our way through the astonished camp (a short moment of glory) and the fall meadows until we reached the Klein-Stein police station, where I was lodged in a little prison cell, the first of many in which I was to sit and sleep in the coming days. I was "on transport," I was told, and I would travel, under guard, from prison to prison to Prague to be interrogated by the Gestapo officer who had signed the warrant.

The next day they put me in a police car and drove me to the town of Oppeln, where they put me in a regular prison, though as a temporary guest, so to speak, with no special privileges. It was an institution run by the Ministry of Justice, not the Gestapo, according to strict and ancient rules. The lunch potatoes were served hot, I participated in the daily walk in the courtyard, spent most of my working time pasting together paper envelopes and keeping my toilet spick-and-span, another basic rule, and when the Kalfaktor—that is, the prisoner bringing the food—introduced himself as an old Social Democrat and asked me if I needed something to read, I told him an English novel would be welcome. He brought me a Galsworthy volume, though in German, and I was grateful for his courage.

Being on transport showed me the underbelly of the Nazi system, and I was not surprised that they marched us from prison to the railway station early in the morning, when few people were about in the streets. I'll never forget the morning at the Oppeln railway station. As I waited there with my guard, an elderly policeman in green, I noticed a group of three British POWs on transport nearby. They were well fed, with ruddy faces, in clean and well-pressed battle dress, especially when compared with the disheveled uniform of the old German infantryman guarding them. Their officer sported a little baton, just as British officers had in the movies, and I told myself that I knew now who had won the war and who had lost.

During the day, alas, I was less hopeful. The old-fashioned train for prisoners (Häftlinge) had minute compartments, each one of us enclosed in a little space of his own, but fortunately there were cracks in the wooden partitions, and I could talk to my neighbor. He said he was an old Communist being sent from the concentration camp of Gross-Rosen to Auschwitz, and that was the place we were going to. He was as good a man as any whom I met on transport, and when I complained of hunger, he pushed little pieces of bread through the cracks. I was still munching these crumbs when we arrived at Auschwitz and I caught a last glimpse of my benefactor being led away by the SS.

I cannot say much about Auschwitz because I was never put in the camp but was marched off to the local precinct in the small town—there was a town—and again put in a little prison cell, and I found myself in a strange idyll, not far away from the inferno. The police precinct personnel consisted of the Polizeimeister and his busy wife, the Polizeimeisterin; three Ukrainian youths; and my comfortable fellow Häftlinge, considered by the police duo as houseguests, slaves, and gofers who did the shopping for the Frau Polizeimeisterin, cut the lawn, and made themselves generally useful. Their solidarity was limited, though. When I mentioned that I was hungry, the Ukrainian in charge let me have half a loaf of bread from his ample reserves in exchange for my wristwatch, which I had received as a confirmation gift from a prominent Prague writer. I never told my father this, not even after the war. I was glad when I was marched to the railway again, leaving Auschwitz behind, and after twelve hours or so of a slow ride I arrived in good old Brno, of all places, and was put in the regional prison well known to everybody as Na Cejlu (on Zeil Street), where, in better times, pickpockets and prostitutes were held.

It was a gregarious place, with an overflow of Häftlinge who were held in large halls, and we, on transport, had a fine chance to meet most interesting local people long under investigation, prisoners of war, officers of the Czechoslovak Army fighting on in the resistance, and black marketeers. I particularly remember a captain of the Soviet Air Corps, who had adventurous stories to tell, and two tall gray-haired brothers, prominent Moravian lawyers whose niece I had once dated in high school; I thought it was too late to tell them now. Once a week a barber came to shave us, unfortunately with blunt, much-used blades, and I liked to sit near the window and look across the street. There was the decaying building of the

Varieté, where as a boy I had gone on many a Sunday to see acrobatic shows and, after the intermission, movies projected on a screen at the other end of the hall. I had sat at a table with my nanny, sipped a Lesněnka (forest lemonade) and then simply turned my head to watch when the Buster Keaton movie started. Na Cejlu was lively, but I had to move on and was duly shipped to the Pankrác Prison in Prague, the part run by the Gestapo, where I experienced the worst days of my life.

Gestapo Encounters

On transport I had ample time to think about my coming encounter with the Gestapo, and in my mind I rehearsed what I would say. The Gestapo, at any rate, had provided me with the key term "illegal activities" (illegale Tätigkeit), neatly inscribed on a black tablet on the walls of my Oppeln cell, but the question was, Which of my so-called activities was important enough to warrant my being transported from the camp in the east to Prague, in the midst of the war? Had somebody informed the police that I had sold a book by Thomas Mann or Bertolt Brecht to an eager reader? Did they know about the poetry readings in our apartment or, perhaps, about the anthology of lyrics I had typed out so diligently? Or did they think I was involved in the activities of my friend Elisabeth, or rather Alžběta, and her group, who had tried to get food to the starving Jews of Terezín? The more I thought about the possibilities, the more I convinced myself that it was this last hypothesis. Elisabeth herself had been arrested in 1943, and I recalled the two Gestapo men visiting the bookshop—why, really?—and I also remembered Markéta, a young Czech woman who had appeared in the bookshop and asked me to continue Elisabeth's efforts, offering me a small printing press to publish leaflets, as Elisabeth had done. I was the literary man after all.

It all had started after I transferred to the Prague Akademické Gymnasium (1939), where, walking up and down the corridor between classes, I noticed a girl who differed from her fellow students, or so it seemed to me. She had reddish blond hair and a high forehead, was dressed in a rather outlandish way, and always walked alone. After class I followed her to her tram, rode with her to the Letná Hill across the river, and immediately addressed her when she alighted there. I walked her home, but we circled a good deal. It so happened that she had come from Vienna, was half Jewish, and lived with her mother; her father had died. She had trouble with her Czech but worked hard, and her grades were improving all the time; as if anticipating my next questions, she said she had little time for dates, dances, or the cinema.

We saw each other occasionally, speaking German or Czech, and one day her mother called me and said that the Gestapo had arrested her and that I should come to their apartment and do something about Elisabeth's little library before they returned to search the premises. Of the volumes of Marx, Engels, Lenin, some I burned on the spot, some I carried away—and just in time, because the Gestapo returned and arrested the mother too.

When a few months later Markéta appeared in the bookstore and introduced herself as Elisabeth's best friend and, vaguely, as a member of her group ready to hand over the printing press, I was confused, but not for long. My instinct told me that something was wrong. Markéta was neat, good-looking, perhaps too much so, but I thought she was definitely not intelligent enough to be Elisabeth's best friend, considering Lenin's volume against empirocriticism in her library. Markéta's habit of uttering provocative statements about the advances of Soviet and Slovak partisans in the countryside was outright foolish, particularly since she did not know me at all. I knew I was going to have to go to the camps soon, so I decided to play a double game. While it was not easy to avoid recurrent conversations (her see-through blouses were as seductive as her news reports), I withdrew into the role of unworldly simpleton, talking about my spiritual interests, especially poetry, and the wide and interior realms of the soul totally untouched by news of whether the partisans were reaching the borders of Moravia or not. I plagiarized Rilke's Weltinnenraum for the occasion, but she did not have the foggiest. I would have preferred to sit with her at the Café Vltava to listen to jazz, but she went on and on, forcing us into conversational situations in which I had to be careful not to stray from metaphysics into politics. I was fortunate that I stuck to my role, because it turned out that she was a Czech agent working for the Gestapo.

In Prague our prison train was shunted to a remote part of the Hybern-

*ská railway station, from which I had left seven weeks earlier, and in the
early-morning hours everything was still, not even a distant locomotive to
be heard. By six o'clock a railway man with a long hammer was slowly
moving along the train to test the wheels, and when I saw him approaching, I quickly opened my window and whispered to him to call my father,
scribbling the telephone number on a piece of toilet paper with a pencil
stub I had hidden in my shirt, dropping my missile through the window.
He continued to bang the wheels for some time but did faithfully what I
had asked him to do because when we were marched through the railroad
station at eight o'clock, my father (plus the inevitable girlfriend) was waiting near the exit, and though I was handcuffed again, we had a chance to
signal to each other that I had come home again, though my home was to
be Pankrác Prison, and my guards were ethnic Germans from Romania
who had volunteered for the SS and behaved accordingly.*

*The subterranean prison cell into which they pushed me had space for
one or two people, but there were six of us, and I gladly recalled my soli-
tary confinement at Oppeln and the large halls of the Brno slammer. We
were constantly hungry, describing or inventing for each other complicated meals we had once enjoyed at comfortable restaurants, but living together was not easy because one of us was constantly urinating or relieving
himself otherwise, or so it seemed to me in my offended and anachronistic
modesty, and running water was minimal. In the morning, when the
guards banged on our door, the oldest of us had to shout "Alles gesund
(All are healthy)," but that did not stop the guards from rushing in to
dunk our heads in the toilet bowls or taking us out to the corridor to do
special gymnastics—that is, standing for hours with raised hands at the
wall or doing push-ups until we dropped or fainted, in which case we
were resuscitated by being kicked and beaten. Waiting for interrogation or
further transport was even worse; on Wednesday mornings the names were
called of prisoners who were to go to the Small Fort at Terezín, a place of
fatal horrors. One of my fellow Häftlinge, an older student who had been
caught in the Austrian mountains trying to cross over to Switzerland,
heard his name read and suddenly turned deadly pale; I shall never forget
how his face terribly changed within a moment.*

*After a few days it was my turn to be brought to the Pečkárna, formerly
the palatial corporate building of the Petschek banking, coal, and iron en-*

terprises, now Gestapo headquarters. We waited on little chairs, guarded by regular SS, and then were marched upstairs to the anteroom of the investigating official. If I were a writer of fiction, I would write that Markéta was in that room doing her nails, but in fact I must report that she was sitting there, whacking away with two fingers at an old typewriter. I was surprised and a little disappointed by the appearance of the Gestapo man behind his desk. He was rather stocky, dressed in a tightly fitting four-button dark suit, shirt and dark tie, and had longish hair, not cut in a soldierly way at all. (After I had read a lot of Kafka, later, in my imagination he came to resemble one of K.'s henchmen, looking like a tenor in a provincial operetta.) I did not have an opportunity to give the little speech I had prepared in advance. He asked me immediately why I thought I had been arrested, and I told him about the "illegal activities" tablet in my Oppeln prison cell and my meetings with Markéta, the very girl now in the anteroom. He did not seem to value her services very highly and virtually shrugged his shoulders, I thought, as if to suggest that he did not believe a word of what I said about my lack of interest in politics.

He did know almost everything about my family—my mother, who had died in Terezín, and my uncle, in the prison in Dresden—and was most interested in the readings in our apartment. Clearly, somebody had told the German authorities about those gatherings (I began to suspect a young actor, but I did not know for sure), and the Gestapo man had already interviewed my friend Kari, from an old Bohemian aristocratic family. I told myself that at least it would be hard for them to conclude that our meetings were organized by the Communist Party. Yet I did not know what he really wanted; he never raised his voice or screamed but queried me, in an almost professorial way, about the poems and poets we had read and discussed. I talked a lot about the poets of past literary history rather than about contemporary ones. There were moments when I suspected that maybe he was performing an elaborate scene simply to demonstrate that he was an old-fashioned policeman and that he would later try to use me as a witness when Gestapo members went on trial. The interrogation, or rather the examination, was repeated three days later. I was returned to Pankrác Prison and told that I would go on transport to another camp for half Jews again, and that was what happened in the first days of January 1945.

Today I am no longer amazed that the Prague Gestapo man did not in-
terrogate me about Elisabeth. He knew much more about her and her
group than I ever did, and Elisabeth's mother, who got out of prison and
went back to live in Vienna, told me after the war that it was the Gestapo
that had organized and run the little group; it would not have been the
only one. Two Czech historians, Alena Hájková and Dušan Tomášek, who
have written an investigative essay about Elisabeth entitled "They Called
Her Líza" (1988), mention the possibility that the Gestapo successfully
"turned" a Communist Party member of long standing and got him to be
an informer; in any event, on August 6, 1943, all members of the group
were arrested, including Elisabeth, who was first held at Pankrác Prison
and later transferred to the women's unit at the Small Fort at Terezín. On
May 1, 1945, her close friend Hanka was suddenly let go from the Small
Fort, but on May 3 Elisabeth was led into the courtyard and shot, one of
the last Terezín victims of the Nazi terror. (The Gestapo messenger who
brought K. H. Frank's execution orders to the fort was none other than
Commissar Georg Friedrich, the "tenor," who had controlled the group.) I
later found Elisabeth's name—in its Czech version, Alžběta Švarcová—
inscribed on a memorial stone in the Terezín ghetto.

Going to Another Camp

In early January 1945 I was sent from Prague to another camp for half
Jews close to the Bohemian-Saxon border, and I worked there until early
May or perhaps late April, when we ceased cutting timber and instead
searched for potatoes to stay alive. When I arrived in that wintry region, I
was vaguely reminded of the descriptions I had read about nineteenth-
century political prisoners in Siberia. It was not a single camp, in fact,
but an entire system of improvised habitations dispersed all over a broad
plain, strangely empty in the freezing cold, with barracks, shacks, decrepit
old inns crowded by the inevitable palandy, and the hills clad in white
snow. The camp was run by the Organization Todt, directing forestry work
from an office at the village of Natschung, but our dwellings were un-
guarded by either men or dogs. I lived with about fifty men in a former inn
and dance hall in the hamlet of Kallich, where the innkeeper's wife gave

us our daily soup, and we knew that the lonely railway stations were watched by police, that any person moving alone in the snow was visible from miles away, a black spot on treacherous white, and that the post office was out of reach because its employees had been instructed, they told us, that we were enemies of the state. Mail was not to be accepted, and telephone calls could not be made.

Every day we trudged for two hours to an opening in the forest, where we cut timber under the eyes of a tubercular Sudeten foreman who generally kept to himself but showed us city slickers how to use our implements and how not to be killed by a falling tree. Two of us were always delegated to tend a fire in which we toasted our sliced bread or rare potatoes. Our tempo was slow, and we constantly discussed the question of how long the Wehrmacht would hold out, especially in the Alpenfestung, before capitulating to the Allies, and whether we did not sin by contributing to the German war effort. Fortunately our council of wise men (the inevitable engineers) assured us in our daily discussions that there was simply not sufficient transport available to move the timber to where it may have been wanted, and it seemed that our Sudeten foreman did not think it would be moved ever. We knew a good deal about the situation on the war fronts; a lucky few of my colleagues had been secretly approached by village women (their men off being soldiers somewhere) to fix electric wiring or radios, and they listened to the news whenever possible. Our gurus, including a few Communists, were of the opinion, accepted at the campfire meetings, that it was important to work as slowly as possible and not to challenge the Germans openly in the last dangerous months of the war because our camp, if indeed it was one, offered us a good chance to survive. The conversations were erudite and important, including those on the latrine, which was a smooth tree over an evil-smelling ditch. I sat there almost every evening with Emil Radok, the future critic and philosopher, talking about Marxist aesthetics, expressionist theater, and Soviet movies we remembered from earlier times.

Roughly halfway between our little former dance hall and a wooden shack in which another group of timbermen, so to speak, slept rose a stone house on a hilltop, the abode of the master forester who walked around in a romantic green uniform with a hunter's gun slung over his shoulder. He was pale, never said a word, looked as if he felt very uneasy, but, if I remember correctly, let us have a sack of potatoes when we were really hungry in the first days of spring. I recall him because he was turned into a character in a movie about the German-Czech borderlands written after May 1945 by a fellow timberman. In the movie, the master forester is the archevil figure, snarling devilishly, almost with blood dripping from his unnatural fangs—clearly a case of the ideological special effects department.

The realities were often far more surprising. One day we were marching to work as usual when about halfway along, where a few trees clustered along the road, a man emerged from the trees and began to look around. It was my father, clad in a city winter coat, black hat, silk scarf, and elegant half shoes, as if stepping out of the Prague Café Savarin. We embraced, my fellow timbermen closed ranks around son and father to protect us from the view of anybody passing, but nobody did, he gave me recent news about my uncle in the Dresden prison and the Allies advancing, and he dug into a little leather bag to hand me a stick of dry salami, which we later sliced thinly at our fire. We walked together for a while, my astonished colleagues and I and my father, the only person from the outside ever to infiltrate our isolation, and at another bend in the road, he jumped into the trees again and disappeared as quickly as he had come.

In the evening we slept on our straw palandy, exhausted more by marching to and from the forest clearing than by actual work, but one evening somebody told us to get out quickly and watch the northern sky; something was burning in the distance, and the clouds on the horizon were red and yellow, in constant and silent change for hours, far into the night and early morning. We walked up and down and stared. Our gurus said it must be Dresden on fire after an Allied air raid, and they were right: it was the night of February 13, 1945. We were watching the conflagration from a distance of more than a hundred miles, and found out only much later that Allied planes had also bombed Prague then. I did not know that Uncle Karl had escaped from the Dresden prison that night or that W. W. in Prague was killed instantly by a bomb during the raid on February 14. We were convinced the Dresden conflagration signaled the coming end of our camp time, and then another event showed us that our forests were not outside history.

One day in March the police and the Todt people made one of their *rare appearances. They marched in, ordered us to line up (some of my fellow timbermen, fearing the worst, discreetly withdrew to the nearby edge of the forest), and a police officer and a local woman looked us over closely, one by one. The woman had been raped in the forest, and we were the prime suspects, but she was honest enough to admit that she could not find the perpetrator among us. We were dismissed, and we assumed that the deed had been done by one of the German deserters hiding in the nearby border mountains.*

Spring came in sputteringly, the sun was warm sometimes, the snow was slowly melting, and we were hungrier than ever. The daily soup was terribly thin, sans noodles, and the wise men were talking about Allied airplanes flying low and strafing trains everywhere, disrupting the transport of German soldiers and goods (potatoes). We had many discussions around the fire about how to organize something to eat. Some people advanced the idea that at night we should break into a few outlying houses and take what we needed by force, but others objected that it was too early to do that: the German system was still dangerously intact, and Franz, our lonely, wispy Hamburg Communist, who prided himself on having been a member of a revolutionary KPD nudist group, absolutely refused to use force against people who were obviously poor and our potential allies in the class conflicts yet to come.

I held on to the theory that our best potato source would be the village parishes and the cooks of village priests. Clergy would possibly sympathize with our plight, and equally important, they lived in stone buildings with cellars full of potatoes. Unfortunately there were only two parishes close to our shacks, the one down in the village and the other about three miles to the north. One March Sunday I walked through the forest to the neighboring village of G., where I arrived after mass, knocked at the door of the stone manse, and was welcomed by two women, the cook and her sister, who were just sitting down to an early lunch. Their vegetable soup was wonderfully thick, I told my story (possibly somewhat overstating the number of believing Catholics in our shack), and they gave me a paper bag full of potatoes. It was pretty heavy, and on my way back I sat down near a little pool to rest. The water was calm, a bird was flitting up and down, a few clouds were scattered across the blue sky, and I suddenly had a curious feeling, a hesitant first foretaste of peace, almost.

Of course I also went a-begging to the parish house down in the nearby village, where I was immediately invited to a simple evening meal. The village priest turned out to be well informed about us and about the decaying regime. He had two bicycles, and he needed one to visit his parishioners, but he offered me the other on a kind of lend-lease procedure if I wished to go home at one point in the future. He listened to the radio constantly, he said, and warned me that the army of Field Marshal Schörner was marching from the north toward Prague. I was eager to leave, and when the priest told me a few days later that Hitler had committed suicide in his Berlin bunker, I asked him for the bike to prepare for my return. It was a mistake. When I was pushing the bike up the hill to reach our barracks, I was overtaken by a band of SS men who declared that I was their prisoner, to be shot within three hours. They locked me up in a shack on the hill and threw the bike in after me.

I sat there remembering our wise men, who had always said that the last days of the war would be the most dangerous ones. Since I did not have any watch, time went by very, very slowly. It was ridiculous, I thought, to be picked up by a chance band of SS men, after so many adventures. When about three hours must have passed, I looked through the fissures of the wooden boards only to discover that the landscape was empty. There was not a soldier in sight. Using the clerical bike to ram the flimsy door, I stepped out into the open.

It is difficult to say when we half Jews and occasional timbermen were really free again, for in the mountains close to the border change came on cat's paws and day by day. There was no single Technicolor scene with tanks rolling in, music playing and liberated people embracing. We knew, though dimly, from second- and thirdhand reports about radio bulletins, that the regime was crumbling and that the Allies were triumphantly advancing everywhere. As desperate April came, we marched off to cut timber a few times, our tubercular Sudeten foreman dozing at our fire, but then a Wehrmacht battalion suddenly appeared in our village, and we had to build some tank traps on the mountain road, barricading it with heavy trees, though the unkempt Wehrmacht contingent was not particularly interested in our efficiency. After forty-eight hours it disappeared again without a trace.

We heard from the central camp office that a few of the Organization

Todt bureaucrats had left rather abruptly, and in our endless discussions two groups began to form, one believing that we should immediately march to Prague and the other, the Realpolitiker, *arguing that the road to Prague was still blocked by Schörner's army and we had little chance to get through. Something had to be done, and when we got hold of our papers, which had been taken from the central office where our fellow timbermen had hanged the last remaining Todt man by the neck, or so we were told, I returned the bike to the priest and decided to walk to the little town in the valley to see what would happen there.*

The Prague Uprising

The Prague uprising of May 5–9, 1945, in the last moments of the war, had been expected and prepared for by many military and political groups as well as by Prague citizens from every walk of life. Plans were not unified, at least not in the beginning, and the headiness of the days of the liberation was an element in the tumult of resistance, as people responded to surprising changes in the situation: to the ongoing, improvised negotiations of Czech and German institutions, both legitimate and far less so, through the days and nights; to the unexpected appearance of General Andrei Vlasov's troops, Soviet soldiers who had joined the Wehrmacht but now suddenly changed sides and wanted to fight the Germans; to potential conflicts between Czech liberals and Communists who had well-defined, if not dogmatic, ideas about how an "anti-Fascist" fight of the "people" should proceed; and, ultimately, to the differences of viewpoint between the Prague revolutionaries and the Czechoslovak government, which returned from its London exile on May 10.

Prague did not give the signal for a great uprising against the German occupying forces. The Soviet Army entered Brno on April 26; Ostrava on April 30. Then, on May 1, an open revolt flared up in the Moravian town of Přerov, between the two, where a national council took over but was overwhelmed by returning Germans, who shot some of its members. In Prague, preparations to unify different resistance organizations, or what was left of them after they had been decimated

by the Gestapo, which had informers in these groups, had been substantially progressing in the winter of 1945, and by late February the
Česka národní rada (Czech National Council) emerged as an inclusive, if fragile, political body to guide the uprising.

The ČNR originally consisted of people from the Rada 3, Council
of Three, continuing the traditions of the Obrana národa (In Defense
of the Nation, DN) and PVVZ (Petitions Committee), which favored a
liberal and national republic; representatives of the Central Council of
Trade Unions, who were nominally left Social Democrats but for all
practical purposes Communists; and delegates of the Fourth (interim)
Central Committee of the Communist Party, quickly established after
the Gestapo had arrested the entire Third Central Committee in a surprise raid as late as March 7, 1945. The ČNR was originally on the left,
at any rate more so than the returning Czechoslovak government, and
its members were taken aback to hear that the latter was insisting that
the future republic would restore the democratic party system (perhaps with the exception of the conservative Agrarians) and was somewhat reluctantly deciding to widen its membership. In the absence of
weapons, which were never delivered in sufficient numbers, though
Philip Nichols, British ambassador to Beneš's government and later to
Prague, heroically intervened with Churchill, attitudes were rather
hesitant, and even the Communists asked the comrades, on May 3, to
keep their powder dry and wait.

Military affairs were no less complicated than political ones. At
least two command groups, established independently of the ČNR,
were ready to strike. The Alex Commando, the last remnant of the DN,
waited until late April to move General František Slunečko from the
Bohemian countryside to Prague, but Alex established its own civilian
National Committee, which quickly withered away; Slunečko recognized the authority of the ČNR, which at a meeting on May 2 appointed General Karel Kutlvašr to be military commander of Prague.
The groundwork was laid for the taking of radio stations and telephone
exchanges. Commando Bartoš was busy mobilizing the former cus-
toms officers and other uniformed units, but in the meantime the
ČNR had organized its own military commission, chaired by Captain
Jaromír Nechanský, who in January 1945 had been dropped in the

parachutist group Platinum-Pewter from England to run the radio connection to London. The problem was that the Prague citizens began to rise up without much regard to military planning or the orders of the hesitant ČNR. From the confusion, and with the willingness of the military groups and commissions to work with one another, a military command structure emerged, with General Kutlvašr in charge and František Bürger as his chief of staff, by which time the uprising was exploding on the streets.

It all started in the most old-fashioned way when on May 4 post office and railway employees, possibly upon orders of the Ministry of Transport, began to remove signs and announcements written in German and tram conductors refused to take German coins. Then, in a first step taken away from the old habits of the occupation, a transport of returning camp prisoners going through the suburb of Vršovice triggered open public protests in the streets. On May 5 events took a more decisive turn, though many groups and the ČNR still hesitated to call for immediate action. In the morning Czechoslovak flags went up on most public buildings, including the National Theater, restless groups demonstrated all over downtown, and at the convenient hour of 9:00 a.m. Commando Alex met to consider its orders.

At the Fochova Street building of the radio station, announcers had begun to broadcast solely in Czech, but by 11:45 a strong group of SS had arrived to strengthen the German guards there. Simultaneously, the Czech protectorate police command gave orders to occupy the radio station. Around noon a group of armed policemen drove from headquarters to Fochova Street, where fierce fighting erupted, and shortly after 12:30 the Czech announcers called for help: "Czech people are being murdered at the radio station!" Their call was heard all over Prague, and at this first public signal of a military uprising against German forces armed men came over the roofs and from neighboring houses to help. Ninety Czechs died there in battle. Strangely enough, Alex and Bartoš were still waiting for General Kutlvašr, who appeared on the scene only at 2:40, but at City Hall power changed hands. Not until the evening did the ČNR, encouraged by a broadcast from London recognizing its legitimacy, introduce itself over the airwaves to the city's fighting citizens. Professor Albert Pražák, representing the "cultural world," was chairman, his first deputy the Communist Josef Smrkovský, his second the Social Democrat Josef Kotrlý; three deputy chairpeople represented "revolutionary peasants," Catholics, and National Liberals (this was the sociologist Otakar Machotka, of Beneš's party). A radical trade union man functioned as general secretary.

The Germans were in the beginning as hesitant as the Czechs to engage in ultimate battle. The Wehrmacht had more than eight thousand and the SS more than four thousand men in Prague itself, but that morning they were mostly intent on holding their positions and resolving the issue of who would be responsible for their operational decisions. (It was General Rudolf Toussaint.) Frank and the SD, together with the Gestapo, played out their final attempts to negotiate with what was left of the protectorate government or quickly to create a last one, but Richard Bienert, who had been chief of government since January, was arrested at City Hall. And when the Gestapo tried to assemble a group of prominent Czech political prisoners to discuss the situation with them, it failed utterly because none of the prisoners was willing to be used in this way. Negotiations between German and Czech groups went on all day and far beyond midnight. The ČNR failed to establish contact with Frank for purely technical reasons, while other groups and commanders sent delegates to their German counterparts to discuss aspects of a local armistice. Late at night an important Czech delegation, including General Kutlvašr and Captain Nechanský, confronted SS General Karl Friedrich von Pückler, but they refused to accept his brazen ultimatum.

The real battle for Prague started a few hours after midnight on May 6, when four columns of Wehrmacht and SS troops were moved from outlying districts toward Prague. Czech broadcasts vainly called on U.S. and British aircraft to bomb the road from Benešov to Prague, on which SS tanks had begun to move, and barricades went up all over the city in heavy rain. The dawn brought brutal fighting on the suburban roads, ongoing negotiations between Frank's office and the ČNR, and recurrent Luftwaffe raids on the city center. In the late afternoon a bomb practically destroyed the Fochova Street radio station, but broadcasting continued from the Strašnice transmitter.

Then, suddenly, the Russian troops under General A. A. Vlasov,

called the Russian Liberation Army, which since 1943 had collaborated with the Wehrmacht to fight the Red Army, switched sides. The
returning Czechoslovak government broadcast its utter disapproval of
the Vlasovci, however, and this created almost insoluble problems for
the ČNR. It commenced hectic negotiations with Captain R. L. Antonov on behalf of General S. K. Buňačenko representing Vlasov, the
result of which was that the Vlasovci agreed to fight the Germans "in
full accordance" with Czech command, and immediately and valiantly
engaged the advancing SS, especially near the outlying towns of
Chuchle and Zbraslav. First Deputy Chairman Smrkovský declared
that American troops were only fifty kilometers away from the fighting
city, and American tanks were expected momentarily. But Commando
Bartoš, charged with gathering and evaluating information, was not
and could not have been informed about U.S. intentions.

On May 7 the Prague uprising entered a critical phase. Though
most of the German battle groups were positioned on the approaches
to Prague, columns from Milovice, including tanks, fought their way to
Karlín, a district in the west of the city close to the Vltava River, and
advanced to a line from the Hybernská railway station to Poříčí Park. In
the city center, heavy fighting continued at the radio building, nearby
at the National Museum, and at the main railroad station, where the
Germans succeeded in taking prisoner all the Czechs working there in
the traffic department while Czech defenders in the freight yards held
their positions against deadly machine-gun fire.

The Vlasov soldiers fought on bravely, but conflicts within their
command, and between their command and the ČNR, intensified.
When a Vlasov emissary was able to ascertain that the American Army
would not proceed toward Prague, General Buňačenko gave the order
to withdraw to the west, leaving behind a small group of his soldiers
fighting with the Czechs on their own. Three hundred men had died,
and many hundreds were wounded; these latter were not treated mercifully by Soviet soldiers later on. Frank and the ČNR continued their
talks, Frank hoping for a political solution, the ČNR insisting on capitulation. In faraway Reims, however, Field Marshal Alfred Jodl, acting
on behalf of the government of Grand Admiral Karl Dönitz (charged by
Hitler, before he committed suicide, to rule Germany after his death),

signed the unconditional surrender of all German forces, with fighting
to end entirely on midnight of May 8.

People in Prague could not understand why the Americans did not
come, but at least Captain Russell Hill of *The New York Herald Tribune*
appeared to write an article about the situation, and late at night an
American delegation under the command of Major C. O. Dowd and
including a captured German officer arrived, not as an advance guard
of General Patton's Third Army but in search of the German headquarters, in order to communicate to the Germans the terms of the unconditional surrender. Later it turned out that the American intelligence
had a few men working in Prague, but when one of them, Sergeant
Kurt Taub (who happened to be the son of a prominent member of the
German Social Democrats in Brno), suggested to the ČNR that it send
a delegation to the American command, nothing came of it. The Americans already knew that the Soviet armies were rapidly approaching.

The citizens of Prague fighting in the streets did not know that the
question of who would move first to Berlin or to Prague had been an
incisive issue of political and military significance, involving the general staffs of the Allied armies, as well as Churchill, Truman, and
Stalin personally. Churchill was untiring in his efforts to push the
Americans to occupy Prague before the Soviets because he believed
(as did many Czechs) that the American presence would change the
entire postwar situation of Czechoslovakia. He turned to Truman, but
the American president was inclined to leave what he considered a
military matter to his generals, and George C. Marshall, U.S. Army
chief of staff, was unwilling "to hazard American lives for purely political purposes." His view was fully shared by the five-star general
Dwight Eisenhower, who agreed with Soviet Chief of Staff General
A. I. Antonov that the advancing American forces would respect a stop
line in the west of Bohemia and not advance toward Prague. Churchill
once more turned to Truman, but in vain, and when, on May 4, 1945,
General Patton received orders to move onward to Czechoslovakia, he
was also told that he had to respect the line agreed upon earlier
by Eisenhower and the Soviets, which ran from České Budějovice
(Budweis) and Plzeň (Pilsen) to Karlové Vary (Karlsbad). Patton noted
in his diary that Eisenhower evidently did not wish to be involved in

international complications but that he personally would not have minded moving on eastward to the Vltava River. Yet Patton followed orders (this time) whatever he privately thought about them.

The Prague uprising had started spontaneously, and the Allies were no less surprised by its force than the Czechoslovak government-in-exile or the Communists, who could not believe that citizens had rebelled without being guided by party operatives. When Communist ministers in the Czechoslovak government first heard about it, they were primarily concerned whether events really conformed to the prescribed idea of an anti-Fascist revolution of the people. Only after recurrent confirmation that the American Army would not proceed beyond the Plzeň-Karlové Vary line did Stalin give orders on May 7 to start Operation Prague immediately. The First, Second, and Third Ukrainian armies, after fierce fighting in Prussia, Saxony, and Moravia, changed course to advance to central Bohemia, then still under the control of the German Armee-Mitte (Army of the Center).

In Prague, fighting went on through the early morning of May 8, with German tanks pushing their way through Holešovice and Karlín to the city center. By morning they had arrived at the Old Town Square. The City Hall and other historic buildings went up in flames. Dispirited Czech fighters, lacking ammunition, ceded their positions, while many citizens, in panic, tried to escape to Czech-held parts of town. Yet General Toussaint knew that he could save his men only by leaving Prague immediately for the West and for U.S. captivity. A German and a ČNR delegation met at 11:00 a.m. and for five hours worked on a formal agreement concerning the German withdrawal, which would begin immediately; light and heavy weapons were to be left to the Czechs, and German civilians who did not join the exodus were entrusted to the care of the International Red Cross. The capitulation agreement was signed at 4:00 p.m. and broadcast in both Czech and German; the exodus of thousands of German soldiers and civilians—healthy and sick, men and women, old and young, among them Frank with his wife and children—began within a few hours and lasted through the night.

Shortly after midnight, tanks of D. D. Leljushenko's First Army reached Prague's outlying suburbs, followed by General P. S. Rybalko's troops, and throughout the morning and afternoon of May 9 tanks of the Second and the Fourth Ukrainian armies streamed into the city and, together with Czech units, in often fierce battle defeated the last SS groups holding out at the Barrandov and elsewhere. The historian Stanislav Kokoška says that 1,694 Czechs died in battle and suggests approximate numbers for German (1,000), Vlasov (300), and Soviet (20) losses.

Prague's citizens celebrated the arrival of the Soviet soldiers in an overwhelming wave of emotions, flowers, embraces, flags, and sincere gratitude, and they had little reason to heed the rumors of the misconduct of Soviet troops in distant Moravian villages. Ancient Pan-Slav hopes merged with the sudden joy that the occupation and the war had ended. On the streets and in official celebrations poets, politicians, and generals dedicated themselves to the idea of Czechoslovak-Soviet brotherhood.

On May 10 the Czechoslovak government, firmly organized along the lines of a national front of selected political parties, including a powerful group of Communists, arrived at Prague Airport, and the diminishment of the uprising and resistance started right away. President Beneš, who was expected a few days later by train, had consistently praised the heroism of the uprising, but his chief of government, Zdeněk Fierlinger, nominally a Social Democrat yet in the service of the Stalinists, immediately expressed the nation's gratitude to the Soviet Union, which had liberated the city and rescued its ancient glories, threatened by fire and destruction.

On May 11 a series of meetings brought together members of the government and the ČNR, but it was a foregone conclusion that the latter would be transformed into a kind of regional council (zemský výbor) of rather uncertain jurisdiction. Professor and Chairman Albert Pražák wisely preferred to return to the university and to start his lectures again; ČNR members met with increasing distrust.

It was V. A. Zorin, Soviet ambassador and Stalin's watchdog in Prague, who on May 31, defined in a formal note the principal accusations against the ČNR members, saying that it "had prepared in advance the rescue of the German Army" and therefore deprived itself of "the sympathies of the Soviet Army" as well as of "the Czechoslovak government." This last was a curiously inappropriate statement. The accusations were directed principally against Comrade Smrkovský and those who had signed the German capitulation; within a week Smrkovský and Kotrlý were stripped of their new functions in the regional council and five officers were soon stripped of their commissions in the Czechoslovak Army. Yet everything was done secretly: Smrkovský "resigned for reasons of health," Kotrlý was sent on a diplomatic mission to Canada, and of the five officers, at least three (Kutlvašr, Bürger, and Nechanský) were saved, though the other two had to suffer the consequences. On October 10 Smrkovský launched his own attack against his ČNR colleagues, accusing them of having started the uprising too early, but he was a marked man; later he was imprisoned on charges of being a Gestapo agent and shunted into administrative jobs in rural farm collectives and ministerial bureaucracies.

A year later, when Augusta Müllerová, the only woman member of the ČNR and a loyal comrade, wrote about her experiences, she programmatically ignored General Kutlvašr and Kotrlý and paved the way for another prominent Communist, who declared that the uprising was really directed by the Central Council of Trade Unions and not the ČNR at all. It was piteous to see the ČNR, or rather the regional council, now clad only in the tatters of its moral authority of yesteryear, supporting the demands of the Communists (for instance, the fulfillment of a Two-Year Plan). On February 21, 1948, the ČNR members were asked to sign a declaration in favor of the Communists' taking power, and three members refused; among them was Otakar Machotka, who went into exile and published an essay about his experiences. The ČNR had outlived itself, and the Communists did not see any reasons for its further services.

Between War and Peace

Descending from the border mountains to the valleys, I had a certain advantage because I knew where I was going. My school friend Kari suggested that if I needed to, I should try to reach the castle of Prince H., his distant relative, who, it turned out, owned the forest in which we were working. When Kari mentioned the name, I was rather skeptical and had an inkling that I would be utterly out of place in that upper crust. I was right but not entirely; when I knocked at the stately back door kitchen entrance, I was welcomed by two motherly Czech cooks, who by that time were used to feeding people wandering in from the woods. I told them about Kari; one of them left to speak to the lady in charge, returned, apologized for the prince, who could not see me because he was busy packing before leaving for western Bohemia, now occupied by the Americans, and told me that a room was ready for me right away. It was small and adjacent to theirs, but there was a real bed, with a cover and a pillow, they pressed a cup of real coffee into my hands, and it felt like paradise.

Not for long, though. I had hardly closed my eyes when one of the cooks returned, told me that there was a German soldier positioning a machine gun in the kitchen garden and that I should tell him to move elsewhere. That's exactly what I tried to do. He was about my age. I told him that firing his machine gun would certainly attract an enemy response that would endanger the two women in the kitchen. He insisted he had orders, like a good pupil, yet when I came back to the kitchen, he had gone, and the two patriotic cooks, who I noticed were beginning to put together Czechoslovak flags on their rattling Singer sewing machine, thanked me profusely.

The machine gunner from Schörner's army had moved off, but that was still not the end of a long day. I was tired from the march down the mountains and half asleep when a white-haired thin old lady came into my room quietly. She introduced herself as Countess So-and-So (I forget the name), said she was a refugee from Silesia, where the family estate had been lost to the advancing Soviet Army, and told me she was set to join her host, the prince, the next morning on the trek to the American occupation line in the west. She was concerned about a few things left to her and asked me whether I would be willing to protect the family jewels overnight in my room. She handed me a little leather pouch. At first I did not know what to do. Take the pouch and requisition everything in the name of the Republic soon to be reestablished, or help her? Later it occurred to me that my business-minded father would have suggested a convenient deal, or cut, of 10 or 25 percent. As it happened, my political ideas gave way to a more basic instinct to help the old woman, who looked like my grandmother, and in my ideological incapability to live up to the historic moment, I put the pouch under my pillow and slept on it, undisturbed, during that last night of the war.

In the morning the lady came again and took back the pouch. Soon a few automobiles crowded with feudal refugees speedily left for Karlovy Vary and the U.S. occupation zone. The motherly cooks had ready an ample breakfast, even eggs, now that the prince was gone, and they told me that the nearby radio factory was opening up and would distribute its radios, which had been produced for the Wehrmacht, free to the local citizens. I should run and line up to get one of them.

It was a strange day, or so it seemed to me. Definitely spring, but the air was cool, the shops were closed, and only a few people were on the street, scurrying back and forth. I found the radio factory, waited for my turn, nobody asked any questions, and I received a Wehrmacht radio of the latest design and carried it back to the kitchen, where the cooks were serving a second breakfast to Tanja, the Ukrainian household help, who was afraid of what would happen to her after the Soviets arrived, and Vladimír, a young man of my age who had worked as a bookkeeper somewhere close by. Vladimír insisted that something had to be done to show that the spirit of the Czechoslovak Republic was alive and well even before the Soviet troops came, and he convinced me that we should go to the marketplace and watch or possibly take over the police station there if it could be done. We packed our tricolor flag, which the cooks had sewn, marched off, and took up position at the fringes of the marketplace, totally empty. On the way we had picked up two infantry guns and some ammunition that retreating German soldiers had left in the ditches—there were enough weapons for entire battalions—and Vladimír, the more military mind, began to fire at the police station. After he showed me how to handle the ammunition and pull the trigger, I followed his example.

We made a good deal of noise, and our fire was returned from the windows. We fired from a ditch and were well protected, but a ricocheting police bullet hurt Vladimír's hand. Though he bled profusely, it was only a superficial wound, but he could no longer pull a trigger, so I had to bang away as fast as possible, as if I were an entire group of partisans descended from the mountains. The police responded sporadically, and ultimately a white rag was shown through the door. After I stopped firing, two middle-aged Schupos or Schutzpolizei—that is, ordinary policemen—waving white rags, appeared in the door and then quickly disappeared between the houses. I would have fired at them in spite of the white rags if they had been SS, but I was not sufficiently trained to shoot two potbellied Schupos, so we let them go. We would not have known what to do with them anyway. After a while Vladimír and I went into the police station, destroyed the Führer and Himmler portraits on the wall, and immediately looked for a first-aid box to bandage Vladimír's hand.

All afternoon we heard faraway artillery fire, which toward evening came nearer, like sudden thunder. We had raised the tricolor on our precinct and were about to lock the door when we heard a knock and women's voices. We opened, and there stood three nurses, in full starched regalia, asking us to hide them for the night. The Russians were arriving, other women had fled into the forests, smearing ashes all over their faces to appear old and haggard, but they had to work the next day in the hospital. Vladimír, who suggested to me that we would perhaps be rewarded for this later, decided we would hide them in the cellar, where they took care of his hand with expert precision, and then we closed the trapdoor behind them. Upstairs we listened to the police radio, with military news and jazz coming from an American station not so far away. Then we heard terrible noises, explosions, commandos, small-arms fire, the screeching and clanging of many tanks moving. We assumed this was the Soviets fighting the rear guard of Schörner's army.

Toward morning everything calmed down and somebody knocked at our door. It was a Soviet officer, possibly attracted by our tricolor in a sea of white cloth hanging from German windows. He greeted us formally, addressing us as comrades and partisans, and we were so moved that we promptly and conveniently forgot the three German nurses in the cellar. He gave me a big pistol, which was fully loaded, the ammunition being visible because the magazine was made of some kind of translucent stuff. We stepped out, into the world of peace, and the first thing I noticed was the corpse of a man, or a woman, completely flattened under the chains of a heavy tank, the brains spattered into the dust of the marketplace.

Revolutionary Retribution?

Patriotic images of liberation from the Nazis easily celebrate flags, flowers, and courageous citizens in jackets, ties, and steel helmets, leaning over barricades to take aim at advancing tanks. But they tend to ignore what happened on the streets and squares of Prague, Paris, and other cities when disheveled real collaborators or suspected ones, as well as German soldiers and civilians, were killed indiscriminately. The last battles of the war were a school not of humanity but of bloody retaliation. The German troops, especially the SS, fighting their way into Prague from outlying training camps fought with medieval brutality. At Psáry, thirteen Czechs were shot, the youngest sixteen years old; at Březany another thirteen prisoners were killed; at Pankrác SS men of Group Jörchel murdered thirty-seven persons in a cellar, including ten children from six to fifteen, ten women (two of them pregnant), and seventeen men; and at one of the railway stations Czech defenders were taken prisoner and then mowed down by by machine guns.

In early April, K. H. Frank had issued a proclamation allowing German women, children, and old people to leave Prague if they did not have to work and if they knew where to go in the Reich, but tens of thousands of refugees from the east or from bombed-out regions within the city did not know where to turn. The German command was then relying on twelve thousand men in the city and thirty thousand more in the training camps and small garrisons nearby. During the night of the capitulation, possibly as many as twenty-five thousand soldiers and civilians left Prague, but the paragraph of the capitulation agreement that put German women and children under the protection of the International Red Cross was illusionary. (There was an ICRC delegate in Prague, but his few people were busy in Terezín.)

The end of the occupation was the beginning of the expulsion of German civilians, if they had survived the first hours and days of brutality. Retaliation was blind. An old woman was defenestrated; a member of a visiting German orchestra was beaten to death in the street because he could not speak Czech; others, not all of them Gestapo members, were hanged, doused with gas and lit, as living torches. Enraged mobs roamed through hospitals to find easy victims there. One was a Czech patient, who happened to be the father of the writer Michal Mareš, but his papers listed a Sudeten birthplace. From May until mid-October official statistics listed 3,795 suicides of Germans in Bohemia.

Germans were evacuated to dozens of different places in Prague—

cinemas, schools, sports stadiums, garages—and from there expelled
to interim camps in the countryside nearby; by June nearly thirty thousand had been transported out of the city. Revolutionary Guards (RG,
often called robber guards by some skeptical fellow citizens) did not
differentiate between *Reichsdeutsche*, Germans who had come with
the occupying forces, and native Prague Germans whose families had
been living in the city for generations. (In Prague's municipal elections
of May 22, 1938, one-quarter of the twenty thousand German-speaking
voters had voted for the anti-Nazi Bloc of Democratic Citizens, and
not all of them were Jewish.) Some groups were transported to occupied Germany within months, while other families had to survive in
different camps for a year or more before being expelled from the
country in cattle trains.

Sigrid John-Tumler, a Prague native who is now a Berlin psychoanalyst, in a radio talk some years ago described her experiences, shared
by many Germans. She carefully noted that the expulsion of Germans
from Prague was not a singular "act of willfulness" but "the consequence of the preceding Nazi aggression," and though she herself was
one of the Germans expelled, she insisted on the distinction between
the "cold-blooded Nazi liquidation of millions of people" and the "expulsion following an aggressive war." The John family spent the last
days of the war in their cellar, though actual air raids were rare, and after their Czech maid, Tonča, left on the morning of May 8, Frau John
and her three daughters prepared little bags for themselves with a few
necessities; this was none too early, because on the next day the
concierge appeared with his inevitable wife (who immediately swiped
an old clock) and announced that they had to leave their apartment
right away and join the Germans of the district who were assembling
on Štrossmayerovo náměstí (Strossmayer Square). Fortunately Frau
John was able to leave the apartment keys with an uncle (of partly Jewish origin who had survived in the apartment above) and, with the help
of a friendly Czech guard, to return to the apartment later to fetch
clothes for the children.

At Strossmayer Square, busy men walked around with paint in
buckets, painting swastikas on the backs of each of the Germans; the
prisoners were then packed off to a local cinema, where they spent

several days and nights on the seats and in the corridors. A man in the balcony committed suicide and, falling over the railing, hurt the people below. In the darkness and flashing their lights, Soviet soldiers came to pick and rape women on the spot. Frau John rescued her older daughter by offering the soldier her wristwatch. From the movie house the prisoners were moved to a school and later to the Loreto Monastery; and from there to the Letná Sports Stadium to spend six weeks under the open and hot sky, with little food, and skin disease; the children were eager to see the corpses carried away each day, not completely covered on the trucks.

Rumors were rife that prisoners would be delivered to the Americans, but one day the prisoners were marched off to the railway station and transported to the Small Fort at Terezín. There women, children, and men were separated; the women afflicted by lice were shaved by female guards and pushed into a room with showers. One young woman, kicking and screaming that now all of them would be gassed, calmed down only when the water began to dribble from the showerheads. In the fall of 1946, after another four weeks in a quarantine camp, the John family was finally transported to the German border, where they threw away the white armbands that signaled they were German before crossing over. They were "free but homeless," they said.

The policies, if not the practice, of massive expulsions were, if one looks closely, the only victory of the home resistance over the government-in-exile, or rather over President Beneš, who had long wavered over what the resuscitated republic would do with the Germans. Both the members of the exiled government and the people in the resistance had shared in the tragedy and utter humiliation of the Munich Conference, but then their ways had parted, and the daily experience in Prague of resisting, of actually confronting the deadly Nazi terror over the next six years, differed profoundly from that of the exiled government, which despite the German air raids on London continued to think and act in an atmosphere of memorandums and negotiations and continued to sustain the European idea of a postwar Czechoslovak Republic as a multiethnic state.

President Beneš long held to his guiding principle of restoring the territorial, if not liberal, integrity of the republic destroyed by Munich, which meant a republic of which Germans were still an integral part. He moved, for a considerable time, between the idea of merely reducing the number of Germans in Czechoslovakia by border adjustments, even giving up several border regions, and that of transferring the guilty Germans to Germany. The situation was complicated by the fact that in the Czechoslovak Army camps in the west—in Agde, France, and in Cholmondeley, England—many young Jewish soldiers were protesting against the anti-Semitism of some of their officers. (Ten percent of all soldiers in the Czechoslovak Army abroad gave German as their mother tongue.) Beneš for a long time continued discussions with Wenzel Jaksch, chairman of the Sudeten German Social Democrats, even holding out the prospect that Germans might take a number of seats in the exiled Czechoslovak State Council, but these were broken off in the spring of 1943, when Jaksch, disappointed and frustrated, told his younger followers to enlist in the British rather than the Czechoslovak Army. Though a few members of the exiled government, including Jan Masaryk, the former president's son, and the Social Democrat Rudolf Bechyně, considered mass expulsions of Germans foolish or wrong, in the days of the Heydrich terror and of Lidice their colleagues listened more to broadcasts from home than to them. Meanwhile the non-Communist home resistance in Prague constantly protested against having any dealings with the Germans, anti-Fascist or not, declared both before and after Heydrich's murder that it would not tolerate any German presence on Czech territory, and late in the war the Council of Three sent a message to London that Germans and returning Jews speaking German would not be welcome in Czechoslovakia.

Many of Prague's German-speaking intellectuals and writers, liberals or of the left and often of Jewish origin, had joined President Beneš in exile or returned from German concentration camps only to see that the new republic wanted to live without them. Prague's German literature, once so famous and productive, was condemned to continue in exile at least for the time being. Of the older poets, Paul Leppin died three weeks before the Prague uprising (his wife was expelled, and died a year later). The expressionist Paul Adler, who had survived (if it is possible to use the term, for he was totally paralyzed) in a mixed marriage, died in

Zbraslav, near Prague, in the summer of 1946 and was buried not far from Franz Kafka. Communists loyal to the party were able to serve in the German Democratic Republic: F. C. Weiskopf, who in exile in New York had published an important anthology of Czechoslovak writing, joined the Czechoslovak diplomatic service and was posted to faraway places, including Beijing; he later edited a literary journal in East Berlin. The poet Louis Fürnberg turned up as deputy director of the Goethe-Schiller Memorial Institute at Weimar. The Socialist and novelist Ernst Sommer, originally from Moravia, continued writing in London until a fatal illness intervened; he died in 1955. And Johannes Urzidil, who did not give up hope that Bohemian Germans could be reeducated in the spirit of democracy, stayed in New York, went on writing his popular tales and novels in German, and died on a lecture tour in Rome, where he was buried at the Campo Santo Teutonico in November 1970. H. G. Adler, who had returned to his native Prague from the camps, in the fall of 1947 left for London, where he completed his pioneering sociological analyses of Terezín, continued to write poetry and novels, and received the distinguished Charles Veillon and Leo Baeck awards. He died in 1988 in his London exile.

Přemysl Pitter was among the very few Czechs who lived through the years of the protectorate and continued to believe that Germans or, for that matter, any nation should not be judged collectively. After the last day of fighting, he set out for Terezín and the new Czech internment camps for Germans to rescue children and to direct attention to the inhumane conditions in both the old and new camps. Pitter was a Protestant Christian in the Hussite tradition; he philosophically tended to Tolstoy, Masaryk, and the Czech philosopher Emanuel Rádl, but he was a practical rather than an erudite man, and after he had visited Hitler's Germany in the early 1930s, to learn more about the situation there, he opened a home for neglected children, including those of German political refugees streaming into Czechoslovakia. By 1938 he had established a children's sanitarium at Mýto, near Rokycany, ready to care for the children both of Sudeten refugees and of Jewish parents, and in his periodical *Sbratření* (Brotherhood), which was published between 1924 and 1941, he unerringly wrote against the vice of nationalism and, quoting Masaryk, against anti-Semitism.

Right after the liberation of Prague, Pitter and his Swiss wife, Olga, together with a few friends and helpers, including the physician Emil Vogl and H. G. Adler, who had only just returned from concentration camps, convinced the government that the four largely devastated castles of Olešovice, Kamenice, Štiřín, and Lojovice, just south of Prague, should serve as homes for abandoned children, wherever they came from. Pitter brought in twenty-five children from Terezín, then a group of German children and three German mothers from one of the new internment camps. Within three years nearly eight hundred children were cared for in these places by professional nurses, teachers, and social workers.

The ČNR, as long as it lasted, appointed Pitter to a social commission, and in this capacity he visited twenty-five of the many new internment camps, including the worst of them, the one at the former Loreto Monastery; the Hagibor field, where the Gestapo had concentrated the partners in mixed marriages; and the one at Letná in a sports stadium, carefully noting the number of children and the absence of medical assistance. Pitter was the first to deplore publicly what happened after the liberation. "The waters have receded, but the earth remains covered with dirt," he wrote, and in a one-man publication of September 1945 he proclaimed in less than metaphorical terms: "Again today, innocent people suffer. Too bad for us that the people committing lawlessness, brutality and these wrongdoings belong to our own nation. Imitating what the SS people have done, we are sinking to their level. It does not behoove the nation of Hus and Masaryk, and it runs counter to our spiritual tradition."

Pitter clearly recognized the aberrations of what was later called Czech Gestapism. But the Communists railed against him, and when they came to power in 1948, he faced arrest. He escaped through East Germany to the Federal Republic, where he worked as a preacher and social worker in the Valka refugee camp, near Nuremberg, and spoke to his home audience by way of Radio Free Europe. After the Valka camp was closed, he moved with his wife to her native Switzerland, where he remained active in the local communities of the Czech Brethren and in the World Council of Churches. Long before he died in 1976, he had been cited by Yad Vashem, in Jerusalem, as one of the

"Just of the World," and was awarded the West German *Bundesver-dienstkreuz* First Class in 1973. It may be characteristic of his own country that he received the Order of Masaryk Third Class only fifteen years after his demise.

A Taste of Liberation

It is difficult for me to remember what happened, and what I did, in the first hours and days of my liberated life. Vladimír said he would hold on to the police station, while I was practically living on the street, everywhere at the same moment, talking to people at the hospital, negotiating with a Soviet propaganda outfit, acting as a kind of town clerk, hanging around a barbershop, where I got a shave free of charge, and thinking all the time about how I would get in touch with W.W. again and how I would go home to Prague, finally, to start my studies at the university. I accompanied the three nurses to the hospital, and the doctor who ran the place immediately asked me, as if I had any authority, what he should do with the women who had sought refuge there during the night, hiding in hospital beds, which he now needed for wounded Soviet soldiers. An intelligent young Soviet officer, who had studied German at the University of Leningrad, queried me about the local radio and public-address systems, which the Germans had used to announce their victories to the population, and when we had found the answers, I asked him what he wanted to broadcast. It turned out to be a prerecorded speech about the Hitlers that come and go and the German state that lives on. This sounded completely wrong to my ears, considering the time and place—namely, moments after the defeat of Germany and in the Czechoslovak Republic. I asked him to check his maps; it turned out that the speech was to be broadcast to listeners in Saxony, fifty miles north. It was the first and possibly last time that I defended the integrity of the republic against Soviet intentions. The young officer admitted that he had misread his maps, he and his little troop said, "Do svidanja," turned their car, and disappeared up the road to the future East German state, another German state that did not endure.

The Soviet Army was represented by two or three animated female traffic police officers who lived at street corners on little chairs on which they sat all day long, smoking smelly cigarettes and munching apples that I brought them; occasionally they got up to direct traffic with diminutive red flags, which they waved with great verve. This was not an entirely easy job; one day, suddenly, a company of Hungarian soldiers, disarmed and on their way to Budapest, marched down the road, and it was difficult to convince them that it would be better for everybody if they set up camp in the next big city to the south. They vanished as suddenly as they had come.

There were other newcomers, including a mustachioed Slovak from forced labor in Duchcov who immediately requisitioned a horse and, pretending to be a cavalry officer of the old school, artfully rode up and down the streets representing authority. Another newcomer was Emil, or Emilek, returning from forced labor in Germany, who immediately recognized what was needed and established himself as commissioner of food and provisions. He invited me to his apartment, vacated by escaping Nazis, offered me a bottle of Champagne, and introduced me to the two Sudeten girls who had decided to live with him in the midst of plenty. I also met an older Social Democrat who had spent some time at Dachau in the late 1930s and early 1940s; we endlessly discussed the situation in Prague. While I spoke of T. G. Masaryk and the republic of many nationalities, he was skeptical about what he called old-fashioned humanism; his twenty-year-old daughter, a political realist who had carefully listened to the broadcasts from London, told me in no uncertain terms that I foolishly underrated the new Czechoslovak nationalism, that German anti-Fascists would have to leave their homes, in which they had barely survived the regime, with nothing more than fifty kilos of their personal belongings on their backs. She was right, and I was wrong, and I often thought about her when I became, after 1948, one of the exiles deploring (in the Czechoslovak periodical published in Geneva, Skutečnost [Reality]) the sad truth that Masaryk's nation, with which I had identified politically for so long, had unfortunately accepted the Nazi idea of collective guilt as a guiding moral and political principle.

Some telephones functioned, miraculously, and it was time to call W.W., who I knew was working as a medical assistant at the hospital at Podmokly (Bodenbach), in the Elbe Valley, in the shadow of the frontier mountain she came from. I found an old-fashioned telephone exchange

*near the closed post office and opened the door. I think I terribly shocked
the lonely girl on crutches who was running the switchboard manually,
and I was aware that I must have looked awful, with my long hair, my
front teeth missing (the camp dentist had nothing but a pair of pliers, a
bottle of iodine, and a drill operated by stepping on a foot pedal, bikelike),
and the Russian gun in my belt. I told her in my most polite German that
I needed to make a long-distance call to a hospital, and after some attempts she established the connection. I asked for W.W.; the nurse who
answered told me that she would pass the call on to Mother Superior (the
hospital was run by the Sisters of Mercy). I repeated my question, and I
heard a sentence I could never forget in all my life: "Ja, wissen Sie denn
nicht, dass W. im Feber beim Luftangriff auf Prag umgekommen ist?
Didn't you know that W. was killed in February during the air raid on
Prague?" It dawned on me that my father had on purpose not told me anything on the camp road. Later it turned out that he had arranged for
W.W.'s burial, my lonely friend Otakar attending. I do not know how I left
the telephone exchange, the girl's crutches made an awful scratching
noise, I felt empty, and the world I expected to live in had radically
changed.*

*After three older gendarmes, who had few illusions, arrived and took
over the police precinct, I told myself it was time to go home. I packed a
little bag and my new radio, took leave of the motherly cooks, so concerned about their future, and marched three or four hours south to the
next railway station from which occasional trains were dispatched to
Prague. The road was well traveled: trucks with returning prisoners,
heads shorn; Czech working people from Germany; the unavoidable
Hungarian Honveds; German refugees going nowhere; and in the ditches
discarded weapons, burned-out Wehrmacht cars, and a dead horse, penis
erect. I returned by slow train, clad in a U.S. Army greatcoat of uncertain
origin but marked on the back with three big white letters, POW.*

*In front of the Prague railroad station, the very one from which I had
left five months before, I simply took tram No. 14; the conductor, noticing my historical outfit, did not ask me for a ticket. From the tram stop at
Vodičkova there were only a few steps to Příčná Street, and when I rang
the bell, everybody recognized me immediately. There were my father,
limping a little, Aunt Irma, who had just returned from liberated Terezín,*

pale but her old lively self, and later Uncle Karl, a little haggard after three years at the Terezín Fortress and the Dresden Prison. From the pantry, where they had camped for a time, two Polish women appeared; they had been recommended by somebody or other and were getting ready to go on to Warsaw. There was a lot to talk about: my mother, Grandmother, Uncle Karel, his wife, and their younger son, who had perished in the gas chambers, W.W., and Elisabeth, who had been shot earlier that May. Aunt Irma gave me a present from the Terezín warehouses, for summer was coming. It was an outdated bathing suit, and it swiftly gave me a rash, owing to a strong disinfectant, but it served me well because I spent all those summer days on the swimming rafts of the Vltava River, right under the National Theater. I was half dazed by past and present, and I thought, above all, about my future studies of philosophy, as soon as the university would open again.

BIBLIOGRAPHICAL NOTES

INDEX

BIBLIOGRAPHICAL NOTES

My favorite general readings include:

J. W. Brügel, *Tschechen und Deutsche* (Munich, 1967).

G.E.R. Gedye, *Betrayal in Central Europe: Austria and Czechoslovakia* (New York, 1939).

Eva Hahnová, *Sudetoněmecký problém: Obtížné loučení s minulostí* (Prague, 1996).

J. K. Hoensch, *Geschichte Böhmens* (Munich, 1993).

Hillel J. Kieval, *The Making of Czech Jewry: National Conflict and Jewish Society in Bohemia 1870–1918* (Oxford, 1988).

Jan Křen, *Konfliktní společenství: Češi a Němci 1780–1918* (Prague, 1990).

Emanuel Rádl, *Válka Čechů s Němci* (Prague, 1928).

Samuel Harrison Thompson, *Czechoslovakia in European History* (2d ed., Hamden, Conn., 1965).

Christian Willars, *Die böhmische Zitadelle* (Munich, 1965).

Elizabeth Wiskemann, *Czechs and Germans* (2d ed., Oxford, 1967).

Zdeněk Zeman, *The Breakup of the Habsburg Empire* (Oxford, 1963).

CHAPTER I: THE DAY OF OCCUPATION

The Second Republic and the Establishment of the Protectorate

Heinrich Bodensieck, "Die Politik der Zweiten Tschecho-Slowakischen Republik," *Zeitschrift für Ostforschung* 6 (1967), 54–71.

Jan Gebhard and Jan Kuklík, *Druhá Republika 1938–1939: Svár demokracie a totality* (Prague and Litomyšl, 2004). Essential analysis.

Jan Holzer, "Stranický systém druhé republiky: úvod do komparace stranických systémů," in *Politologický časopis* 4 (1997), 330–51.

George F. Kennan, *From Prague After Munich* (Princeton, 1968).

Callum MacDonald and Jan Kaplan, *Prague in the Shadow of the Swastika: A History of the German Occupation 1939–1945* (Vienna, 2001). Remarkable photographic documents.

Victor Mamatey and Radomír Luža, eds., *A History of the Czechoslovak Republic 1918–1938* (New York, 1973).

Vojtěch Mastný, *The Czechs Under Nazi Rule: The Failure of National Resistance 1939–1942* (New York and London, 1971).

Milan Nakonečný, *Vlajka: K historii a ideologii českého nationalismu* (Prague, 2001).

Tomáš Pasák, *Český fašismus-kolaborace: 1922–1945* (Prague, 1999). Eminently instructive.

———, "Vstup německých vojsk na české území v roce 1939," in *Československý časopis historický* 17 (1969), 161–83.

Theodor Procházka, *The Second Republic: The Disintegration of Post-Munich Czechoslovakia* (New York, 1981).

Jan Rataj, "Český antisemitismus v proměnách let 1918–1945," in *Židé v české a polské občanské spolecnosti: Sborník přednášek* (Prague, 1999).

———, *O autoratitivní národní stát: Ideologické proměny české politiky v Druhé republice 1938–1939* (Prague, 1997).

Telford Taylor, *Munich: The Price of Peace* (New York, 1979).

The Question of Refugees and the Demise of Prague's Liberal German Institutions

Peter Becher, "Metropole des Exils-Prag 1933–1939," *Exilforschung: Internationales Jahrbuch,* ed. C. D. Krohn and Lutz Winckler, 20 (2002), 159–77.

Miroslav Beck, Květuše Hyršlová, Gabriela Veselá, and Jiří Veselý, eds., *Azyl v Československu 1933–1938* (Prague, 1983). Close to official point of view, but complete listing of German intellectual refugees in Prague.

Walter A. Berendsohn, *Die humanistische Front* (Zürich, 1926).

Fini Brada, "Emigration to Palestine," *The Jews of Czechoslovakia* II (New York, 1971), 589–98.

Bohumil Černý, *Most k novému životu: Německá emigrace v ČSR v letech 1933–1939* (Prague, 1968).

———, "Emigrace židů z českých zemí v letech 1938–1941," *Češi a svět. Sborník k pětasedmdesatinám Ivana Pfaffa* (2000), 181–89.

Drehscheibe Prag/Staging Point Prague; Deutsche Emigranten/German Exiles 1933–1939. Exhibition Catalog, ed. Peter Becher and Sigrid Canz (Munich, 1989).

Manfred George, "Refugees in Prague," *The Jews of Czechoslovakia* II (1971), 582–88.

Kurt R. Grossmann, "Refugees to and from Czechoslovakia," in *The Jews of Czechoslovakia* II (1971), 565–81. Excellent survey.

Klaus Jarmatz, *Literatur im Exil* (Berlin DDR, 1966).

Ivan Pfaff, "Německá kultura v českém exilu 1933–1958," *Svědectví* 18 (1983), 70–83.

The melancholy book about the demise of Prague's liberal German institutions has not been written yet. But readings would include, on the theater, essays by Veronika Ambrož (Toronto), Adolf Scherl (Prague), and Vlasta Reitterová (Prague and Vienna) in Alena Jakubcová, Jitka Ludvová, and Václav Maidl, eds., *Deutschsprachiges Theater in Prag* (Prague, 2001), and, on the university, Alena Míšková, *Německá (Karlova) univerzita od Mnichova k 9. květnu 1945* (Prague, 2002), especially 37–76 and 193–220.

The pioneering dissertation by Pavel Doležal "Tomáš G. Masaryk, Max Brod und das Prager Tagblatt: 1918–1938" (Frankfurt, 2003) discusses the glory days of the *Prager Tagblatt*. For the agony of the *Prager Presse*, the *Bohemia*, and the *Prager Tagblatt*, it is necessary to turn to their own later files, especially for December 31, 1938, and, for the *Prager Tagblatt*, the issues from March 15, 1939, to early April 1939.

Biographical Studies

Antonín Klimek and Petr Hoffmann, *Vítěz, který prohrál. Generál Radola Gajda* (Prague, 1995).

Tomáš Pasák, *JUDr. Emil Hácha: 1938–1945* (Prague, 1997). Concentrates on the presidency; informative.

Dušan Tomášek and Robert Kvaček, *Causa Emil Hácha* (Prague, 1995).

Václav Machálek, *Prezident v zajetí. Život, činy a kříž Emila Háchy* (Prague, 1998). On the defense.

CHAPTER II: THE BEGINNINGS OF THE PROTECTORATE: 1939–41

Neurath and Early Demonstrations Against the Occupation

Stanislav Biman, "17. listopad," *Dějiny a současnost* 8 (1966), 17–20.

Heinz Boberach, ed., *Meldungen aus dem Reich: Auswahl aus den Geheimen Lageberichten der SS 1939–1944* (Neuwied and Berlin, 1965).

Detlef Brandes, *Die Tschechen unter deutschem Protektorat* (Munich and Vienna, 1969–75), 2 vols. Vol. 1: *Besatzungspolitik, Kollaboration und Widerstand im Protektorat Böhmen und Mähren bis zu Heydrichs Tod (1939–1942)*. From the archives, a magisterial analysis concentrating on Czechs and Germans.

Jan Gebhart and Jan Kuklik, *Dramatické i všední dny Protektorátu* (Prague, 1996).

John L. Heineman, *Hitler's First Foreign Minister: Constantin von Neurath, diplomat and statesman* (Stanford, 1979). Highly instructive.

Josef Leikert, "Černý pátek sedmnactého listopadu" (Prague, 2000). Independent research, essential.

Vojtěch Mastný, "Design or Improvisation: The Origins of the Protectorate of Bohemia and Moravia in 1939," in *Columbia Essays in Foreign Affairs*, ed. A. W. Cordier (New York, 1966), 127–53.

Horst Naude, *Erkenntnisse und Erlebnisse: Als politischer Beobachter im Protektorat Böhmen und Mähren* (Munich, 1965). Another perspective.

Karel Polák, "Máchův návrat," *Kritický měsíčník* 2 (1939), 265–66.

Josef Polišenský, "28. říjen a 17. listopad, persekuce českého studentstva," in *Sedmnáctý listopad* (Prague, 1959), 33–46.

Gustav von Schmoller, "Die deutschen Vergeltungsmassnahmen nach den tschechis-
    chen Studentendemonstrationen in Prag im Oktober und November 1939,"
    Vierteljahreshefte für Zeitgeschichte 27 (1979).
Volker Zimmermann, Die Sudeten im NS Staat: Politik und Stimmung der Bevölkerung
    im Reichsgau Sudetenland (Essen, 1999).

The Formation of the Resistance

Arnošt Bareš and Tomáš Pasák, "Odbojová organizace Zdenka Schmoranze," Historie a
    vojenství 7 (1968), 1003–33.
Jiří Doležal and Jan Křen, Czechoslovakia's Fight 1938–1945: Documents on the Resis-
    tance Movement of the Czechoslovak People (Prague, 1964).
František Fuchs, "Die tschechisch-jüdische Widerstandsbewegung in Theresien-
    stadt," in Theresienstädter Studien und Dokumente, ed. M. Kárný, R. Kemper,
    and M. Kárná (Prague, 1997).
Jaroslav Jelínek, PÚ–Politické ústředí domácího odboje (Prague, 1947).
Radomír Luža, "The Czech Resistance Movement," in A History of the Czechoslovak Re-
    public 1918–1948, ed. V. Mamatey and R. Luža (Princeton, 1973), 343–61. In the
    absence of more recent researches, possibly the most instructive essay.
Odboj a revoluce: Nástin dějin českého odboje (Prague, 1965).
H. Gordon Skilling, "The Czechoslovak Struggle for National Liberation in World War II,"
    Slavonic and East European Review 29 (1960), 174–97. Useful panorama.
Jan Boris Uhlíř, Ve stínu říšské orlice: Protektorát Čechy a Morava: odboj a kolaborace
    (Prague, 2003).

My Jewish and Ladin Family Histories

"Die Juden in den böhmischen Ländern," Colloquium Bad Wiessee (Munich, 1983).
Wilma Eggers, ed., Die Juden in Böhmen und Mähren (Munich, 1986), especially
    90–102, 214–21, 252–93; also the essays by Ruth Kestenberg (161–200),
    Gustav Otruba (209–68), and Ladislav Lipscher (269–90).
Kde domov můj: Wo ist mein Heim?, ed. Helmut Köser, Exhibition Catalogue. Cf. The
    Brod Family, 154–58.
Jana Svobodová and Helena Krejčová, "Sociální a demografická struktura pražského
    židovského obyvatelstva v Praze a její proměny v letech 1938–1945," in Postavení
    a osudy židovského obyvatelstva v Čechách a na Moravě v letech 1939–1945
    (Prague, 1998), 50–85.
Rudolf M. Wlaschek, Biographia Judaica Bohemiae (Darmstadt, 1995), 28 (on Fritta
    and Leo Brod).

Marina Demetz, Hausierhandel, Hausindustrie und Kunstgewerbe im Grödental (Inns-
    bruck, 1987).
Gröden, der Grödner und seine Sprache. Von einem Einheimischen (Bozen, 1864; new
    ed., 1998).
Christoph Perathoner, Die Dolomitenladiner 1848–1918 (Bozen, 1998).
Kajus Perathoner, Adolf Andres Kostner, and Lois Craffonara, Ladinisches Vermächtnis
    (Bozen, 1980).
Cesare Poppi, Ladins: People of the Pale Mountains (Dublin, 2001).

Questions of "Cultural Autonomy" and Literary Discussions

Václav Černý, "Největší z pierotů," *Kritický měsíčník* 2 (1939), 447–55.

František Červinka, *Česká kultura za okupace* (Prague, 2002).

Jiří Doležal, *Česká kultura za protektorátu: školství, písemnictví, kinematografie* (Prague, 1996). Inclusive and particularly useful.

František Kožík, *Největší z pierotů* (Prague, 1939; American version by Dora Round, New York, 1940).

———, *Vzpomínky* (Prague, 1995).

Antonín Měšťan, *Geschichte der tschechischen Literatur des 19. und 20. Jahrhunderts* (Cologne and Vienna, 1984), especially 309–50.

Arne Novák, *Czech Literature*, trans. Peter Kussi, ed. with a supplement William E. Harkins (Ann Arbor, 1976), especially 327–38.

Václav Poláček, *Kniha a národ 1939–1945* (Prague, 2004).

Albert Pražák, "Co dělat," *Kritický měsíčník* 2 (1939), 273–76. Against historicism.

Anti-Jewish Measures and Policies, Economic Rationing

Christopher R. Browning, with contributions by Jürgen Matthäus, *The Origins of the Final Solution: The Evolution of Nazi Jewish Policy, September 1939–March 1942* (Lincoln, Neb., Yad Vashem, Jerusalem, 2004).

Helena Krejčová and Anna Hyndráková, "Postoj Čechů k židům: Z politického zpravodajství okupační správy a protektorátního tisku v letech 1939–1941," *Soudobé dějiny* 2 (1995), 578–605.

Helena Petrův, *Postavení židů v Protektorátu Čechy a Morava* (Prague, 2000). Most useful and detailed.

Marie Durmanová, "Řízené hospodářství a správa Ústředního svazu průmyslu za nacistické okupace," in *Sborník archívních prací* 16 (1966), 366–96.

Food, Famine, and Relief 1940–1946 (Geneva, 1946).

Václav Král, *Otázky hospodářského a sociálního vývoje v českých zemích v letech 1938–45* (Prague, 1957–59), 3 vols. A mass of statistical materials and a strict Stalinist orientation.

Václav Průcha, "Základní rysy válečného řízeného hospodářství v českých zemích v letech nacistické okupace," *Historie a vojenství* 15 (1967), 215–39.

Alice Teichová, "The Protectorate of Bohemia and Moravia; The Economic Dimension," in: *Bohemia in History*, ed. Mikuláš Teich (Cambridge, U.K., 1998).

Information about the introduction of rationing comes from the files of the *Národní politika* (National Politics), Prague daily, September 10 to November 7, 1939.

CHAPTER III: TERROR AND RESISTANCE

Reinhard Heydrich

Shlomo Aronson, *Reinhard Heydrich und die Frühgeschichte von Gestapo und SD* (Stuttgart, 1991).

Édouard Calic, *Heydrich—L'homme clef du IIIe Reich* (Paris, 1982).

Mario R. Dederichs, *Heydrich: Das Gesicht des Bösen* (Munich, 2005).

Günther Deschner, *Reinhard Heydrich: Statthalter der totalen Macht* (Esslingen, 1977). The most useful biographical study.

G. S. Graber, *The Life and Times of Reinhard Heydrich* (London, 1981).

Lina Heydrich, *Leben mit einem Kriegsverbrecher* (Pfaffenhofen, 1976). Mrs. H. speaks.

Charles Whiting, *Heydrich: Henchman of Death* (Barnsley, U.K., 1999). Useful.

Alan Wykes, *Heydrich* (New York, 1973).

Protectorate Jazz

Lubomír Dorůžka and Ivan Poledňák, *Československý jazz: Minulost a Přítomnost* (Prague and Bratislava, 1967). Rich illustrations.

Václav Holzknecht, *Jaroslav Ježek a Osvobozené divadlo* (Prague, 1957).

Josef Kotek and Jaromír Hořec, *Kronika české synkopy* (Prague, 1990). Note especially 9–96, "Swing Under the Swastika," including photographic documents from Terezín.

An Anthology of Czech Jazz 1920–1965. Supraphon DV (1965), 10177–8H, arranged by I. Poledňák and Zbyněk Mácha.

R. A. Dvorský and His Melody Boys. Arranged by Miroslav Černý. Ultraphon (1986), SU 5127–2–301.

Karel Vlach se svým orchestrem. Supraphon Trezor 10 1587–2–311.

Jiří Orten

Jiří Orten, *Elegie* [Elegies], trans. Lyn Coffin, with the help of Eva Eckert (Washington, D.C., 1980). A useful preface by George Gibian.

Ivan Diviš, "Ortenovy Elegie," in *Slovem do prostoru* (Bratislava, 1993).

Jan Grossman, *Nad dílem Jiřího Ortena. Mladá fronta* (Prague), June 8, 1945.

Josef Kocián, *Jiří Orten* (Prague, 1966).

Milena Jesenská

Alles ist Leben, ed. Dorothea Rein (Frankfurt, 1996).

The Journalism of Milena Jesenská: A Critical Voice in Central Europe, trans. and ed. Kathleen Hayes (New York, 2003).

Přes naše síly: Češi, Židé a Němci (Olomouc, 1997). An anthology of her writings.

Margarete Buber-Neumann, *Milena: Kafkas Freundin* (Munich, 1977).

Jana Černá, *Milena Jesenská* (Frankfurt, 1985). Milena's daughter remembers. . . .

Franz Kafka, *Briefe an Milena* (Frankfurt, 1966).

Marta Marková-Kotyková, *Mýtus Milena* (Prague, 1993). Milena without legends.

Alena Wagnerová, *Milena Jesenská: Biographie* (Mannheim, 1994).

H. W. Kolben

Ruth V. Gross, *"Plan" and the Austrian Rebirth: Portrait of a Journal* (Columbia, S.C., 1982).

Jindřich Kolben, Jan Havelka, Václav Daněk, and Vladimír Žák, *Příběh rodiny Kolbenů* (Prague, 2000).

Jürgen Serke, *Böhmische Dörfer: Wanderungen durch eine verlassene literarische Landschaft* (Vienna and Hamburg, 1987), 450.

Heydrich's Policies

H. G. Adler, *Theresienstadt 1941–1945: Das Antlitz einer Zwangsgemeinschaft,* with a preface by Jeremy Adler (Gütersloh, 2005). 1st ed., 1955.

Michael Berenbaum and Abraham Peck, eds., *The Holocaust and History* (Bloomington, Ind., 1998).

Detlef Brandes, *Die Tschechen unter deutschem Protektorat. Part II: Besatzungspolitik, Kollaboration und Widerstand im Protektorat Böhmen und Mähren von Heydrichs Tod bis zum Prager Aufstand* (Munich and Vienna, 1975).

George C. Browder, *Hitler's Enforcers: The Gestapo and the SS Security Service in the Nazi Revolution* (New York and Oxford, 1996).

Jaroslava Eliášová and Tomáš Pasák, *Heydrich do Prahy, Eliáš do vězení* (Prague, 2002). Eliáš's widow speaking.

Saul Friedländer, *Das Dritte Reich und die Juden: Die Jahre der Verfolgung* (Munich, 2000).

Miroslav Kárný, with Jaroslava Milotová and Margita Kárná, eds., *Deutsche Politik im "Protektorat Böhmen und Mähren" unter Reinhard Heydrich 1941–1942* (Berlin, 1997).

Alena Míšková, *Německá (Karlova) univerzita od Mnichova do 9. května 1945* (Prague, 2002), especially 125–92, on the Heydrich Foundation.

Tomáš Pasák, *Generál Eliáš a odboj: Jeden český osud* (Prague, 1996).

———, "Problematika protektorátního tisku a formování tzv. skupiny aktivistických novinářů na počátku okupace," in *Příspěvky k dějinám KSČ* 1 (1987), 52–80.

Livia Rothkirchen, *The Jews of Bohemia and Moravia: Facing the Holocaust* (Lincoln, Neb., and Jerusalem, 2005).

The Case of Moravec and the New Government

Jiří Pernes, *Až na dno zrady: Emanuel Moravec* (Prague, 1997). A detailed biography.

Dušan Tomášek and Robert Kvaček, *Obžalovaná je vláda* (Prague, 1999). The last protectorate government faces the National Court.

Thalia Divided and Theater at Terezín

Richard Billinger, *Die Hexe von Passau: Schauspiel in sechs Aufzügen und einem Vorspiel* (Berlin, 1935).

Franz Hauptmann, *Die Entscheidung* (Eirich Agency, Vienna).

Vítězslav Nezval, *Manon Lescaut* (13th ed., Prague, 1946).

František Zavřel, *Fortinbras: Roman* (2d ed., Prague, 1930), Part II (Prague, 1934).

———, *Polobozi: Dramatická pentalogie* (Prague, 1941).

František Černý, ed., *Theater/Divadlo: Vzpomínky českých divadelníků na německou okupaci a druhou světovou válku* (Prague, 1965).

František Červinka, *Česká kultura a okupace* (Prague, 2000), especially 84–116.

Hans Demetz, *Geschichte des Prager deutschen Theaters,* XI Teil: 1939–1944, 216 ms. pages, on deposit at the National Theater Institute, Prague.

Joža Karas, *Music in Terezín 1940–1945* (New York, 1985). Inclusive, excellent bibliography.

Eva Šormová, *Divadlo v Terezíně 1941–1945* (Ústi n L., 1973).

Bořivoj Srba, "Z osudu českých divadel za nacistické okupace," in *Otázky divadla a filmu: Theatralia et Cinematographica*, ed., Artur Závodský (Brno, 1971), II, 191–234.

The Death of Heydrich

Alan Burgess, *Seven Men at Daybreak* (London, 1960).

Hellmut G. Haasis, *Tod in Prag: Das Attentat auf Reinhard Heydrich* (Reinbek, 2000).

Miroslav Ivanov, *Atentát na Reinharda Heydricha* (5th ed., Prague, 1987). Facts and fictions mixed.

Callum MacDonald, *The Killing of the SS Obergruppenführer Reinhard Heydrich: 27 May 1942* (London, 1990).

RichardStröbinger, *Das Attentat von Prag. Reinhard Heydrich, Statthalter Hitlers: Seine Herrschaft und die Hintergründe seines Todes* (Bergisch Gladbach, 1976).

Jan G. Wiener, *The Assassination of Heydrich* (New York, 1969).

Hangmen Also Die (Hollywood, 1943). Fritz Lang, director; screenplay written in part by Bertolt Brecht.

Hitler's Madman (Hollywood, 1943). Douglas Sirk, director; John Carradine as Heydrich.

CHAPTER IV: THE END OF THE PROTECTORATE

K. H. Frank

Ernst Frank, *K. H. Frank: Staatsminister im Protektorat* (Heusenstamm, 1971). His brother speaks.

Miloslav Mouliš and Dušan Tomášek, *K. H. Frank: Vzestup a pád karlovarského knihkupce* (Prague, 2003).

Marlis Steinert, *Die 23 Tage der Regierung Dönitz* (Düsseldorf and Vienna, 1967).

Zpověď K. H. Franka-Český národ soudí K. H. Franka (Prague, 1947). Trial papers, published by the Ministry of Information.

Prague Movies: The Years of Occupation

Luboš Bartošek, *Náš film 1896–1945* (Prague, 1985). Complete survey but close to the official point of view.

Petr Bednařík, *Arizace české kinematografie* (Prague, 2003). Excellent analysis.

Český hraný film II 1930–1945, Czech Feature Film II 1930–1945 (Prague, 1998). Repertoire of all Czech films of the period, published by the National Film Archives in Czech and English.

Boguslaw Drewniak, *Der deutsche Film 1938–1945* (Düsseldorf, 1987). Hitler's favorite movies are discussed on 632–45.

Václav M. Havel, Sr., *Mé vzpomínky* (Prague, 1993).

Helena Krejčová, "'Jsem nevinen': Süss, Harlan, Čáp, a jiní." *Iluminace* 5 (1993), 65–97.

Stanislav Motl, *Mraky nad Barrandovem* (Prague, 2006).

Ladislav Pištora, "Filmoví návstěvníci a kina na území České republiky," *Iluminace* 8 (1996), 35–59.

Hans Dieter Schäfer, *Das gespaltene Bewusstsein: Deutsche Kultur und Lebenswirklichkeit 1933–1945* (Munich, 1981).

Joseph Wulf, *Theater und Film im Dritten Reich* (Gütersloh, 1965). Official documents.

Lída Baarová, *Života sladké hořkosti* (Prague, 1991). Memoirs.

Aleš Cibulka, *Nataša Gollová-Život tropí hlouposti* (Prague, 2002). A biography.

Vladimír Just, *Vlasta Burian: Mysterium smíchu* (Prague, 1993). A balanced biography.

Adina Mandlová, *Dnes už se tomu směju* (Prague, 1990). The diva's memoirs.

The Prague Uprising

Stanislav Auský, *Vojska generála Vlasova v Čechách* (Prague, 1992; San Francisco, 1982, Russian ed.).

Karel Bartošek, *The Prague Uprising* (Prague, 1965). Conformist interpretation of the uprising as "the People's Democratic Revolution."

Stanislav Kokoška, *Prague v květnu 1945: Historie jednoho povstání* (Prague, 2005). A balanced analysis.

———— and Jaroslav Kokoška, "Česká národní rada a vojenská příprava květnoveho povstání," *Historie a vojenství* 39 (1990), 3–16.

Radomír Luža, "The Liberation of Prague: An American Blunder?," *Kosmas* 3 (1984), 41–57.

Albert Pražák, *Politika a revoluce* (Prague, 2005). Memoirs.

Pražské povstání 1945 (Washington, D.C., 1965). The liberal and social democratic point of view. Contributions by Otakar Machotka, Josef Kotrlý, and others. Important.

Revolutionary Retribution!

Edvard Beneš, *Demokracie dnes a zítra* (London, 1941–42), 2 vols.

————, *Paměti* (Prague, 1941).

Wenzel Jaksch, *Europas Weg nach Potsdam: Schuld und Schicksal im Donauraum* (Stuttgart, 1958).

Jan Masaryk, *Ani opona, ani most* (Prague, 1947).

Přemysl Pitter, *Unter dem Rad der Geschichte* (Zürich and Stuttgart, 1970).

Detlef Brandes, *Der Weg zur Vertreibung 1938–1945* (Munich, 2001).

Tomáš Brod, *Osudný omyl Edvarda Beneše: Československá cesta do sovětského područí* (Prague, 2002).

Benjamin Frommer, *National Cleansing: Retribution Against Nazi Collaborators in Postwar Czechoslovakia* (Cambridge, U.K., 2005). A pioneering analysis.

Erich Kulka, *Židé v československé armádě na Západě* (Prague, 1992).

Radomír Luža, *The Transfer of the Sudeten Germans* (New York, 1964).

Tomáš Pasák, *Život pro druhé: Česko-německé soužití v díle Přemysla Pittra* (Prague and Litomyšl, 1997).

Tomáš Stanek, *Německá menšina v českých zemích 1948–1989* (Prague, 1993).

Alena Wagnerová, *Odsunuté vzpomínky* (Prague, 1993).

INDEX

DATE DUE